UNDERSTANDING THE FAITH

PRESBYTERIAN COLLEGE STUDIES IN THEOLOGY AND MINISTRY
VOLUME 1

To Eric —
hope you enjoy!

12/07

UNDERSTANDING THE FAITH

Essays in Philosophical Theology

JOSEPH C. McLELLAND

CLEMENTS ACADEMIC
Toronto

Published 2007 by
CLEMENTS PUBLISHING
6021 Yonge St., Box 213
Toronto, Ontario M2M 3W2 Canada
www.clementspublishing.com

Library and Archives Canada Cataloguing in Publication

McLelland, Joseph C. (Joseph Cumming), 1925-
Understanding the faith : essays in philosophical theology /
Joseph C. McLelland ; edited by John A. Vissers.

(Presbyterian College studies in theology and ministry)
Includes bibliographical references.
ISBN-10: 1-894667-61-1
ISBN-13: 978-1-894667-61-6

1. Philosophical theology. 2. Presbyterian Church—Doctrines. 3. Pastoral
theology—Presbyterian Church. I. Vissers, John, 1957- II. Title. III. Series.

BT40.M415 2007   285   C2007-902379-7

CONTENTS

PART THREE: THEOLOGY AND CANADIAN SOCIETY

EDITOR'S PREFACE

This collection of essays by Professor Emeritus Joseph C. McLelland is the inaugural volume in a new series of publications called Presbyterian College Studies in Theology and Ministry. The modest purpose of this series is to make available theological material that informs and is informed by the life of the Christian church, especially in Canada. It assumes something that is not as widely accepted today as it once was, namely, that ministry and theology belong together. More specifically, it assumes that ministry precedes and produces theology, and that theological reflection on Christian ministry is crucial to the faith and life of the church. With this in mind, the occasional volumes in this series will include both collections of essays and monographs, authored primarily by those associated with the Reformed tradition in Canada.

The series is sponsored by The Presbyterian College, Montreal. The Presbyterian College is a theological school of The Presbyterian Church in Canada, a member of the Montreal School of Theology (The Joint Board of Theological Colleges), and affiliated with the Faculty of Religious Studies at McGill University. Since being founded in 1865 the College has been engaged primarily in the task of preparing ordained leadership for the church. As a centre of theological education and research open to students and scholars from Canada, the United States, and around the world, it is committed to the essentials of the Reformed faith: the sovereignty of God, the centrality of Christ, the authority of Scripture and the tenets of the Christian tradition as attested to by the ecumenical creeds and Reformed confessions. The historic motto of the College is "Holding Forth the Word of Life" (Philippians 2:16) and its current mission statement is "Shaping Transformational Church Leaders."

That being said, theological schools are often better known by their professors, and this is certainly true of The Presbyterian College, Montreal. In 1955 The Rev. Dr. Joseph C. McLelland was appointed part-time Robert Lecturer in the History and Philosophy of Religion. Thus began an association that has continued to the present day. In 1957 Dr. McLelland became Robert Professor of the History and Philosophy of Religion and Christian Ethics on a full-time basis, and in 1964 he was subsequently appointed McConnell Professor of Philosophy of Religion at McGill University, while continuing to serve as a faculty member at the Presbyterian College. He also served as Dean of the Faculty of Religious Studies at McGill from 1975 to 1985. 2007, therefore, marks the 50th anniversary of Dr. McLelland's full-time association with the College.

In addition to his teaching and administrative responsibilities over many years, Professor McLelland has also found time to write. Among his better known books are *The Visible Words of God: The Sacramental Theology of Peter Martyr Vermigli*, *The Other Six Days*, *Living for Christ*, *The Clown and the Crocodile*, and *Prometheus Rebound: The Irony of Atheism*. As a theologian and philosopher of religion Professor McLelland has always had an eye for what the American Roman Catholic theologian David Tracy has called the three publics of theology: society, academy, and church. In fact, one of the things that characterizes Professor McLelland's books and articles is the sense that one cannot speak meaningfully to any one of these three publics without always keeping the other two in view. That's what makes his work so relevant, inspiring, provocative, entertaining, inter-disciplinary, prophetic, insightful, and sometimes even exasperating, at one and the same time.

The Canadian Presbyterian theologian Walter Bryden, under whom Professor McLelland studied, once wrote that "Scholars, when they cease to be prophetic, and thus fail to be theologians, possess a significance little more than that of scribes." As these essays show, McLelland is no mere scribe. He is a scholar who has never ceased to be prophetic, and he has thus fulfilled the vocation of a true theologian—a doctor of the church.

It is therefore a pleasure, and indeed a privilege, on the occasion of Professor McLelland's 50-year association with The Presbyterian College, to introduce this collection of his essays as the first volume in our new series, believing that these articles deserve to be read again and again, and that they provide an important record of a half-century of theological and philosophical reflection by one of Canada's leading scholars of religion.

John Vissers
Summer 2007

AUTHOR'S PREFACE

Any collection of essays is bound to lack consistency and perhaps relevance at times. Like short stories, they should be approached not as a single but a diverse group. Since this volume covers over forty years in my writing career, it exhibits certain shifts in interest and perspective. I trust that readers will look kindly on these efforts, some betraying a young teacher's ambitious reach as well as personal preferences and recurrent themes.

I am indebted to Principal Vissers for hatching the idea of a Presbyterian College series of publications. My fifty years with P.C. provided an ideal situation to pursue a varied career: teaching our Teaching Elders, working both sides of the street through appointment to McGill University's Faculty of Divinity (now Religious Studies), travelling for lectureships and conferences. Obviously great changes have occurred during that period in theological education, in the church, and in society. The three parts of this collection are a rough guide to this evolution. Some of them are more technical than others (on episcopacy and predestination, for instance), prepared for an audience of theologians. Others are speeches at convocations or elsewhere; an Appendix provides a lighter view of College life. If I were to choose I would take the last two as my favourites, and the final one, "A Serious Playfulness," as a reliable expression of my theological position. I am surprised to see how some themes endure from the first selection to the last (1955-1996), such as faith as union with Christ, and the call for theological humour ("Call me Isaac"). I have not attempted to update the articles, thus leaving some traces of what is taken to be "exclusivist" language: "man" for "human." Occasionally I have inserted a footnote, marked with asterisk, to indicate a new development worth noting.

Besides Dr. Vissers, others are due acknowledgment for their support and influence. My wife Audrey comes first as one who has sacrificed much in order to grace me with the time to prepare not only lectures but books and articles. My students have been an inspiration—enquiring minds, more interested in the new than the old but willing to bear with my historical approach. My colleagues in College and University supplied a sounding board and debating society as well as a source of information about other disciplines. I was blessed to be called to the new Robert Chair in History and Philosophy of Religion and Christian Ethics (Principal Lennox observed, "more a chesterfield than a chair") and so forced to work hard in three fields. The McConnell Chair in Philosophy of Religion at McGill allowed greater specialization, but the foundation at P.C. was invaluable in developing my philosophical theology. The latter involves some themes absent from the present collection and the subject of a volume in the works: a new natural theology, a modal approach to religious pluralism, scientific and aesthetic analogies for theological discourse, for instance. But the following *essais* reflect my attempts at understanding Christian faith and ways of communicating that understanding.

Joseph C. McLelland
Spring 2007

PART 1

Theology and Christian Ministry

1

THE RISK OF OUR MINISTRY

*Inaugural Address on induction to the Robert Chair of the
History and Philosophy of Religion and Christian Ethics,
The Presbyterian College, Montreal, November 1958.*

The word "Professor" comes from the classical Greek educational system, from the Sophists indeed, who drew their pupils by promises. They promised or "professed" ideas which attracted students to them. In this address I am supposed to give you a taste of the future, to deposit a kind of promissory note to your account, that you may judge the quality and the validity of that which is to come.

Yet what can I say about the History and Philosophy of Religion? For everyone knows that the word "religion" is *tabu* today, and we prefer to talk about "going beyond religion." Who would dare take it seriously in face of Karl Barth's declaration (in an appropriate section of some hundred pages) that Religion is now "abolished"?[1] As to Ethics, the literary world is full of books on ethical subjects general and specific. Therefore let me not attempt sweeping claims, but promise this one thing: that I shall consider these subjects committed to my steward-ship as the bridge between church and world, so that Philosophy of

---

1.   *Church Dogmatics* I/2, §17, pp. 280-361.

15

Religion will be approached in terms of *evangelism,* and Christian Ethics in terms of *social action.* Let me now try to explain why I consider this the realistic approach, because of "the risk of our ministry."

THE RIDDLE

Let me propose a riddle. There is a puzzling feature of God's call to the ministry that is especially evident in the lives of certain great historical figures. God addresses someone in call and challenge. But here is a man that answered, "Who am I, that I should go to Pharaoh?" His name was Moses. Here is another who replied, "Ah, Lord God! behold, I cannot speak: for I am a child." His name was Jeremiah. Another desired to serve God in a life of scholarly meditation and devotion, and used to avoid any town with a vacant bishop's chair, for fear the people would force him into it. But he let down his guard at Hippo in North Africa and so St. Augustine became a bishop, despite his protests and tears at the very chancel steps. A parallel is that of the young scholar John Calvin who was on his way to pursue the same career of quiet study and writing, when fiery old William Farel put the fear of God into him if he should refuse ministry in Geneva. Or think of John Knox, sitting in the pew in St. Andrew's Cathedral and suddenly hearing the preacher address him by name and summon him to become a Minister of the Gospel. He fled in tears, but could not escape this call.

Is my riddle clear now? If fear and trembling is the reaction of such saints to God's call, why have we lost this phenomenon from so much of our ministry today? Have we perhaps advanced beyond these former generations? Is it because the ministry has become so acceptable, so socially beneficial, so "professionally" respectable, that we are now able to shrug off the fear and the trembling? After all, the Minister is no longer expected to be a preacher—and never a theologian!—so long as we are good visitors, organizers and administrators.

Our position is something like that of the temperance worker whom Kierkegaard describes. In order to make membership in the Federation more attractive, and to give the worker himself more zeal in his campaign for total abstinence, he is allowed one bottle of wine each day as incentive and aid. So this ministry of doom and resurrection is supported by organizations of dubious relevance, and evaluated by the criterion of "success."

MINISTERIAL MIDWIFERY

I submit to you, on the contrary, that the Ministry is a dangerous business, a mixed blessing, a threat to our security and values, our ambitions and desires, our ideas and ideals. For the Ministry is a calling to perform a certain quite curious task for people. What is this task? To preach the Gospel, we are told, to shepherd the flock, to let people see Jesus. "Not enough" I reply—our task is much more simple and earthy than these high-sounding phrases. In one word, we are called to be *midwives.* Our task is to assist at a birth.

It seems to me that theology in terms of "evangelism" might be described as *the science of new birth and the art of its delivery,* while in terms of "ethics" as *the science of the new growth and the art of its nurture.* We are called to be specialists in the laws that govern the new birth and new growth—justification and sanctification, faith and works, knowing and doing the truth.

It was, of course, Socrates who first described himself as a midwife. As a philosopher, he felt called to assist at the delivery of true ideas which were already conceived in men's minds but awaited birth through the maieutic office and instruments of his questioning and debate. Just one hundred years ago, Kierkegard compared this philosophical method to theology, and declared that because of sin there are no "true ideas" within us, so that one can act as midwife only so far; then one must become a witness to the Truth. By this means Kierkegaard advanced "one step beyond Socrates."[2]

Let us now attempt to advance one step beyond Kierkegaard. Let us take with the utmost seriousness this word of Paul to the Christians in

---

2.   Kierkegaard, *Philosophical Fragments*, 1844.

Galatia: "My little children, with whom I am again in travail until Christ be formed in you." And this to the Christians in Corinth: "I became your father in Christ Jesus through the Gospel."[3] And consider how Paul time and time again says that by faith a man is "in Christ," and that Christ is "in us." This is nothing less than a definition of "faith" as *union with Christ*. I submit to you that this is in fact the classic definition of faith, articulated by Christ Himself, by St. Paul, by the Church Fathers, the medieval "mystical theologians," and the great Reformers of the Sixteenth Century. I submit that without this definition, faith becomes a human work, a subjective distortion leading to a superficial evangelicalism. The familiar carol got it right: "O holy Child of Bethlehem ... be born in us today."

Some folk talk about being "born again." Perhaps you've heard the lovely little story of the man who was converted so roundly at an evangelistic meeting that when he got home and opened the door, his dog met him and bit his ankle! Yes, this is one side of the story: one begins a new life of one's own, in Christ we are a new creation. But this is not the *best* side of the story of new birth. Rather, it is the strange and wonderful fact that Christ Himself condescends to come into a man's life in the form of an infant—that *Jesus Christ himself* is "born again," as it were, whenever the event of faith occurs. What the Holy Spirit conceives and the Church mothers is thus a new union, the birth of a new person in Christ and of Christ in that person. It is this birth at which we are called to assist, this growth we must nurture.

You see the *risk* of our ministry, then? It's this complex nature of the new birth, especially the mystery that our midwifery passes over into parenthood, convulsed with the travail of birth itself. Such is the mystery of our ministry, that we may deliver yea, be parent to—babies in Christ; such is the deeper mystery of Christ's own ministry through ours, that he still comes in gentle accommodation to the weakness of his people. Just because he has ordained this means of his grace, this ministry of his

---

3.   Gal. 4:19; 1 Cor. 4:15.

18

Word and its Sacraments, therefore how real is the hazard of our labour. For what if, by false teaching, or by true teaching at wrong times, we should deliver an abortion, or even stifle an infant heartbeat?

That wise teacher of the Early Church, Origen of Alexandria, expressed the risk by stating: "I often think of the maxim, 'It is dangerous to talk about God, even if what you say about him is true'. The man who wrote that must, I am sure, have been a shrewd and dependable character. There is danger, you see, not only in saying what is untrue about God but even in telling the truth about him if you do it at the wrong time."[4] Such is surely the peculiar risk of our role as *teaching Elders!*

Another form of risk is, in Paul's words again, "I have become all things to all men, that I might by all means save some ... I do not run aimlessly, but subdue myself, lest after preaching to others I myself should be a castaway." Thus let us suppose someone led on by the Gospel to a conviction about the terrible inequality, the sinfulness of the social order. Suppose such a one, however, finds such "spirituality" in the Church that no one cares about these "materialistic" things ("so heavenly minded as to be of no earthly use"). Suppose he therefore feels constrained to break with the Church and its religion, and to join those who fight social injustice apart from all spirituality. That is, he becomes a radical socialist, perhaps even a communist. Now here is the risk—that such a one has become an atheist ... for the sake of the Kingdom of God!

During the days of the McCarthy purge in the United States, it seemed to me that the Church could have proclaimed the Word of God best by setting up its own investigating committee, to condemn any Christian who had not at least considered becoming a communist during the years of Depression! That leading world evangelist, Daniel Niles of Ceylon, has put this thought well: "until Buddhism began to

---

4.   Origen, *Hom. Ezek.* I.11. (See McLelland, *God the Anonymous* (Phila. Patristic Foundation, 1976), p. 135).

exert an influence over me, until I found it fascinated me, until Buddha and his teachings became something that really attracted me—until that happened, I couldn't be an evangelist to the Buddhists ... And it is the same with the Communists. Nobody who would say, 'Communism is all rubbish', nobody who has failed to feel the power of Communism, will ever be able to evangelize the Communists."[5]*

Or yet again, suppose a Minister is called to enter into the fellowship of suffering with someone in grave trouble—moral trouble, let us say, that has brought disgrace and scandal. Must not our "sympathy" be so real that we must imitate our Lord in refusing to cast a stone, but rather must share and bear the very guilt and shame of this sufferer? Such a descent into the depths of degradation, such identification with another's temptation and trial, is no easy experience. Yet it is a necessity if we are to help this other one.

CHRISTIAN HILARITY

Now let me add the note that may sound discordant at first; yet without it, this risk would be too much for any of us. I submit to you that there is one factor that sets the hazard in an entirely different focus. I mean *Christian humour.*

Socrates used "irony" to assist his maieutic task, but we are accorded a different gift, what the New Testament calls "hilarity." The best illustration of what I mean comes from the Old Testament, from the life story of Abraham and Sarah. This old couple are visited by the messenger from God with a promise that they will yet have a son of their own, through whom God's covenant-promise will be kept. And Sarah, who knew the "facts of life," that she was past child-bearing, finds this news so humorous that she laughs at it—and so does Abraham.

---

5.   No doubt Niles has in mind (as do I) the humanism of the early Marx rather than its development into ideological Marx-Leninism. See my *Prometheus Rebound* Ch. 8, "The Practical Death of God: Marx, Engels, Lenin," pp. 147-74.

But then—after nine months or so—a child is born! Once again Sarah can laugh, indeed she names the child Laughter, "Isaac" in the Hebrew tongue. She cries: "God has made laughter for me; everyone who hears will laugh over me." But now she is laughing with God, not at him; now she has seen the mystery of God's unique purpose and power, the prelude to the miracle of virgin birth. So Abraham and Sarah discover the good news about our life and our history, about the "divine comedy" that lies behind it and within it.

Even so shall we discover, especially when we become willing to risk our souls by descending into the hell of our generation's doubt and anxiety and sickness unto death—discover that Jesus Christ is there already, as Saviour and Lord. The risk of our ministry is the risk of evangelism and its social action. Yet these in turn bring us face to face with the secret of Christ's power, that it works through human weakness and service. A few days before he was hanged by the Gestapo, the young theologian Dietrich Bonhoeffer wrote: "This is the decisive difference between Christianity and all religions. Man's religiosity makes him look in his distress for the power of God in the world; he uses God as a Deus ex machina. The Bible, however, directs him to the powerlessness and suffering of God; only a suffering God can help."[6]

When we follow God in his humility and limitation in this way of the Cross, we find what is of critical importance for theology: that just as God has limited himself in Jesus Christ our Lord, so there will be a corresponding limitation about our knowledge of him. This limit will become the creative boundary-line where theology breaks forth in doxology: "O the depth of the riches, both of the wisdom and knowledge of God!"

Here we may close on a note that comes to us from those Early Fathers of the Eastern Church as distinct from traditional Latin or

---

6.　Bonhoeffer, *Letters and Papers from Prison* (SCM Fontana Books, 1959), p. 122.

Western theology.[7]* This teaches that we cannot live simply and solely from the Cross, from a symbol of death and judgment, but rather from its Resurrection side, the symbol of life and victory; and that this is the new age, the age of the new humanity of Jesus Christ, and of our new humanity in him. For this mystery of the new birth and growth means that Christ is alive and at work this day, pushing back the hand of time, renewing, refreshing, rejuvenating the world through his Church. His aim is simple: to make the Church more like himself—that is, younger and more virile with the power of his human perfection. Already the Church is affianced to Jesus Christ. But it is still marred by the old age in which it lives, it does not yet have sufficient hilarity to live entirely, from the future, from its great hope in him who is on his way. Therefore he is busily making it younger, ever younger, so that when he does come, it will be young enough to make a fitting Bride for the New Man.[8]

We are entering a great day in Canada, when the time is ripe for the shaping of a *Canadian* theology, the contribution of this young nation to the Church of Christ in this twentieth century. Surely we especially should be able to help recall the Church—and its world!—to this lost heritage of the dimension of joy, the joy that proceeds from living from our future, as from a Fountain of eternal youth.

---

7.   I develop this theme in later writings, particularly *The New Man* (1973).

8.   See *The Shepherd of Hermas* (2nd Century) for this analogy.

2

ELDERS' HOURS, MINISTERS' LICENSES, BISHOPS' GAITERS

Address to the Synod of Montreal-Ottawa,
15 October 1958, Cornwall, Ontario.

My subject is "Discipline in the Reformed Church." The title (chosen because you wouldn't have come for the actual theme) indicates three main aspects of the problem of discipline in this age of disturbance and revival in the Reformed Churches. What do we mean by "discipline?" It obviously has to do with "discipleship." But in the history of our Church it has played a decisive role, and I submit that we must recover the high Reformed doctrine of discipline, if we are to prove worthy of the challenge of the age.

First let us understand the marks or "notes" of the true Church, according to Reformed theology. (1) Where the Word of God is truly preached and heard; and (2) where the Sacraments of the Gospel are rightly administered. Now to this was usually added—sometimes as a third note—"and discipline duly upheld."[1] Thus the primary marks of

---

1.   Recent research by Robert Kingdon and others show that it was Vermigli who introduced this "third mark"—I argue this in "Vermigli on Penance—a Third

the Church describe the Ministry of the Word and Sacraments, while the whole structure of the Church which supports and expresses this Ministry is called "discipline."

Let me illustrate from our history. In the beginning of the Church's life, our Lord had given a Ministry commencing with the Apostles. In later generations came officers variously called Presbyters or Bishops. Through the need for a more centralized ministry there developed the "monarchical" or single Bishop assisted by Presbyters and an order of Deacons. But we all know the sad story of Church and State from this beginning in the Roman Empire—of Dark Ages and dark practices, of the separation of East from West, of how the Bishop at Rome grew into a Pope, and held the Western Church in thrall for a thousand years. Discipline had become something wielded by the Bishops, with the power of excommunication as a big stick over the people.

In Geneva, those independent citizens had got rid of their Bishop as early as 1519, and had taken the power of episcopal discipline into the hands of their Town Council. When John Calvin was asked to help reform the Church in Geneva, he saw that everything depended on regaining this episcopal discipline for the Ministry of Word and Sacraments. Calvin's great struggle with the Town Council was over this very issue.

Calvin's own doctrine of the Ministry and its discipline may be sketched as follows. Taking his cue from Cyprian, the ancient Church Father, he teaches that Jesus Christ is Bishop of the Church, that he institutes a kind of *sub-ministry* throughout the whole Church body, a common and universal episcopacy. Calvin, of course, was a great Patristic scholar, and took with utmost seriousness the kind of ministry and discipline of that Early Church, existing in unity up to the Sixth Century. He uses examples from that period to prove that the doctrine of "apostolic succession" as taught by Rome is mere "smoke," and does not affect the

---

Sacrament?," Sixteenth Century Studies Conference, Salt Lake City 2006, to be published in *Zwingliana*.

right to true Episcopal oversight. Thus he writes to the King of Poland about the reformation taking place there, and actually recommends that the system of Bishops be continued. For, he concludes, "it is one thing to hold a moderate dignity such as is not incompatible with the abilities of a man, and another to comprise the whole world under one overgrown government."[2]

You see what was happening. In the New Testament, bishops and presbyters are one and the same office. That's fine, we say today, it means there are no bishops, just presbyters. But Calvin and his friends argued the other way—not that bishops are reduced to presbyters, but that presbyters share an episcopal oversight. Not individually, we must add (I know we're all tempted to consider ourselves bishops!), but collectively—a collegiate or *corporate episcopacy*. Thus a group of Presbyters together is "the Bishop"—that is, the Presbytery is the Bishop.

Now this idea took different forms in different places. There were and are individual Reformed Bishops in Hungary. There were many Calvinists involved in the English Reformation who did not object to episcopal government. After all, John Knox was an Anglican priest who was once offered a bishopric! When the office of "Superintendent" was established in Scotland, it was considered replacing a Greek name for a Latin, but the office was the same. Yet at first they were interpreted in terms of corporate episcopacy, the oversight or discipline which derives from Jesus Christ Himself, "the only King and Head of the Church."

My own opinion is that this original, dynamic view of things was soon put out of focus by the successors of the Reformers, as Theodore Beza and others in Geneva stressed the doctrine of predestination in an extreme way. When Andrew Melville replaced Superintendents by the Court of Presbytery, however, it was still the same episcopal discipline that was at stake. And must we not seek for truth despite these

---

2.   Calvin, *Letter to the King of Poland*, 1554—see chapter eight on the same point.

names and titles and changes? Is not the word "bishop" just as firmly embedded in the New Testament as the word "presbyter"?

Let us see how this quick sketch of our history enlightens the three terms of our title.

1. ELDERS' HOURS

The Elders appointed in Geneva and in Scotland were the chief instruments of discipline. They were not intended to be mere disciplinarians, ecclesiastical policemen, wielding the big stick all over again. No; in the beginning—in Knox's First Book of Discipline and Melville's Second, those two blueprints of the Scottish Reformation—the word "discipline" is very broad, involving three kinds of people: Ministers, Teachers of the young from elementary school to University, and (note well!) the *poor*. The scheme outlined in these Books is nothing less than a type of welfare state, deriving from the Kingship of Christ over Nation as well as Church.

The idea didn't last, because it never really began. The nobles were not so convinced as the Church that the money should go to these causes. Therefore, the Elders were left little to concern them except the finding of offenders—did their people spend the whole time (of the Lord's Day) in the public and private exercises of God's worship? for example. They became known as the watchdogs of the community, seeking diligently for immorality in others. Robert Burns has given us the classic type, as Holy Willie prays:

> I bless and praise Thy matchless might,
> When thousands Thou hast left in night,
> That I am here before Thy sight,
> For gifts and grace
>
> A burning and a shining light
> To a' this place. ...
> Lord, hear my earnest cry and prayer
> Against that Presbytery of Ayr. ...

Indeed, Burns' poems give us a good picture of the bad side of the Kirk—its Holy Fairs, its Unco' Guid or Rigidly Righteous, its cutty stools for the penitent.

The old Scots Elder's chief duty was not to assist at the Sacrament but at the Preparatory Season, for he was in charge of the Communion Tokens. He "visited" in the role of spiritual spy and religious accountant. And since the chief sin was "houghmagandie," he must needs be up late to investigate this above all—hence (so tradition has it) the saying arose that someone was "keeping Elders' hours."

In our own *Book of Forms* there is a much healthier view of the Eldership, as in modern Scotland too. "As the pastors should be diligent in teaching and sowing the seed of the Word, so the elders should be careful in seeking the fruit of the same in the people" (§ 111). The outline of the Elder's duties reminds us of the broad and positive sweep of that original "discipline" in the Kirk: Christian education, youth work, missionary outreach, provision for the poor.

Therefore we may well ask ourselves, "Just what is a *ruling* Elder?" And we must answer, "One who rules by measuring or testing the Church against the Rule of the Bishopric of Jesus Christ its King and Head."

2. MINISTERS' LICENSES

The heart of the Reformed doctrine of the Ministry is that Jesus Christ is the chief Minister, who brings His people to new birth through the seed of His Word, and nourishes them by the milk and meat of that same Word. Therefore His Ministers are *teaching* Elders, congregational Rabbis. We do not believe that the Holy Spirit acts on his own, as it were, raising people up here and there to drive them into a "ministry" wherever they can get a hearing. We believe rather that the Spirit works "by and with the Word," and so calls us into Ministry of the Word and its Sacraments. He drives us to the Word of God in its various forms, makes us thirsty for more knowledge of this Word, and leads us to the Church "doctors" set apart to study, cherish and transmit such knowledge.

There was a day when the Presbyterian Church was the Church of "a learned ministry," whose place in the life and culture of the community and nation was accepted as representing serious intellectual discipline, and the mastery of theological science. Now this seems no longer true as a general statement. Partly is the changed situation due to the decline of expository preaching. Nowadays the Minister gets the text from some topic of the day (not bad in itself of course!) instead of the doctrinal event of the Church Year or from the Scripture passage dealt with in an orderly "diet" of preaching.[3]*

A symptom of our sickness is the hypocritical way we treat the languages of Holy Scripture. How many of our Ministers make diligent use of Hebrew and Greek in their weekly sermon preparation? How many consider themselves firstly as called to be *teachers*? In the Scottish Kirk of the Sixteenth Century however a Minister's needs were listed in the following significant order: "books, clothes, meat, fish, fuel and other things necessary" (*First Book of Discipline*).

Now as to the license to preach: its origin is somewhat foggy, but the principle is clear: that no one can arrogate to themselves the office of preaching, but must have the consent of the Presbytery—not of the people, mark you—they have a rightful voice in whom they call, but not in whom the Presbytery shall license and ordain.

Trials for License before a closed meeting of Presbytery remains the chief bulwark of our Ministerial discipline. Perhaps the low esteem into which these have fallen is the most obvious sign that the Presbytery has forgotten its episcopal office.[4] For "It pertains to the Presbytery to take heed that the Word of God is purely preached within its bounds, the sacraments rightly administered, the discipline rightly maintained, and the

---

3.   Nowadays the Lectionary has become popular even among Presbyterians.

4.   The Trials have now been transformed into a system of examination that removes the Presbytery from such direct responsibility.

ELDERS' HOURS, MINISTERS' LICENSES, BISHOPS' GAITERS

ecclesiastical goods uncorruptly Distributed"(*Book of Forms* 198). More about this in a moment.

The two exceptions we make to licensing are significant and of great practical importance for our Church. First, theological students are granted "certification" to a College, a kind of temporary license or "learner's permit" we might say. This is in order as an anticipation of their future licensing. But its danger is that our students tend to develop deplorable habits of preaching manners, and often, such pride in their practical success as to create serious problems for the College charged with homiletical instruction.

Second, what about "laymen" who preach? There are many with definite gifts of oratory—should not the Church somehow incorporate these more regularly within her structure? Is the problematic office of Catechist sufficient? Now these men fulfill a genuine calling by meeting the need of small vacant congregations throughout our Church. But here is the danger—there is too much of this unlicensed (illegitimate!) preaching, which often blinds such laymen to their legitimate vocation—witness in their daily work, in the workaday world. "Laymen's Sunday" was never meant to be a sounding-board for frustrated preachers, but rather an opportunity to teach this true "ministry of the laity" which our Presbyterian Men's organization is stressing so well.

3. BISHOPS' GAITERS

I put it like this to emphasize the fact that our usual mental picture of a Bishop is of an old gentleman in frock coat and gaiters, smoking a pipe and telling the latest story about the Archbishop of Canterbury. This is as naive a portrait as the one we have of what a Communist is like. (Come to think of it, don't Church of Scotland Moderators wear the same oldfashioned garb?)

A bishop, in our Reformed sense, is not an individual at all, but a group of Presbyters, a Presbytery. As we saw, our *Book of Forms* states its duties in the precise terms of the classic Reformed "marks of the

Church," so that it forms the essential structural core of its discipline. The Presbytery has the episcopal oversight and responsibility for all Ministers and Congregations within its bounds. We address it in petition as "The Reverend the Presbytery."

Just here, I submit to you, is the key to our urgent problem of discipline—in getting Presbyteries to exercise their episcopal function once again. One thinks of the decisions of the General Assembly that are given but lip service in Courts of Presbytery. One thinks of the distressing cases where discipline is required but sidestepped because difficult and distasteful. One thinks of the brethren who are always ready to insist that the "business" of the Courts is not theological but merely administrative. Yet the idea of Presbytery began in the Scottish weekly "exercise," a Bible study!—and the French *classis*, while the first Canadian Presbytery consciously established itself to deal with doctrinal material equally with the rest of its "business."

Yet the real crux of the rehabilitation of Presbytery, it seems to me, is the problem of the Boards and Committees of the General Assembly. Just what is their relationship to this episcopal discipline we have submitted as the right and responsibility of the Presbytery? We sometimes feel that certain Boards develop a kind of episcopal authority in the matter of expenditures and appointments. There is sense in which this is both necessary and orderly, within limits. Yet there is also the dangerous natural tendency towards authoritarianism in an increasingly centralized Church such as ours. But notice that one Board is actually singled out in our constitution as having some kind of archiepiscopal status: "The Board of Administration shall coordinate the activities of the existing Boards ... (and) shall take concern for and initiate action helpful to the life and work of the Church" (*B. of F.* App. 2). How far is this rule practicable without interfering with "the government of this Church by Sessions, Presbyteries, Synods and General Assemblies"?

Finally—what can we do about *Synod*? Is this Cinderella of our ecclesiastical household perhaps the answer to some of these questions? Synod is not really legislative, it has no share in the doctrine of government represented by the Barrier Act, for instance. Nor has it any real supervision over the Presbyteries within its bounds. Therefore should it not be guided into less spectacular but more foundational ways, ways of study, conference and the like? Such theological moulding of Synod agenda might well be a partial answer to our need of refreshment, recreation and rejuvenation. For the Church Reformed is a Church always in need of being re-formed: *ecclesia reformata semper reformanda.*

3

THE THEOLOGY OF THE PREACHING OFFICE

Address to Conference of Professors of Homiletics,
Toronto, May 1960.[1]

The office of preaching has been captured in our day by "practical, theology." As a result it is the problem of method or technique that dominates the homiletical landscape. This approach depends on a very significant assumption, namely that the nature and the purpose of preaching are so well understood that most of our time can be spent on the "practical" question of methodology. But what if one is mistaken about this nature and purpose? Then all methodology will be as highly impractical as the behaviour of the athlete who turned out for the tennis tournament dressed in rugby uniform.

To avoid any such confusion, we shall be well advised to explore the background of homiletics, the doctrine of the preaching office. First let us consider preaching as a form of the Word of God. Then let us examine the nature of communication. Finally, let us turn to some. suggestions about the ministerial office.

---

1.   Published in the *Canadian Journal of Theology*, VII (1961), No. 1, pp. 4-12.

1. PREACHING AS A FORM OF THE WORD OF GOD

It was a dictum of the Reformers that "the preaching of the word of God *is* the word of God."[2] There is a sense in which every Christian, especially every Christian theologian, has to begin again and again with the doctrine of the Word of God. For Christianity is not a religion, something to be approached exclusively in terms of comparative religion or the philosophy of religion; it's a *Gospel*, a revelation through the divine Word that became incarnate in Jesus Christ our Lord. This Word was "handled" by Apostles (1 John 1:1)—just how can one "handle" a *word*? That is the stinging question with which the Gospel faces us.

It is Karl Barth who has given us the most searching analysis of the doctrine of the Word, which he treats as prolegomenon to Church Dogmatics. Barth begins with the fact that the Church exists in and through proclamation.

> The language about God to be found in the Church is meant to be proclamation, so far as it is directed towards man in the form of preaching and sacrament, with the claim and in an atmosphere of expectation that in accordance with its commission it has to tell him the Word of God to be heard in faith.[3]

Barth analyses the doctrine of the Word according to its three forms, as preached, as written, and as revealed. The first form includes both preaching and sacraments; they are (existentially) first because this is the actual starting place for sinful humans, when we hear the Word of God addressed to us in preaching and sacrament. From there we may be led to the second "form" of the Word, namely the written Word of Scripture, and thence to the third. The last is primary in an ontological sense, the Word as revealed in past and future and therefore in the present too.

---

2.   Praedicatio verbi dei est verbum dei, attributed to both Luther and Bullinger.

3.   K. Barth, *Church Dogmatics*, 1/1, § 3, p. 51.

It is preaching that constitutes the growing edge of the Church; it is the form in which the Word presses in upon us, convicts us and blesses us, judges and saves. Therefore, when we speak about preaching we are speaking about a form of the Word of God, and by implication we are speaking dogmatically, about a datum that must be enlightened by theological reflection and understanding. That is why Barth completes the section heading referred to by adding:

> So far as, in spite of this claim and this expectation, it is *man's* word,
> it becomes the material of dogmatics, i.e., of the investigation into
> its responsibility, measured by the Word of God which it means to
> proclaim.

Now the eternal, original and unique Word of God is the "second person" of the Trinity, incarnate in Jesus the Christ. According to the classic Christology of the Church, he is both divine and human, "very God and very man." The other forms of the Word must correspond proportionately to him if they are to be valid forms of the Word. Therefore they too will partake of this divine-human relatedness, and will be both truly divine, a Word of God, and truly human, a human word. One must not transubstantiate preaching (or scripture) into a pure and simple divine Word; neither can one so emphasize the human element that oratorical splendour becomes the measure of the office. A christological heresy lurks behind both errors; preaching must be understood in the light of christology. Dogmaticians on several fronts have been reminding us of this truth, that divine and human are together in Christ as a matter of fact, and that we must consider proclamation under the twin rubric, "The Word of God and the Word of Man in Christian Preaching." As it happens, this formula is the title of another of Barth's subsections, but lest we imagine that it denotes a peculiarly modern approach, let us turn back to Luther.

Luther was nobody's fool. When he said that the preaching of the Word of God *is* the Word of God, he was quite well aware that many sermons are not worthy of such a description. This is why he stressed preaching of the *Word of God*. Let us listen to Luther's typically bold words:

> A preacher must not say the Lord's Prayer, nor ask forgiveness of sins, when he has preached (if he is a true preacher), but must confess and exult with Jeremiah: Lord, thou knowest that what has gone forth from my mouth is right and pleasing to thee. He must boldly say with St. Paul and all the apostles and prophets: *Haec dixit dominus*, Thus saith God himself; or again: In this sermon, I am a confessed apostle and prophet of Jesus Christ. It is neither necessary nor good to ask here for forgiveness of sins, as though the teaching were false. For it is not my word but God's, which he neither will nor can forgive me, and for which he must always praise and reward me, saying: You have taught rightly for I have spoken through you and the Word is mine. Whoever cannot boast thus of his preaching repudiates preaching; for he expressly denies and slanders God.[4]

Luther's doctrine of preaching is this: these two facts are entirely logical: that those who preach the Word of God must necessarily be sent by God; and, conversely, that those who are sent by God cannot proclaim anything but the Word of God. Therefore he can stress the unity of the divine-human event of preaching:

> 'Tis a right excellent thing, that every honest pastor's and preacher's mouth is Christ's mouth, and his word and forgiveness is Christ's word and forgiveness. . . . Therefore, we do well to call the pastor's and preacher's word which he preacheth, God's Word. For the office is not the pastor's or preacher's, but God's. . . . On the last day God will say to me, Hast thou also preached that? I shall say, Yea, exactly. Then God will say to thee, Hast thou also heard that? And thou shalt answer, Yea. And he saith further, Wherefore hast thou then not believed? And then thou sayest, Oh, I held it for a word of man, since a poor chaplain or village parson uttered it. So shall the same word which sticketh in thine heart accuse thee and be thine accuser

---

4. For quotations from Luther, see *Luther's Works* (ed. J. J. Pelikan), voL 22 (St. Louis, 1957), pp. 370ff.; 482ff. Cf. K. Barth, *C. D.* 1/1 (Edinburgh, 1949), pp. 101ff.; 1/2 (Edinburgh, 1956), pp. 746f.

and judge at the last day. For it is God's Word, 'tis God himself thou hast heard. . . . See to it, how thou standest.

Luther is an excellent guide in any talk of preaching. Preaching is a form of God's own Word, not human words about God's Word, but a unique kind of speech that is at once human and divine. A doctrinal problem emerges, of course, parallel to that found in the great eucharistic debates between Lutheran and Reformed in the sixteenth and seventeenth centuries. It is largely our failure to push back this debate to the more basic problem of the office of preaching considered in relation to christology that has caused us to continue fruitless discussion about problematic issues. Is not Christ himself present "in, with and under" the preacher's words? This is Luther's question. Are not these words to be judged in terms of their faithfulness to the textual exposition? This is the Reformed concern.

2. THE PROBLEM AND THE MYSTERY OF COMMUNICATION

Gabriel Marcel has forcefully expressed the important distinction between *problem* and *mystery*. The one may be rationally solved, but the other demands personal decision and commitment, for genuine mysteries "remain mysterious even when understood, because, though understood, they exceed our comprehension."[5] The communication of truth between persons is perhaps mystery as well as problem, as Augustine maintained in his dialogue *De Magistro* ("The Teacher") which served as textbook for medieval pedagogy. Certainly for Christian truth "mystery" is the proper category; it forms the "proper domain" of theology.[6] Linguistic philosophers today tend to miss the distinction; but at least they serve to force theology back upon prior questions of the validity and appropriateness of language about God.

---

5.   M.B. Foster, *Mystery and Philosophy* (London. 1957), pp. 18, 20; see G. Marcel, *The Mystery of Being* (Chicago: H. Regnery, 1960).

6.   Cf. M. J. Scheeben, *The Mysteries of Christianity* (St. Louis, 1946), p. 18.

Communication is a problem because it involves a discipline of submission or conformity to the truth one seeks to learn. The mind must be accommodated to the nature of its "object." Christian truth, however, is not simply personal but a Person, this person who is also Lord. He has chosen to be identical with his message, he comes to us as "Christ clothed with his Gospel" (Calvin). That is to say, Christ gives himself through his word of address, what he communicates is *himself.* This is why one cannot really "communicate" this truth as if it were truth "about" Christ, as if one comes to "know" this truth apart from one's conversion. Beyond the problem of understanding lies the mystery of the Saviour's redeeming encounter with his people.

How different must *preaching* be from *oratory,* then! Indeed, oratory may become a major stumbling-block to "good" preaching, a confusion of vocations. (Of course, in classical times the art of rhetoric served to communicate truth in the elegant and persuasive speech appropriate to high matters.) It was Kierkegaard who stressed this fact of the personal being of Christian truth. He also stressed its historical factuality; you do not learn this as you do the timeless truths of mathematics. For this Christian truth is nailed to the scheme of history, to Jews, to Church Fathers and Doctors, to teachers in time and space. It addresses us in history, through historical means. This is why some people hear it very badly put to them, and many do not hear it at all. Every church school pupil recognizes this problem, while mature theologians must still argue the point.

This historicity is not a defect of Christianity; on the contrary, it is one of those peculiar problems that are signs of its mysterious character. When the Word became incarnate, he submitted himself to all that history means: limitation, dependence on historical communication, the contingency of space and time. God has entered time, has become human, has exchanged heaven for earth—or even, briefly, for "hell." This unsettling fact means that our preaching ought to proclaim:

God's in his *hell,*
All's right with the world!

37

Such a reversal of roles is the heart of the Gospel. It prevents Christianity from becoming a religion of a heavenly deity known by spiritual attainments. If God is to be known in his singular humanity, then the decisive thing is the Word in its forms, the proclamation of Christian preaching and sacraments. And this involves the other aspect of the scandalous Gospel, namely, that God acts like this because he is reconciling the world unto himself, so that man cannot "know" this truth without being caught in its reconciling power. This communication "solves" the problem of knowing by the mystery of being.

The unity of knowing and being is seen in the strange and wonderful Hebrew usage according to which the same verb (*yada*) is used for God's knowledge of his people and for sexual union. It is seen also in the fact that church proclamation demands both preaching and sacrament. The liturgical revival has helped us here. In Britain, for instance, it used to be said that in Scotland one always knew what the preacher would say in his sermon but never in his prayer, while in England a clergyman's prayers could be fully anticipated, but certainly not his sermon. Today the two emphases are held together in creative tension, so that although the balance of the two is no easy matter, yet there is a growing recognition that the sermon belongs in a proper liturgical setting, while liturgy involves the preaching office. (Incidentally, it needs to be stressed that there is no such thing as "non-liturgical" worship. *Leitourgia* means service, the "people's work," and any order of worship is liturgical. The order may be bad or naïve liturgy but it cannot be *non-* liturgical.)

In reality, therefore, preaching has not only an outward sacramental relationship, but an inner sacramental structure. Ronald Ward's book, *Royal Sacrament*, describes preaching as "the sacramental offering of a Person. . . . The ultimate aim of preaching is to give Christ. He is offered in words; He may be received in Person. Thus preaching is a sacrament."[7] On this view, there is memory, *anamnêsis*, and re-presentation, not only

---

7.   R. A. Ward, *Royal Sacrament* (London, 1958), pp. 14, 22.

in the Eucharist but also in preaching as well; in its turn, eucharistic prayer includes the tremendous proclamation of the kerygma. This sacramental prayer is a kind of preaching, just as preaching is a kind of sacrament. We must add that such a position involves a broader definition of "sacrament," or perhaps the category of "sacramental." (Strictly speaking, the two dominical sacraments of baptism and eucharist preclude extending the term, although Ward's point about the kerygmatic dimension of sacrament is excellent.)

If oratory may obscure the preaching office, so may the misuse of odds and ends of liturgical cosmetics, so to speak, which hide and distort the true face of divine worship. The old term "diet of worship" signified something deeper—the balanced meal of orderly progression both in the liturgical year and in expository preaching from week to week, a solid diet of meat rather than milk (Heb. 5:11-14).[8]

What we are recovering today is the dimension of *dramatic encounter* in both preaching and sacrament. In these two forms of proclamation, Christ himself confronts us. Just because he was and is the Word incarnate, he confronts us in the flesh, with words that seek to be deeds. That is why we may use the term *drama* with some degree of correctness and fruitfulness. Drama, after all, began in religious liturgy. Two and a half millennia ago, in the cultic worship of Dionysos, the classic form of the dramatic art, Greek tragedy, was born. This was a "mystery religion;" its theme was death and resurrection; its liturgy involved ritual singing and dancing, entrance and exit, light and darkness, pantomime and revelation. And one day—so legend has it—a chorister named Thespis turned from his part in the chorus to address the worshippers in the very name of the god. Even the developed art did not lose this elemental conviction that drama is a liturgical act in which the power of the god himself is present. Drama is a peculiar sort of dialogue in which players and spectators, through pathetic and empathetic encounter, represent the basic facts of life. Together they enter the dimension of suffering

---

8.   See "Where's the Beef?" below.

and fate in order to win through to hope and immortality. The drama is a meeting of lives in a ritual of contest and struggle, *agon*, in the crucible of death.

How much of all this can we or should we apply to preaching? Is there a parallel to Greek experience in the wholeness of worship restored in preaching and sacraments, in word and deed, in things said *(kerygma)* and things acted *(drama)?* Are we perhaps dealing with a pagan grasp of that parabolic "sign" which is so central to the biblical understanding of comrnunication? The *mysterion* of the Kingdom of God is mirrored in the mystery of parable and miracle by which Christ brought it in. These were signs *(semeia)* of the divine-human Sign himself.[9] Communication involves a unique kind of human language and human work, and so the office of preaching involves a unique kind of function.

3. MINISTERIAL MIDWIFERY AND MOTHERHOOD

The old method of catechetical instruction by question and answer has recently been investigated by T. F. Torrance, who defends it on the ground that theology is bound to be *dialogical:* "It is concerned throughout with the address of the Word of God and the obedient response of faith."[10] Preaching is part of the dialogue between God and man; but this dialogue has already received a definite completion in Jesus Christ, the one true God "who loves man and calls him in grace, and the one true Man who loves God and follows him in faith."

---

9.   It is a pity that Paul Tillich has redefined "sign" and "symbol" to the confusion of the biblical concept of *semeion*. Cf. *Systematic Theology,* Vol II (Chicago, 1957), p. 9. For Tillich, sign is "only a sign," whereas symbol "participates in the reality which is symbolized." Although this has some weight in view of the traditional understanding of theological symbolics, nevertheless the classic Scholastic and Renaissance discussions of *signum* and *res* presupposed the participation of the "sign" in the "reality" signified; this was decisive in the eucharistic controversies, at least. Cf. T. F. Torrance, "A Study in New Testament Communication" (*Scottish Journal of Theology,* September, 1950), for the concepts of *lalia* and *logos* in Christ's parabolic teaching.

10.   T. F. Torrance, *The School of Faith* (London, 1959), p. xliii.

The Preacher witnesses to this event named Jesus Christ, but he is also part of the event. This involvement is inherent in the mystery of communication, but it reaches a peculiar intensity in Christian communication. An excellent analogy to assist us here is that of the Virgin Birth—or of Mary's office of handmaiden, if we wish to by-pass the problem of the place of the Birth in the Gospel records. I am convinced that the Protestant failure to appreciate the significance of mystical theology for its doctrine of faith, despite the clear emphasis of Luther and Calvin, is reflected in its suspicion of the person of Mary. (This suspicion, of course, is not quieted by the expansion of Mariological dogma in the Church of Rome.)

Mary is a picture of humanity dedicated to the doing of the Spirit of power, whose visitation engendered the Word like seed within her. He comes and goes, this Spirit; such is his freedom. But the coming and going are according to the Word, for he is the Spirit of Jesus Christ. The office of preaching cannot be spoken of fruitfully or realistically except in terms of the office of the Holy Spirit. There is much talk these days about our neglect of the doctrine of the Spirit. It is true that the Church has never articulated a consistent doctrine of the third person of the Trinity as it has of the first and second, but does not one reason for this omission lie in the very nature of the Spirit? He is not "objective" in the same sense as Father and Son (I speak improperly); no one witnesses to him for his own sake. His work consists in witnessing to our Lord, in bringing him to birth in men, and in bringing men to birth in him. This is why the doctrine of the Spirit is a kind of postscript to the doctrine of Christ, rendering it vital and relevant. Pneumatology is applied Christology.

In such a context, the ministerial office is seen as a kind of midwifery. It was Socrates who described himself as a species of midwife, a maieutic philosopher assisting at the birth of ideas. Just a century ago, Kierkegaard compared the Socratic method with theology. Because of human sinfulness there are not "true ideas" within, already conceived. We can act as midwives only to the point at which our dialogue is no longer effective, when we must become direct witnesses to the truth that is outside man, in Jesus Christ. By this means Kierkegaard advanced one step beyond Socrates.

Let us advance one step beyond Kierkegaard. We should take with the utmost seriousness Paul's words to the Galatians, "My little children, with whom I am again in travail until Christ be formed in you," and to the Corinthians, "I became your father in Christ Jesus through the Gospel."[11] And we must also consider how Paul says, time and again, that by faith someone is "in Christ," and Christ is "in us." This is nothing less than a definition of faith as *union with Christ*. I submit that this is the classic and normative definition, enunciated by our Lord himself, by St. Paul, by the Fathers, by mystical theologians, and by the Reformers. Without this definition, faith becomes a human work, a subjective distortion matched by a false kind of preaching.

In Christ a human being becomes a new creation. But the other side of this miracle and mystery of the new birth—Christ's side as it were—is the fact that our Lord himself still condescends to us in the humility of his revelation, still comes into one's life in the form of an infant, is "born again" whenever the event of faith occurs: "O holy child of Bethlehem … be born in us today." What the Holy Spirit conceives and the Church mothers is a new person in Christ and Christ in that person. It is at this birth that we are called to assist in our maieutic office of communicating the Word through preaching. Here too is the *risk* of our ministry. The complex nature of the union of faith, especially the mystery of its motherhood, means that our midwifery passes over into parenthood, that our ministry is convulsed with the travail of birth itself. To deliver—yea, to be parent to—babes in Christ; to share Christ's own ministry as he communicates himself to men through his ordained ministry of word and sacrament; this labour involves great hazard. For what if, by false teaching, or by true teaching at wrong times, we deliver an abortion, or stifle an infant heartbeat?

---

11.   Gal. 4:19; 1 Cor. 4:15.

That wise teacher of the early Church, Origen of Alexandria, expressed the risk when he said:

> I often think of the maxim, "It is dangerous to talk about God, even if what you say about him is true." The man who wrote that must, I am sure, have been a shrewd and dependable character. There is danger, you see, not only in saying what is untrue about God but even in telling the truth about him if you do it at the wrong time.[12]

According to this view, preaching requires both identification and nonidentification with those to whom we preach. In writing of "the gift of ministry," Daniel Jenkins has described the true preacher:

> All the doubts and difficulties and terrors which confront mortal men as they face the temptations and hazards and ambiguities of existence should be his familiar ground. Life at its grimmest and harshest should have an almost morbid fascination for him. Wherever there is trouble he should be found. He is the one man among all men who cannot be permitted the luxury of a sheltered life. . . . Of all men, he has to be the freest thinker, allowing the most dangerous of facts to lead him wherever they will, without regard to personal safety or comfort or professional prestige, offering himself on the altar of God's truth, that God's glory might be made manifest in his weakness. [13]

Such identification is the secret of genuine dialogue, in which the preacher does not confront his fellowmen as someone "religious" addressing sinners, but simply as *"man to man."* Both stand in the common humanity that Christ seeks and saves. At the same time, the preacher must recognize that his message is not identifiable with the standards and the assumptions of his hearers; surely it is a prime responsibility of homiletics teachers today to stress this non-identity, this radical break, this disturbing two-edged sword of preaching. There is too much conformity today; there are too many domesti-

---

12. *Hom. Ezek.* I.11.

13. D. Jenkins, *The Protestant Ministry* (London: Faber & Faber, 1958).

cated parsons, too many preachers who have made themselves "homiletical eunuchs" for the sake of a heavenly kingdom. This will not do; only authentic humanity will do in the pulpit. Otherwise we fail to let the genuine *scandalon* of the Gospel confront our hearers. Bultmann is trying to make this clear, when he insists that "Christ meets us in the preaching as one crucified and risen. He meets us in the word of preaching and nowhere else. The faith of Easter is just this—faith in the word of preaching."[14] And Paul Tillich also speaks of overcoming the wrong stumbling blocks ("our inability to communicate") in order "to bring people face to face with the right stumbling block and enable them to make a genuine decision."[15]

Once again the problem and the mystery of communication emerge to challenge us. The problem is complex: to revive biblical preaching as something more than mere "concordance preaching" which strings together thematic texts and thinks this is exposition; to find ways of using the Christian year and the lectionary as practical guides for a diet of preaching; to define methods of evangelism and teaching within the preaching office; to venture into new forms of dialogue and conversation, lest we define preaching too narrowly in terms of a pulpit message once a week, thus missing that "holy worldliness" to which Christ is calling us outside.

But too much concentration on the problems creates pessimists, experts of despair, ecclesiastical beatniks. We must cultivate a lighter touch. The maieutic task of Socrates involved the concept of *irony*; ours involves theological *humour*, the effect of justifying grace. When Abraham and Sarah received the promise of a son they laughed quite rudely, for they knew the facts of life, and so realized that this promise was humanly impossible. Then a son was born. Once again Sarah laughed; indeed she named her son "Laughter," *Isaac*. Surely it is in the Church alone that we can find such hearty humour at the good news

---

14.   R. Bultmann, "New Testament and Mythology," in H. W. Bartsch (ed.), *Kerygma and Myth* (London, 1953), p. 41.

15.   P. Tillich, *Theology of Culture* (New York, 1959), p. 213.

of what God has done and continues to do in his overruling kindness. This is the secret of faith, and pre-eminently of the preachers caught up in the dynamics of its actuality. Shortly before his execution by the Gestapo, Dietrich Bonhoeffer put it like this:

> This is the decisive difference between Christianity and all religions. Man's religiosity makes him look in his distress for the *power* of God in the world; he uses God as a *Deus ex machina*. The Bible, however, directs him to the powerlessness and suffering of God; only a suffering God can help.[16]

---

16.   Bonhoeffer, *Letters and Papers from Prison* (London: SCM Press, 1953) p. 122.

4

THE AUTHORITY OF
THE CANON

Paper read to The Canadian Theological Society, 1958.[1]

M y appointed task is to address the topic of this paper from the
point of view of the philosophy of religion. We all know that this
science has fallen upon bad times over the past decades. But a few years
ago it changed its name to Philosophical Theology, accepted Paul Tillich
as chief spokesman, and now happily pursues linguistic analysis, asks
existential questions, and perhaps—at night and in private—reads a little
of Karl Barth.

In view of this situation, how is the philosopher of religion (or the
philosophical theologian) to approach the subject of the authority of the
canon? I propose to begin with Kierkegaard's idea of revelation and apostolicity, then to relate this to the problem of canonicity and tradition, and
finally to show the inadequacy of Barth's christological analogy and the
need for a reformulated doctrine of inspiration. If it is somewhat ominous

---

1.   *Canadian Journal of Theology*, Vol. V (1959) No. 1, pp. 35-43.

to begin with Kierkegaard and end with Barth, to attempt all this in one paper is a kind of lunacy. On both counts I crave your indulgence.

1. THE DIFFERENCE BETWEEN A GENIUS AND AN APOSTLE

Adolph Peter Adler, *Magister Artium*, Lutheran priest in Denmark, and author of four books in the Hegelian vogue, experienced in 1842 a "vision of light" in which Jesus bade him burn his books, and dictated the substance of a new one. Adler was deposed after an enquiry in which he admitted that "revelation was perhaps too strong an expression" for his experience. Adler's contemporary, Søren Kierkegaard, rejoiced at first that perhaps now Christendom had what it required, someone to claim divine authority in such a way as to scandalize it into a Socratic confession of its ignorance of Christian truth. But Adler lacked sufficient naïveté to maintain the ironic situation. Therefore Kierkegaard writes:

> We will stop here and look carefully before us, for it seems clear
> enough that the upshot of Adler's whole story is that he is a genius.
> *Quel bruit pour une omelette!* All honour to genius. In case Adler is
> a genius, in God's name! I certainly shall not envy him for that. But
> he began by having had a revelation—though *summa summarum* by
> this we are to understand that he is a genius.[2]

Kierkegaard's thesis is that between an apostle and a genius there is a qualitative distinction, the decisive factor being divine authority. The genius is born, the apostle is made. The genius develops from his potential possibility, while the apostle's existence is contingent upon the historical actuality of the divine revelation which constitutes him such. Kierkegaard goes on to satirize that "clerical ignorance" which prostitutes Christianity by eulogizing, for instance, the genius of St. Paul—his style and artistic use of language. Why not rather "maintain

---

2.   Kierkegaard, *On Authority and Revelation* (NY: Harper, 1966) p. 102.

that his work as an upholsterer must have been so perfect that no upholsterer either before or since has been able to equal it?"

The episode of Adler and Kierkegaard points up in a striking manner
the basic problem of our philosophy of revelation: that the historicity of
Christian truth involves a unique, contingent and unrepeatable factor
that constitutes a scandal to philosophers—most notably Lessing. He
claimed that "accidental truths of history can never establish necessary
truths of reason," and refused "to dream of suspending nothing less than
all eternity by a spider's thread," meaning the words of the witnesses of
Christianity's first period.[3]* Now we cannot avoid offending Lessing and
his friends. Although Christianity learns much from people of genius,
it is not built upon their teaching, upon the fruits of human wisdom,
however lofty. Its one foundation is an Apostle sent from God, namely
Jesus the Christ (Heb. 3:1); and with him in this foundational Apostolate
are those whom he in turn has sent (Eph. 2:20).

Theological students are taught that an apostle is "one sent with a
commission." But the decisive character of apostolicity is its relation to
the Incarnation, indeed to the forty days between Christ's Resurrection
and Ascension. Just as Christ was sent into the world at a certain time
and place—so that Caesar Augustus and Pontius Pilate become involved
in the event—even so are the apostles called and sent because of this
space-time phenomenon, this singular coincidence of time and eternity,
this *historical* figure. Revelation as Incarnation of the Word means a distinction of times: the time of Christ, the time of the apostolate, the time
of the church that received its canon, and the continuing time of church
proclamation.

This radical nature of apostolicity is best illustrated by the thorny
problem of St. Paul's conversion. We may begin from a text like Mark
3: 14: "and he appointed twelve, to be with him, and to be sent out to
preach." After the Ascension, Peter set forth the criteria of apostolicity

---

3.   See G.A. Michalson, *Lessing's "Ugly Ditch:" A Study of Theology and History*
(Un. Park: Penn,. State U.P., 1986).

quite explicitly: "So one of the men who have accompanied us during all the time that the Lord Jesus went in and out among us, beginning from the baptism of John until the day when he was taken up from us—one of these men must become with us a witness to his resurrection" (Acts 1: 21f). Justus and Matthias fulfilled the criteria, and the lot was cast between them. Since this was after the Ascension, after the event which sealed the resurrection with its veil of a hidden dimension, with its infinite recession into the being of the Godhead, therefore the criteria could apply only retroactively, to a limited (and diminishing) number of men.

On the Damascus Road, Saul the Pharisee claims to have received the commissioning of an apostle. His claim has nothing to do with religious genius, but with the fact that the nature of his vision united him with the apostolate, crowned him, in a unique yet valid sense, with the criteria of the witnesses to the Resurrection. Thus he describes himself as one born too late for normal apostolic vision, but nevertheless, like an abortion unnaturally alive, to be added to the list of witnesses: "Last of all, as to one untimely born, he appeared also to me" (1 Cor. 15: 8). In effect and in kind, this is a pre-Ascension vision: "Am I not an apostle? Have I not seen Jesus our Lord?" (1 Cor. 9:1).

It is this meaning of apostolicity that the religious philosopher misses in much of today's research. To take an illustrious example, C. H. Dodd finds the authority of the Bible in "the authority of experts in the knowledge of God, masters in the art of living; the authority of religious genius," and describes Jesus as one "in whom religious genius reached its highest point and passed into something greater still."[4] Dodd's basis is the primary authority of truth itself, and he sees clearly that the real problem is the way God conveys his truth to us. Yet his concept of "genius" compromises the constitutive orientation of the apostolate, and surely of Christ himself. The canon was closed because the relation of the New Testament authors to the apostolic witness

---

4.   Dodd, *The Authority of the Bible* (New York: Harper & Bros., 1929), pp. 24, 27.

was thought to form a closed circle, like the relation of the apostles themselves to Christ. Paul could be referred backwards into this circle, but not forwards into the category of religious genius. The latter would have meant an extension *ad infinitum,* so that a Teresa in the sixteenth century or an Adler in the nineteenth might be considered equally authoritative.

2. THE CANON AND TRADITION

The formal criteria of canonicity have proved complex in the history of the church, and have combined with the working of some internal criterion as well. The Old Testament canon was not closed finally until early in the Christian era. The rabbinic tradition of the post-exilic community demanded that a prophetic book be written in Hebrew and before the time of Nehemiah. Yet *Ecclesiasticus* fulfils both tests and was not accepted. The New Testament case is similar. Some twenty books were universally recognized by the second century church as a basic canon. The two chief marks appear to have been apostolic origin and general usage, with Marcion as a negative test. The *Shepherd* of Hermas, although referred to by Irenaeus as "scripture," was rejected at Rome because Hermas wrote "quite recently, in our own times." The famous listing of Eusebius in the fourth century indicates seven disputed books, if we include Hebrews and Revelation, which were accepted in certain parts of the Church. The five generally disputed were James, II Peter, II and III John, and Jude.

The term *canon,* meaning staff, rule, pattern, originally signified the whole rule of faith, the apostolic doctrine. When the fourth century church applied the term to its official list of writings, was it making a particular application of a general principle, or perhaps narrowing the meaning of the term? This is the question at the heart of our contemporary problem of Tradition. I submit in answer, however, that the church from the second to the fourth centuries was a church in reaction, forced to define and to declare its authoritative rule of faith and life, and that it was able at last to say that its canon was a written, finalized, prophetic-apostolic word.

In equating its canon with scripture, with a group of writings, the church was acknowledging a certain independence or autonomy, a "freedom towards her and power over her," of this canon. Thus the church cannot be said properly to "create" her canon, but rather to recognize and declare the nature and bounds of the rule created and given by her Lord. The closing of the canon corresponded to the closed circle of historical revelation on which her existence depended.

Yet the closing of the canon was a "church" event, and therefore not simply transcendent or divine. The formal and material criteria remain operative, so that each generation must accept the canon by its own decision of faith. This truth was illustrated in the sixteenth century, when the canon was modified in two ways. In the first place, the problematic Apocrypha were declared to be uncanonical in the proper and therefore authoritative sense, by the Reformed party at least. Secondly, the seven New Testament books which had been suspect in the Early Church (the *antilegomena)* were once again questioned, by Luther, Calvin, Brenz—not to mention Erasmus and even Cardinal Cajetan!

Luther's stress falls on the *content* of scripture: it preaches or treats of Christ; that is its office, and so its test *(was Christum treibet).* He calls the Bible "in truth the spiritual body of Christ," and Christ the "mathematical point of holy scripture." He makes an interesting distinction between the Old Testament as scripture proper because of its written form, and the New Testament as properly a *preached* Gospel. His radical emphasis on the criterion of the preaching of Christ led him to write, in the familiar passage from the *Preface* to James and Jude:

> All the genuine sacred books agree in this, that all of them preach
> Christ and deal with him. That is the true test by which to judge all
> books, when we see whether they deal with Christ or not, since all
> the scriptures show us Christ, and St. Paul will know nothing but
> Christ. What does not teach Christ is not apostolic even though
> St. Peter or St. Paul taught it; again, what preaches Christ would be
> apostolic even though Judas, Annas, Pilate and Herod did it.

Thus Luther can state that "John's Gospel and St. Paul's Epistles, especially that to the Romans, and St. Peter's First Epistle, are the true kernel and marrow of all books." As early as his September Bible of 1522 he had separated the books of Hebrews, James, Jude and Revelation in the table of contents, thus preparing for Lutheranism's distinction between a proto- and deutero-canon. The book of James, that "right strawy epistle," is on occasion called "a good book," but Luther also declared, "One of these days I'll use James to light the fire!"[5]

With John Calvin we take a careful step forward, which will have mixed effects in later years. Calvin suggests one valid "proof" for the authority of the canon, the justly famous "inward witness of the Holy Spirit" (*testimonium internum spiritus sancti*)—not originated but best articulated by him.

> Let it be considered, then, as an undeniable truth, that they who have been inwardly taught by the Spirit, feel an entire acquiescence in the scripture, and that it is self-authenticated, carrying with it its own evidence; it ought not to be made the subject of demonstration and arguments from reason; but it obtains the credit which it deserves with us by the testimony of the Spirit [*Inst.* 1.7.5].

But in the next chapter he proceeds to give "arguments from reason" as a kind of secondary "proof" to those experiencing the Spirit's prior witness. Calvin's method here presents a like problem to that of his doctrine of predestination. Unfortunately, historic Calvinism has managed to place the emphasis in both doctrines on the secondary rationalizing rather than Calvin's primary grappling with the mystery of the Spirit's office. Thus Scripture becomes itself instrumental, object of the Spirit's witness only in a secondary and derivative way.

The *Westminster Confession of Faith*, however, is faithful to Calvin on this point. After indicating those qualities of Scripture "whereby it doth abundantly evidence itself to be the Word of God," the Confession con-

---

5.   *Luther's Works*, ed. E.T. Bachmann (Phila: Muhlenberg Press, 1960), Vol. 35, p. 396.

cludes, "Yet notwithstanding, our full persuasion and assurance of the infallible truth, and divine authority thereof, is from the inward work of the Holy Spirit, bearing witness by and with the Word in our heart" (1.5).

Perhaps these notes from Luther and Calvin illustrate their conviction that the authority of the canon partakes of an absolute character. For them, this is not a question of a primary source of authority within a relative context of complementary strands of tradition, such as "the shape of the liturgy" as Dom Gregory Dix outlined it, or the rule of truth or faith as Tertullian and Irenaeus use the terms. And even if the Reformers, like Athanasius before them, argued for certain foundational doctrines as contained in scripture only indirectly or implicitly (an argument *de re ipsa* but not *de vocabulo)*, this was not felt to question the "sufficient authority" of scripture in the church. It was their consistent and insistent enunciation of this principle that led to the erection of a counter-church beginning with the Tridentine decrees. For it was the Council of Trent which built a new structure on largely unformed ideas. It brought the old Vincentian Rule up to date: now there were to be two explicitly marked channels by which revelation is transmitted, scripture and tradition, each to be heard *pari pietatis affectu.*

When one considers the unfortunate direction of post-Tridentine Rome, and the new form of the question it poses, the debate about Tradition carried on between Anglicans and those they call "Protestants" seems decidedly *demitasse.* I refer to the concept of "the development of doctrine," by which Tradition no longer merely draws out what is implicit in scripture and oral apostolic doctrine (the old idea of "logical explication"), but now is an instrument for the progression and production of new doctrine. This has led Karl Adam to contrast the "dead word" of scripture with the "living voice" of the church.

The Tübingen school's Johann A. Mohler seems to be the key figure in this story. His relation to John Henry Newman has been treated most recently by Owen Chadwick in his book *From Bossuet to Newman.* From this line of ancestry came M. J. Scheeben, most influential at the time when Pius IX declared that the Pope, speaking *ex cathedra,* possesses the infallibility which Christ wished the doctrinal definitions of faith and life to possess in his Church. The classical concept of tradition as the unwritten apostolic testimony and the process of its Church transmission was now left behind. There was to be a third source of revelation, the creative, vital authority of the Church of Rome, as gathered up in one head, its *papa*. For the same Vatican decree of 1870 states that the papal words, by themselves and not by the consent of the Church, are *irreformable*—whoever contradicts them, *anathema sit*.

It seems to me that this movement above all others presses us for an answer to the problem of Scripture and Tradition, and in particular to the authority of the Canon, in terms of a new doctrine of inspiration.

3. CHRISTOLOGY AND THE DOCTRINE OF INSPIRATION

The unhappy history of the doctrine of the inspiration of Scripture in the post-Reformation Church is familiar to all. Where Luther and Calvin talked of the preaching of Christ and the witness of the Spirit, Protestant Orthodoxy talked of dictation and inerrancy. The ground of authority was shifted so that the doctrine of scripture became related directly to theories of inspiration rather than of revelation. Thus the 17thC Abraham Calov could state, "The form of divine revelation is inspiration *(theopneustia)*, through which divine revelation is what it is."[6]

A complication emerged in the nineteenth century when the influence of ideas of exact science contributed towards a theory of literalism based on a materialistic notion of truth. It is this phenomenon that has led writers such as J. K. S. Reid to describe the doctrine of verbal infallibility as peculiarly modern, and not simply a continuation of the doctrine of inspiration held by Protestant Orthodoxy.[7]

---

6.   See H. Heppe, *Reformed Dogmatics* (1950) II.6 on the shift in the concept of inspiration from connection with revelation to its own authority (*certitudo*) as essentially the divine wisdom.

7.   J.K.S. Reid, *The Authority of Scripture* (London: Methuen, 1957).

The shift to a pseudo-scientific ground proved fatal. For a new but less *pseudo* science of Biblical Criticism was already surveying the ground and beginning to excavate here and there. It led to a complete undermining of the new edifice of an infallible book. It was after the collapse of this edifice, when Kantian moralism seemed the only recourse for theologians in both Europe and America, that an address was delivered in Switzerland entitled "The Strange New World Within the Bible." A young Swiss pastor examined the kind of speech found in scripture and concluded, "It is not the right human thoughts about God which form the content of the Bible, but the right divine thoughts about men . . . The word of God is within the Bible." That was 1916; and the speaker was, of course, Karl Barth.[8]

It was not yet the theology of crisis in its classic lines, where biblical authority derived from the "transparency" of the intervening centuries between the biblical authors and ourselves. Our concern is with a more mature Barth, who emerged from the "egg-shells" of crisis theology by publishing his crucial book on Anselm in 1931. And we are especially concerned with his Prolegomena to the *Kirchliche Dogmatik*—prolegomena which amount to 1444 pages of English print! This doctrine of the Word so carefully expounded by Barth represents the decisive step that modem theology has taken in rehabilitating the doctrine of holy scripture and its authority.

Let us attempt the madness of summing up Barth's doctrine in a few lines. He traces a threefold form of the Word: the eternal Word, the written Word of scripture, and church proclamation. But the decisive thread running through his analysis is the christological analogy so familiar now in all his theology: the divine-human nature of Jesus Christ is the God-given (revealed) analogue for our understanding of revelation. Thus scripture has an analogical correspondence to the person of Jesus Christ, according to "the analogy of proper propor-

---

8.   Barth, "The Strange New World Within the Bible," in *The Word of God and the Word of Man* (New York: Harper, 1957).

tionality" worked out in its logic by Aristotle, and in its "theo-logic" by
Thomas Aquinas. This involves a likeness and unlikeness of proportion
on each side of the relationship. The Bible is not another hypostatic
union, but *resembles* the divine-human unity of our Lord in that it also
has two elements, a true divinity and a true humanity.

> When we necessarily allow for inherent differences, it is exactly the
> same with the unity of the divine and human word in Holy Scripture.
> . . . As the Word of God in the sign of this prophetic-apostolic word
> of man Holy Scripture is like the unity of God and man in Jesus
> Christ. It is neither divine only nor human only. Nor is it a mixture
> of the two nor a *tertium quid* between them. But in its own way and
> degree it is very God and very man, i.e., a witness of revelation which
> itself belongs to revelation, and historically a very human literary
> document.[9]

Since the WCC Assembly at Lund we have been seeking to let our
ecclesiology become informed by our christology. But is it not true also
that since 1938 these words of Barth have been a summary of what we
have been doing, consciously or not, in our doctrine of scripture? We
have been treating scripture as both divine and human, for a Word of
God along with words of men in one and the same book at one and the
same time has seemed to be the answer. Let biblical criticism have free
rein within the Bible, for it is word of man; let dogmatic theology have
free rein with the Bible, for it is Word of God. This reconciliation has
given a measure of peace to those of goodwill on both sides, for the Book
now seems to be patient of the best that dogmatic theology can do with
it as well as of the worst that biblical criticism can do to it.

I submit that the peace is too easy. It fails to honour the truth that
we acknowledge in our use of scripture—that we cannot and must not
divorce divine from human words, dogmatics from criticism. Else we
breed a schizophrenic theology: exegetes buried under a mass of minutiae
and dogmaticians floating above the results of modern criticism. The

---

9.   *C. D.* 1/2, pp. 499, 501

problem seems to be that on the christological analogy, the unity of the divine and human elements now depends on the inspiration and genius of the exegete or interpreter! Yet it is not the principle of christological analogation that is wrong, but the manner of its application. What if Karl Barth had carried further his analogy, as he has worked it out in earlier sections (notably § 15) and applied it so fruitfully in later ones, such as those on ethics and election? I refer to his emphasis on the true humanity of Jesus Christ as the *new* humanity, his appeal to the post-Chalcedonian doctrines of *anhypostasia* and *enhypostasia*, for instance. This places the stress on the positive, the enhypostatic nature of the new humanity, its definite and concrete existence within the assumption by the Word.[10]

The miracle of the incarnation of the Word is such that the sovereign divine decision creates the possibility and actuality of a reactive/responsive free human decision, to render perfect obedience, to be the second Adam, the new man: here is a humanity both true and new, both "fallible" and yet "perfect." The two Patristic doctrines at issue here were formally adopted as dogmata by the Second Council of Constantinople in 553. In christology they were meant to guard against the error of a double Christ, leading to docetism on the one hand and ebionitism on the other. As to scripture, must we not follow these signs in order to prevent the corresponding error of a "double" Word, leading to docetic dogmatics and ebionitic exegesis?

Let us be careful. The "fundamentalist" doctrine of verbal inerrancy raises a christological question: what kind of human nature did the eternal Word assume? and answers it by saying, the flesh of Adam before the Fall, nay rather the flesh of a second Adam who could not fall: *non posse peccare*. The position is expressed in the well-known encyclical of Pope Pius XII: "Just as the substantial Word of God became like to men in all things, sin excepted, Heb. iv. 15, so the

---

10. See Barth, *C.D.* IV/2, pp 48f, 91f. These twin doctrines spell out the subsistence of the human Jesus within the Word, thus "enhypostatic," and the continuing divinity of the Word distinct from Incarnation, thus "anhypostatic."

words of God, expressed in human language, became in all things like to human speech, error excepted."[11]

We need not follow such identification (which is therefore no longer a proper proportionality!) in order to agree that some explanation in terms of "new human words" is in order, some doctrine of "inspiration." Is it not to be expected that the divine economy of a Word that completed Himself in a new humanity, an enhypostatic reality visible in his own Body, should involve as part of this Body a People named Israel? He raised up a holy nation and peculiar people, and led them to this graphic form of witness, a holy Scripture and peculiar Canon. Form and content are unified here; we cannot have this witness except in this form. Thus scripture is not a duality of divine and human "elements," but offers itself as *one* Word, not the words of men but of these men of Israel, both truly human and therefore fallible, yet also newly human and therefore in some positive sense "perfect." To quote Professor James Barr of Edinburgh: "The finger of John the Baptist should be given a rest; he is simply not an adequate analogue for the whole range of biblical statement . . . the true analogy for the scripture as the Word of God is *not* the unity of God and man in the Incarnation; it is the relation of the Spirit of God to the People of God."[12] Inspiration is a mean between divine revelation and human faith: it is our theological sign that God's Word to man has taken a way within history, characterized by the contingency of history as well as by the interpretive nature of historical records. It points also to the reason for the "sufficient authority" of scripture as the canon of the Church. Authority for the canon derives from the actuality of revelation itself, of the God who chooses to address us by Word and Spirit. And authority for revelation cannot be sought outside the circle of God's grace and Israel's faith, Israel old and new. This is a self-authenticating circle, yet not vicious because it is closed not logically but factually, in the faith and the doubt of this People. The written nature of the Church's

---

11.   Pius XII, *Divino Afflante Spiritu*, 1943.

12.   Barr, review of J.K.S. Reid, *The Authority of Scripture*, in *Scottish Journal of Theology*, March, 1958, pp. 88f.

canon is itself a marvellous sign, reminding us, as it serves by ruling and rules by serving, of the One who is the servant-lord, the Canon of our canon itself.

5

THE CONCEPT AND CONCEPTION OF GOD IN THE SEMINARY

Address to the Special Convocation, Knox College, 18 September 1984.

On this signal and happy occasion congratulations are in order to our two distinguished recipients of the honorary Doctor of Divinity, Stanley Glen and David Hay, as well as to Knox College itself; for its history, its achievements, its place as chief educational institution of The Presbyterian Church in Canada. These sentiments come also from your sister The Presbyterian College, Montreal and from the Faculty of Religious Studies, McGill. Let me congratulate also and more personally Principal Charles Hay, for his leadership and enthusiasm in these days of budgetary problems for institutions such as ours.

It is with a distinct sense of privilege that I stand before you tonight—privilege at having studied theology here, at being an alumnus of this College.[1] My class, of '49, arrived at a period when difficult days seemed to be over for our church and its colleges, when Walter Bryden was principal, with a small but select group of colleagues. Bryden, Hay, Glen

---

1. Diploma 1949, B.D. 1951, D.D. 1976.

and Andrews: they appeared to us on entering (remember that authority was still obeyed in those days, there was little fraternization between staff and students, and certainly no first-name basis anywhere)—they appeared like the four horsemen of the Apocalypse, sweeping down the corridor with flowing gowns, classes attentively waiting. A small group of teachers, joined by Donald Wade in our second year. We owe them so much, as I learned on proceeding to doctoral studies at Edinburgh and discovering what a good preparation this was for advanced work.

Walter Bryden dominated things, of course, with his prophetic words and serious tone. He *could* unbend a little. When he learned that I had married during the summer he called me into his office to tell me of his displeasure. But at the end he remarked: "At least you appear more sensible than another student in similar circumstances. When I asked him why he had married before graduating, he replied: 'Oh Dr. Bryden, wait till you see her!'"

In those days theological education covered the ground. All the ages of church history were at least touched upon by Bryden, all the books of the Bible by Andrews and Glen, all the chief heads of doctrine by Hay—including a critical introduction to Karl Barth for which I remain most appreciative. And as for the impossible dream appointed for Donald Wade—"The History and Philosophy of Religion and Christian Ethics"—I applaud the brilliant way he handled it. He was in fact a role model for me, since the new Robert Professorship at Montreal was patterned after his. As Principal Lennox, later to join this Faculty, commented, "It's not so much a chair, Joseph, as a chesterfield!"

So, let gratitude be on record. And a special word to David Hay, teacher and mentor and friend—congratulations on this added honour tonight. He once said in class, "theologians should read more poetry," and his own touch has always been light and poetic. As for Stanley Glen, our thoughts are with him on this occasion, and our memories are of the man we knew in his strength and health.[2] He was a scholar

---

2.   Dr. Glen was absent because of ill health, receiving the degree *in absentia.*

and teacher for whom this honour from his beloved college is most fitting. Thirty years ago this very month my own teaching career began as Tutor in Greek, his assistant.

This college has maintained a special place in Canadian theological letters. A recent history of Canadian philosophy begins with two Knox professors—William Lyall, tutor for two years at mid-nineteenth century before moving to Halifax, and his successor George Paxton Young, most famous for his struggle with doubts which led to his leaving the Christian Ministry. His obituary in the Knox College Monthly stated, "nothing but the poverty of a College can justify the laying of so much work upon one teacher." That lament continues to some extent, for our Church has measured its theologians against standards other than that of the University, expecting much busyness from them, with little appreciation of the need for research. But Knox today is in the midst of a campaign already promising, as one result, a new professorial chair. Let us hope that this is a sign of good health and of the confidence of our church in this primary educational endeavour.

Now let me turn from reminiscence. The title "Concept and Conception" is deliberately ambiguous.[3] It means of course the way the seminary *thinks* of God—the "concepts" of theology. But it also means something more, what I take to be the heart of Christian faith, although much neglected in recent theology. I refer to the powerful symbol of faith as implying our being joined to God: faith is more than an assent of mind and a yielding of will—it is *union with Christ.* A somewhat "mystical" idea, no doubt; yet after all, we are dealing with a *mystery;* something is going on that's more than meets the eye. It is crucial for Paul, for the Church Fathers and the Reformers. John Calvin was fond of this notion. He took the Psalms, for instance, as a mirror of life in God, of following the Way of God's Word. It's also called *sanctification.* And in that crucial turn at the beginning of his *Institutes* Book Three he states clearly:

---

3.   Indeed, so ambiguous that when published in the Knox newsletter the "conception" was omitted.

as long as there is a separation between Christ and us, all that he suffered and performed for the salvation of mankind is useless and unavailing to us. To communicate to us what he received from his Father, he must, therefore, become ours, and dwell within us.

The way that the Word takes is seen best because seen uniquely in Christ Jesus. Therefore to follow *this* way is to share *his* journey, *his* life. It is as if Christ is *conceived within us* by faith, to repeat his experience of incarnation, to grow and to mature as our hidden life. Or as if *we* are re-born in him, to grow into his likeness more and more.

The supreme Mystery, of course, is God himself. A God whose will toward us is love, who communicates to us not a message about himself or a declaration of his intention. Rather, he communicates *himself*. Thus we are given not so much concepts as *conception*. From this kind of "knowing," the heart becomes pregnant with an expectation of birth, the very birth of Christ himself. God is not inhuman, as if he grants decrees and issues laws for our obedience. He is Emmanuel, God with us, a presence and a power never divorced from his people. For this reason, Karl Barth used to call theology "the most thankful and *happy* science ... the most beautiful of all sciences." For the great Reformers, especially John Calvin and Peter Martyr, the very definition of faith is "union with Christ." Every concept of deity falls short, because of what Calvin called our "improprieties" of reasoning; but a genuine conception may come despite it. See, then, what awesome responsibility the seminary has! What if our poor concepts lead to *mis-conceptions*? Then are we poor midwives indeed.

Knowing God is a kind of experimental venture: there are words, signs, symbols, which allow a foothold on our journey upward toward the heights. But then a curious thing happens—the rarefied air causes dizziness, vertigo, and we are shown a different route. This way leads *downward*, a ladder of descending orders of humility and repentance. Bernard of Clairvaux, one of Calvin's favorite authors, wrote much of this ladder of twelve degrees, which traces the pattern of Christ himself in his incarnate form. Calvin himself was fond of warning us that all our language about God is bound to suffer from *improprietas*. If we cannot describe God *properly* what hope is there? Ah there's the rub—theology is not a speculative science but a *practical* one for *amateurs*, "lovers." Its hero is not—to take two medieval theologians of note—Thomas Aquinas the Doctor of Light, but John of the Cross, Doctor of Night. For faith is not so much a learning as a being acted upon, a suffering. Not a light going on in the mind so much as a rescue from darkness, what used to be known as "the dark night of the soul."

I emphasize this because these days, as it seems to me, theology stands in grave danger of being dissipated into something other than itself, the beautiful science of the Word of God. Instead of union with Christ, the mystery of our being reconciled and sharing his ministry of reconciliation, we are tempted and challenged and provoked to substitute righteous indignation, despair over evil, and a sort of religious entrepreneurship to keep things going. God, it would appear, no longer judges and saves; our socalled "Divine Parent" is too busy being "supportive" in absolutely everything.

I mean that we are no longer committed to setting aside time within the seminary for apprenticeship to scholarly pursuits, to the difficult concept and the more difficult conception of God. We teachers have been cajoled by the modern spirit, corrupted by enticing theories of education—and also ordered by General Assemblies telling us what to add to our curriculum and how to provide ministers who are organizers, administrators, counsellors, enablers, supporters, conflict managers, and so on.

Oh where is the basic and the classic theological curriculum that grounded us in biblical languages and literature, in history and doctrine—that taught us the cost of biblical theology and exegetical preaching? Why does the church ignore the tradition that made Knox College, for instance, worthy of its central place among us? a tradition that stressed the centrality of preaching in the Ministry of Word and Sacraments? We are all to blame; we have accepted dubious communication theories that breed, not solid sermons which edify and nurture, but brief meditations too often subjective, anecdotal, trivial. We have the kind of preaching, the kind of ministry, we deserve. The church will not be edified, nor the world saved, by fifteen-minute sermons beginning with a five-minute anecdote. But let me try to suggest a more excellent way.

Dr. Bryden used to teach a course entitled "The Cultural Logos and the Divine Word." It compared and contrasted the philosophical and religious ideas of culture with what he called "the judging, saving Word of God." As students we caricatured his theme as "no grace in Greece." But his was a solid and passionate thesis: as Christians we claim to serve One whose word and work judges all human efforts, prone to pride and selfserving as they are, and who offers his grace as the meaning of our lives; his is the gift of freedom to love.

The Presbyterian Church in Canada, in Bryden's estimation, is called to set aside pretensions to greatness, as well as the trivial pursuit of organization, structures, every secondary preoccupation. For only as we focus on this one thing needful—the proclamation and the theology of God's sovereign grace—will we be heard in this modern welter of competing philosophies and technological manipulation. His vision for our church, shared in particular by my good friend Allan Farris, his student and successor as historian, was to work at quality, to accept our Reformation heritage and cultivate *theological learning,* to accept our unique place in Canadian society and make *prophetic preaching* our trademark. To probe more deeply, one might say that *Trinitarian* theology was the hallmark of Bryden, his colleagues and successors.

It seems that, yet once again, our church is plagued by doubts about its identity, the socalled "Presbyterian distinctives." Here, in this building with its long shadow of history—the shades of sober divines, near heretics, linguists, historians, Systematikers, philosophers and preachers—surrounded as we are on this auspicious occasion by such a cloud of witnesses to the "most beautiful of all sciences"—can we not, must we not!, confess with our fathers and mothers, and on behalf of future generations: that this one thing is our calling, our "distinctive" witness ? Namely, that Brydenesque witness of a people neither afraid nor ashamed to proclaim their faith in a living God, one who judges our sins of mistaking licence for liberty, busy-ness for vocation, good intentions for peacemaking; and one who saves the humble and needy, those who trust in his truth and in his kingdom. Such witness will not divide us from fellow Christians, only from falsehood.

And one thing more: such witness demands a Seminary where God is conceived in such theological terms, but also allowed his own way of *conceiving himself in our midst.* That is surely what our college tradition of proclaiming a "living" God means. Here is the point of my title: concepts are not conception, nor is knowledge the same as wisdom. The Reformers were strong on the point that when the Logos became incarnate it was not just into a man named Jesus but into *every human being,* a universalism we forget, especially in our ethics. How dangerous a game we play indeed, we who take on ourselves the name of Jesus Christ, an outcast, a rebel, a martyr! Even more: his presence is a sharing of his own humanity with every follower, a birth and a growth will result from faith, as this same Christ is reborn in countless mangers of our being.

So ours is a vocation to be *midwives,* assisting at a birth, to be practitioners in the beautiful science of new birth, new life, rejuvenation. After all, the word "seminary" means "seed-bed." "My little children, with whom I am again in travail until Christ be formed in you"—may these apostolic words, this cry of the theologian, mark our students and teachers, our colleges and congregations; that Christ may dwell in our hearts by faith, that conception may come through true concepts, and true concepts may follow true conception.

6

WHERE'S THE BEEF?
Theology for 21st Century Adults

Convocation Address, The Presbyterian College, Montreal,
6 May 1993, on retirement.

The title of my address is *not* an attack on vegetarians; in fact it comes from the Pauline literature. The church in Corinth is told: "do not be children in your thinking: be babes in evil, but in thinking be mature." To the Ephesians: Christ gave such gifts as pastors and teachers "until we all attain maturity, the measure of his own fulness." And to the Hebrews: milk is for infants, solid food for adults. Notice that the examples of milk include resurrection and eternal judgment! But solid food, the meat of Gospel, has to do with "the powers of the coming age" which are already upon us.[1]

I feel somewhat like the older businessman in that '60s movie "The Graduate," advising Dustin Hoffman about the future. "In one word," he says, "it's in *plastics*." I give you *three* words, as our homiletical/ rhetorical tradition dictates. Your future vocation lies in becoming

---

1.　1 Cor. 14:20; Eph. 4:13; Heb. 5:11-6:5.

prophets, mystics, aliens. A ministry for the coming century must be pro-phetic, mystical and alienated: so I believe.

1. PROPHET

Not someone who foretells the future. You know the saying, "I don't believe in prophecy, especially about the future." In fact it means someone who speaks on behalf of God, and warns of the consequences if present belief and conduct do not improve. The Old Testament Prophets used to be regarded as our model. Recently theological education—reflecting both church and society—has displaced the "three marks of the church," preaching, sacraments and discipline, so that prophetic preaching is no longer primary. Sometimes I think we're not so much the conservative party at prayer as the Rotary Club.

The Academy has gone along with this drift. Higher education, reeling from budget cuts, like any institution now emphasizes planning, fund-raising, advertising. A desirable image for consumers must be projected. That is, we're now part of a market economy where entrepreneurial skills are the highest priority for our management (that is, teachers) and our products (that is, students). We think what is needed is functioning professionals, possessed of market skills and contemporary technique. Naturally we have to downgrade creativity, originality; "Masters of Divinity" are something like those strange degrees in "creative writing." The great American novelist Flannery O'Connor complained that such odd expertise results only in "death by competence." That is, technique at the expense of spontaneity and imagination may eliminate risk but it also settles for a planned and limited professionalism, one that is *safe.*

Can we fit those ancient Prophets into our model of "competence for ministry"? Amos or Jeremiah or Nathan? They were originals, defiant and antisocial. (You could call a prophet a preacher with attitude.) They suffered the consequences—Hebrews chapter 11 is an honour roll of what their faith led to, because, as the author states, they all "desired a better country." They saw God's Kingdom in their future, and called their people to conform to that vision and that dream. By definition they were revolutionaries, subversives.

We too live among a people that "do not honour God or give God thanks" as Paul put it. All around us is violence, licentiousness, hatred, inhumanity. A new barbarianism seems unleashed around the globe. "They became futile in their thinking and their senseless minds were darkened" he continues.[2] Now that was pre-Christendom; today we are experiencing "post-Christendom." Our New Age religion and culture and lifestyle is powerful in its self-serving and trivial narcissism. It's an age that cries out for subversion. Scholars now regard the parables of Jesus as agents of radical change, subverting the social order in behalf of a visionary Kingdom. Only prophets in our pulpits will do for such a time as this.

2. MYSTIC

This isn't a popular word among Presbyterians. It suggests ecstasy, intuition, possibilities beyond mere thinking—and certainly beyond doing things "decently and in order"! Moments of wonder in an otherwise dull and unbroken Flatland. Now I don't pretend that we either have or should have mystical *experiences;* only mystical *consciousness.* Otherwise we miss that dimension which theologians from Paul to Calvin to Barth have insisted on as absolutely essential. The crucial question in theology is: how do you get from God's electing love to our vocation and stewardship? Answer: only by passing through *adoption,* being joined through our Elder Brother Jesus to the lifegiving Family of God. If you miss that, religion becomes a matter of working things out on your own, trusting your own powers. It becomes bad news and hard work, not the joyful release of Gospel.

And suppose we relate the three classic moments of mysticism to the three marks of the true church? Purgation, illumination, union with God—how's that for prophetic preaching, sacramental celebration and

---

2.   Rom. 1:21.

congregational solidarity? (Or the three years of theological studies?) Suppose moreover that we stop thinking in *labels* and ask what this is, this kind of consciousness or awareness of a hidden dimension whose name is Love? Here is the Ultimate Reality, which we hardly touch in education. As Professor Wisse said to us at our closing service of the term, theology maps the sides of the mountain; but the top is lost in fog. Yet "mountain-top experience" is surely the goal of religion. Of course, on that mount of transfiguration, Jesus didn't stay long, he had better things to do down in the valley. Peter wanted to stay and build a shrine; Jesus said "Suit yourself, but I'm leaving."

Here we see that the mystic is not someone who *dwells* on mountaintops, but someone who lives according to the *rhythm* of mountains and valleys. You can build a church on top of the world but if you don't descend to the valley of suffering and injustice you won't keep company with Jesus. The one is church work, the other is Kingdom business—justice issues, peacemaking, reconciliation. Or again: this is not about *knowledge;* we're talking *wisdom* here. The difference between them is the difference between your reason and your imagination. Reason needs a teacher, someone who knows ideas and history and texts; imagination requires a Master, someone who's been there and knows the way. Prophets hear a Word from God, they warn their generation; mystics see the divine, they invite and persuade. If the *beginning* of wisdom is 'the fear of the Lord,' what is its *end,* the *goal* of Wisdom? Is it not something like this: to be united with God in the congregation of faith and of hope and of love? To become a member of this peculiar people, this odd Family?

3. ALIEN

To be a prophet demands a theology of church and society. To be a mystic involves a theology of experience. To be an *alien,* however, requires a theology of "possible worlds." Recent studies of the church, such as "The Once and Future Church" and "Resident Aliens," recall the history of God's People as aliens, the enduring phenomenon of the Jew above all. That "Utopian Pessimist" Simone Weil understood this personally and deeply. In *The Need for Roots* she analyzes "uprootedness," stressing the need "To exile oneself from every earthly community ... [because] by uprooting oneself one seeks greater reality." This sense of alienation, beloved of sociologists and existentialists, reminds us of our calling as bearers of good news. Is not the motto of our College "holding forth the word of life"? Alienation marks the reign of death, the power of negation; ours is a proclamation of Gospel—reclaiming, renewing, healing. But at present theology looks a mess, lacking consistency and punch and humour: a kind of "grunge" theology.

To this sort of alienation a new dimension has been added through technology. We've had the cultural revolution of the 'sixties and now the technological breakthrough of the 'eighties. Our graduating class will minister in an age shaped by the powerful exploration of possible worlds. (Here I have a confession to make: I've given up playing Nintendo with my grandchildren—even the four-year olds always win. It's their environment, not mine.) But think of what's coming for their generation! Not just those 300 television channels already in place and waiting for commercial contracts, but what is called "virtual reality." Two comic strips this week mentioned this, so it must be serious. This will take off from interactive TV and computer games to offer all sorts of experiences. What a scene! Individuals sitting at home alone, outfitted with headgear and gloves, operating a sophisticated machine that simulates what you choose—thrills, sex, even (no doubt) "peak" experience, mystical experience, religious experience! Here is one meaning of "alien:" someone able to move out of our human and social world into a private possible world of their own choosing, to dwell in "virtual reality" without tasting reality itself. It's a technological, and sinister, form of autistic behaviour, and religion must learn how to handle it.[3]

---

3.   This prediction seems not to have come true, except in the form of interactive television and playstations, which in fact do offer the privative scenario suggested, and are perhaps even more destructive of relationships.

71

This word "alien" has also come to denote *creatures of outer space.* Both fantasy and science fiction use the imagination to explore possible worlds. They envision utopias as well as dystopias—not only E.T. but Darth Vader. "Extraterrestrial" means that whatever we say and do about our global and human affairs and concerns will suffer a quantum leap in the coming century. As soon as the first human encounters a true alien all our theologies will be out of date. If you don't believe there's anyone besides ourselves in this vast and expanding universe, you're simply gambling. Your theology is based on a kind of intellectual bet. Your God is limited, global rather than universal.[4] You can't minister to the coming generations who will learn more about the possibilities of space and time than we can even guess. Don't force a replay of the Copernican revolution, please! Venture your theology, push it into possibilities already being discussed by our scientific and technological gurus.

Think of the new paths of communication, those invisible highways of inaudible sounds that span the globe and probe outer space. They warn us that it's too late for provincialism, nationalism, every divisive split within humanity. We continue to tear ourselves apart so that most of our news is bad news. I have a dream beyond this divisiveness, a dream of genuine universalism. Young men, it is said, see visions but old men dream dreams. Mine is that Christian theology will recapture its total dimensions, will see the whole universe as God's created order; will reach even farther than our radio telescopes, and claim the expanding universe as its rightful playground, Calvin's "theatre of glory."

My life and ministry have been spent entirely within the Twentieth Century; yours, graduates and students, will enter the 21st, a new century

---

4.   Consider that strange doctrine labelled by Lutherans "the *extra-Calvinisticum.*" Calvin claimed that the Logos maintained his separate existence (*an-hypostasia*) even while joined to Jesus (*en-hypostasia*), and therefore was able to continue his proper role in the Trinity. Does this not entail that Logos is capable of uniting with other and all forms of life in the universe, without denying the enhypostatic nature of Jesus the Christ? See my "A Theory of Relativity for Religious Pluralism," *Journal of Religious Pluralism* Vol. I (1991) 1-19.

and a new millennium. I dream dreams of what *might* be and what *should* be, in YOUR future! I want *your* visions to match *my* dreams.

The vocation of a Christian intellectual is to think through the Faith in ways that show its credentials, that is, its credibility in face of sceptics and enemies. To show how someone both modern and educated may hold these truths and live this way with intellectual honesty and integrity. Not everyone has this vocation; only a few are required to spend their hours in such exploration in depth. It's a vicarious calling on behalf of the whole People of God. That's why I call Presbyterian ministers not just Teaching Elders but "congregational Rabbis." Your calling is to help convince them of the validity of their own commitment, and to excite them into sharing a little of this "exploration into God." Otherwise we leave them like children, satisfied with soft food and simple notions; not mature adults subsisting on a diet of beefy truth, therefore fit and able to face new possibilities for thought and deed.

Go then, holding forth the word of life; accept and celebrate your vocation of risk and riotous loving: prophet, mystic, alien too. For every such journey takes you farther into the true Reality which those who know the Way name ... *God.*

PART 2

Theology and the Reformed Tradition

7

THE REFORMED DOCTRINE OF PREDESTINATION ACCORDING TO VERMIGLI AND ZANCHI[1]

The doctrine of predestination—particularly in its extreme double form (*gemina praedestinatio*)—is commonly regarded as the normative dogma of Reformed or Calvinistic theology, but the contemporary demand for christocentric theology is held to prove that this norm is not fully Christian. The impressive critical analysis of Karl Barth, for example, shows how the Reformed doctrine, especially as worked out in the centuries following the Reformation, becomes reduced to "double predestination." This unscriptural teaching, Barth argues, derives from the misplacement of the doctrine in Reformed theology, since its proper position *(Stellung)* in dogmatics is in the context of christology, and "not directly following the doctrine of God."[2]

---

1.   Published in *The Scottish Journal of Theology* 8/3 (1955), pp. 255-71.

2.   I.e., *Kirchliche Dogmatik*, II/2.7 ("The Election of God"), pp.16, 83: Praedestination heisst in Luthers *De servo arbitrio*, in Zwinglis *De providentia*, in den Schriften Calvins unzweideutig doppelte Praedestination, doppelt, in dem Sinn, dass

Here let us submit two propositions. First, the normative dogma of Reformed theology, that is, of the theology of the Reformation, is not so much the doctrine of predestination as the doctrine of *union with Christ*. Second, the Reformers' doctrine of predestination (or better, "election") was both scriptural and christological in its essential pattern, despite the other emphases that developed in the rationale of sixteenth century polemics. We shall elaborate these propositions by an analysis of the doctrine of predestination of Peter Martyr Vermigli, one of the original Reformers, whose theology was ranked by contemporaries alongside that of Calvin himself, and of his disciple Girolamo Zanchi. It is significant that Barth notes two examples of the proper christological placing of the doctrine of predestination: Calvin's first draft of the *Catechism* of 1537, 'and after him Peter Martyr, in his *Loci Communes* (1576)'.[3] Now this statement is historically misleading, since Martyr died in 1562, and the material which Robert Masson gathered into the *Loci* comes from a period not 'after' Calvin at all. The heart of Martyr's own doctrine of predestination, for instance, lies in his 1555 Oxford lectures on *Romans*, which include a lengthy excursus on the topic.[4] Let us first examine further Peter Martyr's place in the Reformation, before offering his teaching as a valid key to the Reformed doctrine of predestination.

Born in Florence in 1459, *Pietro Martire Vermigli*—named after a thirteenth-century martyr—became a leading figure in the Italian Church, rising to a share in the episcopal oversight of Lucca, until his zeal for reform forced his departure (one step ahead of the Roman Inquisition formed in his honour) from his native soil. In December 1542 he was

---

Erwählung und Verwerfung jetzt als die beiden Species des durch 'Praedestination' bezeichneten Genus verstanden werden.

3.   *K.D.*, ibid., p. 90.

4.   *Commentaria … ad Romanes* (Basel, 1558); the two scholia from the lectures have now been published as *Predestination and Justification*, trans. F.A. James (Kirksville MO, 2003; Peter Martyr Library, vol. 8).

appointed Professor of Theology at Strassburg,[5] colleague of Martin Bucer, thus beginning a career of twenty years in which, by teaching, preaching and writing he struggled for the cause of Reformation in the whole of Europe. During this period he resided in three cities that were focal points of Reform—Strassburg, Oxford and Zurich. He was a close friend of Bucer, Calvin, Cranmer, Bullinger, Melanchthon and Jewel.

Peter Martyr's place in the Reformation has yet to be properly acknowledged.[6] While at Strassburg he was a central figure in that debate with the extreme Lutheran party which served to form—for good or ill—the decisive Reformed emphases as against the Lutheran.[7] As Regius Professor of Divinity at Oxford during the reign of Edward VI he was the leading theologian in England at the very time when doctrine and liturgy were being formed; it was Peter Martyr that Cranmer named as associate to defend the Prayer Book and "the whole doctrine and religious order established" by Edward VI, in his challenge from Lambeth on 5th September 1553, when the cause of Reformation was all but lost by the new regime of Mary.[8] Martyr's closing years at Zurich saw an increase in the ties binding him to John Calvin as well as Bullinger and the other successors of Zwingli; this fact indicates a

---

5.   I use the German spelling current at the time rather than the modern French "Strasbourg."

6.   The English translation series "The Peter Martyr Library" is attempting to overcome this oversight; since 1994 nine volumes have been published.

7.   The debate involved the Lutheran doctrine of the ubiquity of the body of Christ as necessary to a proper doctrine of the sacraments, and the Reformed doctrine of the perseverance of the saints as necessary to a proper doctrine of predestination. There is a deep truth contained in each, although perhaps we should ask ourselves whether Martin Bucer was not correct in thinking he could hold both Lutheran and Reformed together in good faith. See J.P. Donnelly, S.J., trans. and ed., *Dialogue On The Two Natures in Christ*, PM Library, vol. 2, 1995.

8.   See Burnet's *History of the Reformation of the Church of England* (London, 1681), Vol. II. n, App. II.8, for text of Cranmer's statement.

basic falsity in the charge of 'Zwinglianism' leveled at the theology of Zurich.[9]

Although Peter Martyr's writings are concerned chiefly with biblical exegesis and sacramental theology, his teaching on justification and predestination is deserving of study. For this is the man whom Calvin termed *optimus et integerrimus vir*, claiming that the Reformation controversy over a local presence in the Eucharist "was crowned by Peter Martyr, who has left nothing to be desired."[10] For his part, Martyr regarded Calvin as 'the most eminent and noble expositor of holy Scripture of our times'.[11] During the Strassburg controversy, he wrote to Calvin:

> I want you to know that this sadly grieves me, along with others, that [the Lutherans] spread against truth and against your name, very foul and false reports concerning the eternal election of God. . .. We here, especially Zanchi and I, defend your part and the truth as far as we can. . . . [12]

During the years 1556-62, Peter Martyr was engaged in two separate debates concerning predestination. One was with his ageing fellow-teacher in Zurich, Theodore Bibliander, the other and more important one, his defence of his friend and one-time disciple in Italy, Girolamo Zanchi, against the attack of the Lutherans in Strassburg. We shall present Martyr's teaching in three parts: first, his foundational treatment of the doctrine in his Commentary on Romans, which contains the treatise *De Praedestinatione*; second, his statements in the Bibliander and Zanchi affairs; and third, his doctrine in the context of his whole

---

9.   In fact our Vermigli research team is pressing the fact that "Calvinism" is misleading as denoting the Reformed churches, since Zurich was as influential as Geneva, more so in some part of Europe, including England. See J.P. Donnelly, "Calvinist Thomism, *Viator* 7 (1976), pp. 441-55.

10.   Letter to Cranmer: *Epistolae et Responsae Calvini*, 127; *True Partaking*, etc.— *Tracts*, II, p. 535.

11.   *De Votis Monasticis (*Basel, 1559), 1424D.

12.   From Strassburg, 9th May (1553 *?)—Loci Comm., Epist.*

theology, as a concluding estimate of his significance for historical theology.

THE DOCTRINE IN THE EXEGESIS OF ROMANS

Writing to Henry Bullinger from Strassburg in 1553, Peter Martyr states:[13]

> But whereas I recollect that in a former letter you wrote me
> somewhat upon predestination, I will now content myself with
> replying, that in the treatment of that subject I have been especially
> on my guard lest men should cast all their faults and sins upon God,
> or derive from the will of God an excuse for their wickedness: and
> for the rest, I so treat it, as to follow the holy Scriptures as far as
> possible. But I have neither room nor opportunity to dwell longer
> upon the subject. You will perceive the nature of what I have taught
> as soon as I shall have published my commentaries on the Romans,
> as I shall do this year. I must however candidly confess that I cannot
> but lament that our Churches are agitated from time to time by new
> controversies: we have had, I think, quite disputing enough. May
> God of his goodness grant us all so to feel respecting predestina-
> tion, that what ought to be the greatest consolation to believers,
> may not become the painful subject of pernicious contention! As far
> as I am concerned, I am not of such an obstinate opinion in these
> matters, as that if an opinion differing from my own were pointed
> out to me from the sacred writings, I should refuse to yield to the
> truth.

The *Commentary on Romans* was delayed by the Strassburg turmoil and Vermigli's subsequent removal to Zurich. It appeared in 1558; its Epistle Dedicatory acknowledges modern expositors such as Mel-anchthon, Bucer, Bullinger and Calvin. His comments on 1.16 strike a chord familiar in Martyr's theology: the Gospel is 'properly' *(proprie)* salvation, but may cause harm through external causes or *per accidens*. This is repeated in 8.2: both Law and Gospel are instruments of death

---

13.   *Original Letters*, 1537-1558 (2), (Parker Society, 1847), p. 506.

per accidens, not *per se* or *proprie.* Introducing the key section Chapters 9-11, he indicates their dependence on what has preceded. They take up two questions deriving from Paul's doctrine of justification by faith: the efficacy of the promise made to Abraham's (carnal) seed, answered by Chapter 9, and the legal righteousness of the Jews which ought to be recognised, answered by Chapter 10. On 9:10 Peter Martyr observes that "human reason greatly abhors" the doctrine of election, and desires to appoint the ground of salvation rather in the human will. But the distinction between Jacob and Esau, for example, must be "attributed wholly unto the will and election of God as to a higher ground and principle." Although attempting no compromise of the doctrine, he reminds us that "the holy Scriptures everywhere frame themselves to our infirmity," so that Paul's language is an attempt to convey to our creaturely minds "the constancy and immutability of God's will." His will means "purpose and election"; and in examining this will we dare not go beyond the *scopus* of Paul's doctrine.

The question is this: does the scriptural "scope" include within the will of God a genuine *hatred* as well as *love*? Writing on 9:13 Martyr notes this problem, and concludes: "I affirm with the holy Scriptures that God truly and indeed loves and hates, and from this follow the effects we have now mentioned. And since we cannot understand the force and power of the love and hatred of God in themselves, we consider them by the effects: namely, either by his gifts or by his punishments. But the ground of the question is, whether the love comes of our merits, or freely." This passage reminds us that in the sixteenth century the question of "double" predestination was not at issue so much as the subtler problem of the relation of predestination to divine *foreknowledge.* Martyr termed it "the weightiest matter of all, namely to what we should attribute our salvation and election, to works foreseen or to the free mercy of God."

The commentary on 9:13 includes a scholium on Patristic teaching, in which Martyr acknowledges himself to be Augustinian in regard to the doctrines of grace, election and free will.[14] He rejects the distinction between the divine effective will and permissive will as ultimately invalid, because "I am somewhat doubtful whether it can thus occur in God." The question here is the origin of evil, and he concludes: "if we would speak properly and simply, we cannot say that God either wills sin or is its author."[15] He now turns to his own positive definition:

> First I understand that to love is nothing else than to will a man
> well. And to hate is nothing else than to will a man ill, or not to
> will him well. Wherefore God is 'said to love them to whom he wills
> eternal salvation, that is, the chief felicity, and those he hates, to
> whom he wills it not. Now this being so, the controversy is, whether
> God wills felicity to the elect by works foreseen or not, and how he
> wills it not to the reprobate.

In his treatment of the problematic terms, Martyr articulates a doctrine that comes precariously close to the classic "double predestination," (*gemina praedestinatio*), placing positive and negative in parallel (as Beza would do in his famous diagram). Yet he groups together God's love, election and predestination: "predestination follows love and election." Here is the key—he seems to give a normative meaning to the word "predestination" as *referring only to the elect*. Even though he argues analogically from this sequence, "as love is to election, so hatred is to reprobation," yet he refers reprobation to *hê eudokia*: the purpose of God is the pleasure of his will, and is taken as the general word to define predestination and reprobation. This denial of the generic nature of election and rejection is consistently carried through in the Treatise.

---

14.   He elsewhere qualifies this by rejecting the doctrine of irresistible grace—*Comm. in Iud.* 9.25 (Zurich, 1561).

15.   Two treatises in his *Comm. in Samuelis Proph. lib. duos* (Zurich, 1564) deal with this question at length: I, 2.26 and II, 16.22: *An Deus Sit Author Peccati*. See my translation in *Philosophical Works* (PM Library, vol. 4, 1996).

On 9.2 Martyr notes that the opposite of election and predestination is not damnation, but simply reprobation.[16*]

Does the doctrine of predestination deny *justice*? On 9:14 Peter Martyr suggests that Christ's parable of the penny wage points to a distinction between "distribution done from justice and that giving which proceeds from mercy." But if everything is willed by God, are not humans then "stocks and stones"? This question is answered in the comment on 9:6-19: "our will is so made by God that it cannot be compelled"; "He moves things only according to the condition of the nature which each has"; we are moved by God according to our nature, namely to work by reason and will, in such a way that choice or will is not compelled. Martyr can therefore say: "Each part is true: both that God hardened the heart of Pharaoh, and also that Pharaoh himself hardened his heart." This "both-and" is Peter Martyr's solution to the problem of divine election and human choice: no "violence or coaction" is brought to human will by divine grace, for "by a pleasant moving and conversion" the will is altered, "willing yet so willing that the will thereof comes from God."[17]

Here is a dynamic view of grace: the selfsame thing is willed by God and us through the operation of the Holy Spirit in the faithful, without confusion and without separation (the doctrine of concurrence). Although Peter Martyr does not carry his analysis further here, his doctrine of the real presence of Christ in the Eucharist presents a like problem. There he answers as follows: the Person of Jesus Christ is the architectonic of theology, the archetypal analogue; therefore the "both divine and human"of his own Person, the "without confusion and without separa-

---

16.   In recent years Frank James has studied and written on predestination (*Peter Martyr Vermigli and Predestination: the Augustinian Inheritance of an Italian Reformer* [Oxford University Press, 1998]), and presses the opposite view, that Martyr clearly enunciates the doctrine of *gemina praedestinatio*. While acknowledging the force of his argument, I continue to regard it as moot, not least in view of the material in this essay. See my reply in *Philosophical Works* (PM Library vol. 4), 265-70.

17.   *In Iud.* 9.25; *II Sam.* 16.22. The rejection of *coactio* (coercion) on behalf of persuasion resembles the modern "Process Thinking" of Whitehead, Hartshorne, Cobb and others.

tion" of the Chalcedon creed, is reflected analogically in the sacramental relation, as well as in the relation of faith between divine election
and human decision.[18] He deals with the problem of *necessity* against
such a background. The necessity which the Divine will involves is not
one of compulsion but of infallibility, or as logic phrases it, of the consequence or composite.[19] And here he gathers up his material in a clear
statement in the treatise *De Praedestinatione,* inserted after Chapter 9.
(It may be of some significance that all of Martyr's major Treatises, on
knowledge of God, justification, resurrection, repentance, are written
in the body of his scriptural commentaries).

The treatise *De Praedestinatione* is divided into four parts: the
nature and definition of predestination; its causes; its effects; and a
final section on the nature of its necessity. An introductory paragraph
acknowledges the opposition to Augustine's doctrine, by "many of the
brethren in France, and not of an inferior sort." Against this opposition,
Martyr suggests two of Augustine's works, *De bono perseverantiae,*
especially Chapters 14, 15 and 20, and *De correptione et gratia,* 5 and
14-16.

The primary orientation of the doctrine of predestination is this: *it
confirms justification by faith.* "Free justification should perish, if we
were not rightly taught of predestination." To teach this doctrine is to
give God His due: "By this doctrine men are brought to glory not in
themselves but in the Lord." It manifests "the certainty of our salvation"
and leads to a proper acknowledgment of God's gifts (see below, p. 89).
Many consolations derive from knowledge of this doctrine:

> May all our speech be directed to this, namely that they that are of
> Christ should not have confidence in their own power and strength
> but in God; and that they should acknowledge his gifts, and glory in
> God and not in themselves, and to be aware of the grace and mercy
> given them, being freely justified by Christ. Let them also under-

---

18.   Cf. particularly his 1549 *Oxford Treatise and Disputation* (PM Library vol.
7), and his *Defensio de vet. et Apost. de ss. Euch.* (against Gardiner).

19.   See below, end of Part II.

stand that they are predestinate to be made to become like the image of the Son of God, to the adoption of children, to walk in good works (§ 4).

To conclude: "nothing more advances the glory of God than does this doctrine." Predestination is to be sharply distinguished from the pagan *fatum,* since it does not lead to necessity but to freedom. It is to be received because it is part of the Gospel *(pars quaedam Evangelii)* (§ 5).

"Part of the Gospel"—here is the dominant theme of the whole Treatise, echoed most clearly in section 10: "in this Treatise, under the name of predestination we shall comprehend the saints only." For this he has historical precedent: "for that reason I think Augustine entitled his book *On the Predestination of the Saints* ... the Schoolmen also affirm that the elect only, and not the reprobate, are predestinate." These precedents are significant. Calvin could not have been one in this regard, since as early as his 1539 edition of the *Institutes* he had written, "some men are predestinated to salvation, others to damnation" (XIV.I). The scholastic doctrine, to which Karl Barth has also made favourable reference, does indeed treat predestination as *pars providentiae,* yet succeeds in preserving its evangelical nature to a remarkable degree.[20]

In section 14 Martyr further explains his position:

> I separate the reprobate from the predestinate, because the Scriptures nowhere that I know of, call men that shall be damned predestinate.

That this is not merely a linguistic cavil, Martyr shows by his further analysis. God's *praescientia* extends further than his *praedestinatio*—he has knowledge of all creatures, but a *will* only to the saints.

> We ought also to remember that the love, election and predestination of God are so ordered in themselves that they follow one another in a certain course.

---

20. *K.D., loc. cit.,* pp. 16, 47. Aquinas, *S.T.* I, Q.22: Huiusmodi autem est providentia quidem respectu omnium; praedestinatio vera, et reprobatio, et quae ad haec consequuntur, respectu hominum; specialter in ordine ad aeternam.

Augustine therefore defined predestination as "a preparation of grace" and "a purpose of mercy." Martyr now gives his own fuller definition:

> I say therefore that predestination is the most wise purpose of God, by which from the beginning he has constantly decreed to call all those whom he has loved in Christ, to the adoption of his children, to justification by faith, and at last to glory through good works, that they may be made like unto the image of the Son of God; and that in them may be declared the glory and mercy of the Creator (§ 11).

Two aspects of the definition should be noted. First, it is *eschatological:* "predestination has a respect unto things to come." (§ 11); "predestination has a regard unto those ends we cannot by nature attain, such as justification, good life, and glorification" (§ 14). Second, it is *christological:*

> 'Whom he has loved in Christ'—we add this, because whatever God gives, or decrees to give, that he gives and will give through Christ. And as we have often affirmed, Paul says to the Ephesians that we are elected and predestinated in Christ, for he is the prince and head of all the predestinate; yea, none is predestinate, but to this end alone, to be made a member of Christ (§ 12).

This statement alone indicates a doctrine of Christ as much more than merely instrumental to the purpose of the Father; it also shows the relevance of the foundational doctrine of union with Christ to the doctrine of predestination.

The first main division of the Treatise ends with a definition of reprobation:

> Wherefore reprobation is the most wise purpose of God, by which before all eternity he has constantly decreed, without any injustice, not to have mercy on those whom he has not loved, but has overlooked them, that by their just condemnation he might declare his wrath towards sins, and also his glory (§ I5).

Although in his treatment of reprobation Martyr, like the other Reformers, disappoints us by not dealing with what is surely the basic issue, namely just how the Christ has borne our *rejection* in bearing our sins, yet his consistent use of the negative in relation to reprobation, and his separation of this as a different order from predestination, recall us to his christological doctrine and context.

The second division of the Treatise, concerning *causes,* begins with a consideration of causality in terms of the Aristotelian fourfold distinction of ends. Although the divine will is its own cause, yet scripture attributes a *final* cause of predestination, to show God's power and glory, *material* and *formal* causes such as vocation and justification, and a type of *efficient* cause, the way our minds work and respond. The ambiguity of ends must be before us in this matter: "It is possible indeed that the effects of predestination may be so compared together, that one may be the cause of the other" (§ 16). A first principle is this, that divine and human election do not share the same ratio: "Divine and human choice have different modes *(ratio)*" *(§* 23).

The problem of the relation between the death of Christ and our predestination forms a transition to the third section of the Treatise, since Martyr holds that "Christ and His death is the first and principal effect of predestination" (§ 25). Christ is given to the elect, he is the road or channel through which God gives us all his gifts *(per hanc viam et quasi canalem),* and is "the image of our predestination."

> The first effect, therefore, of predestination is Christ himself; for the elect can have none of the gifts of God, unless it be given them by our Saviour (§ 37).

Paragraph 39 teaches the perseverance of the predestinate *(Necesse est praedestinati maneant),* and 42 notes that "outward calling is common to the predestinate and the reprobate." The next two paragraphs consider the extent of the Atonement:

> The scriptures do not teach that God has now decreed to deliver all men from misery, and through Christ to have them blessed; therefore, not without just cause do we say that he has decreed to deliver some and leave others, and that justly, yet the causes of this justice are not

88

to be sought by our own works, since they are known to God only through his hidden and unspeakable wisdom.

The universal propositions of scripture are to be read in terms of the two societies, godly and ungodly, which scripture presupposes (§ 45). God's mercy towards all people is shown by his restraining the Devil and by his providential care (§ 47).

The final division of the Treatise concerns necessity. This is first distinguished into outward and inward, only the former having relevance. A further distinction is that between a "violent" compulsion (the scholastic *necessitas consequentis)* and a more humane necessity of supposition or *ex hypothesi (necessitas consequentiae).*[21] Since the former would refer to objective circumstances in the manner of pagan Fate, we are left with the latter. With the ground thus cleared, he proceeds to the positive statement. Predestination involves a necessity *ex hypothesi:* "the necessity falls upon the connexion and conjunction of the predestination of God with our works" (§ 50). Such necessity involves "certainty or infallibility" as against "compulsion." Therefore:

> In the predestinate it provides that nothing be committed by them which may overthrow their salvation. And in the reprobate he takes away from them no natural power pertaining to their substance or nature, nor compels them against their will to attempt anything (§ 52).

The final question of the relation of divine necessity to divine justice is answered as follows:

> We have hitherto in this third article seen what necessity comes of the foreknowledge and predestination of God, namely such a necessity as is not an absolute but *ex hypothesi,* which we can term

---

21. These scholastic distinctions serve to clarify the scriptural depiction of the divine will, which acts through concurrence with the humans in terms of the necessary consequences foreseen but not dictated. Martyr further notes the dialectical distinction of sensum compositum et divisum.

consequentiae, infallibilitatis et *certitudinis,* but in no way *coactionis.*
And this being so, it is evident that no injustice is committed by God
when he condemns sinners and glorifies the just. For to every man is
rendered according to his works. . . . (§ 58).[22]

Second causes may be doubtful, but God's will is certain: his foreknowledge hinders not "the power of a man's will," and truly "we obtain
liberty through Christ." The conclusion of the matter is this:

> Let no man be offended with the doctrine of predestination, when
> rather by it are we led to acknowledge the benefits of God, and to give
> thanks unto him alone. Let us also learn not to attribute more unto
> our own strength than we ought: and let us have a sure persuasion of
> the good will of God towards us, by which he would elect his before
> the foundations of the world were laid: let us moreover be confirmed
> in adversities, knowing assuredly that whatever calamity happens, it
> is done by the counsel and will of God, and shall at last by the gov-
> ernment of predestination turn us to good, and to eternal salvation.

THE DOCTRINE IN CONTROVERSY

When Peter Martyr went to Zurich in 1556 as Professor of Hebrew,
Bullinger and the other theologians of the *schola Tigurina* were engaged
in debate about the doctrine of predestination. Bullinger, advising that
one should handle "this great mystery" *(dieses grosse Geheimniss)* with
moderation and caution,[23] had renounced Calvin's harsher teaching in
his debate with Bolsec, refusing to sign the *Consensus* of 1551 on predestination. Another Zuricher, Theodore Bibliander, was a declared
adversary of Calvin's doctrine, and as early as 1535 had been accused
of teaching free will in the sense of Erasmus. Bullinger restrained him
from attacking Calvin's doctrine, but in June 1557, despite the influence
of Bullinger and Martyr, he began to oppose the doctrine of predestina-

---

22.   See my comments on the distinctions in *Philosophical Works,* pp. 265ff.

23.   C. Schmidt, *Peter Martyr Vermigli, Leben und ausg. Schriften,* Elberfeld, 1858,
p. 215.

tion in his lectures. At this very time Peter Martyr was lecturing on 1 Samuel, and in connection with the rejection of Saul, discoursed at length on the assailed teaching. He wrote to Calvin:

> I have read your book (the two works against Castellio) with the greatest delight; God redounded your defence unto honour and to the defence of the orthodox faith— so I hold for my own part, I concur with you in all points. I have begun to treat of predestination, and shall continue with it the whole week. Not only does the inducement of the passage move me to declare it, but also because my College, as you know, is widely separate from me in regard to this, and has spoken against the doctrine in lectures the past week.[24]

By this time Bibliander had brought both scorn and pity upon himself, being excused on account of his age. He began to ask whether Martyr himself were really predestined, and in December 1559 challenged him to a duel! In January 1560 Martyr issued a formal statement in defence of the doctrine, and the following month the Council relieved Bibliander of his position, allowing him to retain his salary. Schmidt comments: "Bibliander was not pensioned off on account of his teaching, but because he was of unsound mind" *(geisteskrank)*.[25]

Peter Martyr's statement in this controversy, *De Libero Arbitrio*,[26] advances one main thesis, that "the natural man" has a certain freedom of the will, which extends to "knowledge moral, civil and economic," but that in regard to things divine, he is as dead. "The dead have no power to prepare themselves, nor to regenerate themselves." Conversion is "utterly ascribed to the Spirit of God, and not to our own strength." The necessity of the natural man's sinning, however, is not absolute but the *necessitas suppositi seu consequentiae* of the Treatise. The decisive point is this:

24.　Quoted in Schmidt, p, 216.

25.　Schmidt, p. 218.

26.　Included in the 1583 edition of the *Loci, App.* See my translation of Vermigli's public lecture of 1560 in *Philosophical Works*, 271-319.

> Wherefore we determine that before regeneration the will or choice
> can do nothing by itself regarding divine and spiritual things, but that
> the Spirit of God is necessary.

The Spirit works through calling, either the external Word which is common to all, or the effectual Word which has justification joined to it. The purpose of election is to "conjoin, justify and bless in Christ," to incorporate the elect in Christ (*sunt Christo insiti*). And at this point the Christian doctrine of free will enters:

> ... no small power should be attributed to free will, that is to the
> will now reformed. Therefore I affirm that the regenerate can know
> spiritual things, that they also can choose them, and in a way perform
> them: for they are not now merely human, but men of God: they are
> incorporated in Christ, they are his members, and so partakers of his
> freedom.

The debate with Bibliander serves to do two things. It shows us something of the sixteenth century climate, which was neither so homogeneous nor so rarefied as we often imagine; and it reflects, in Martyr's case at least, the concern for Christian life, and this as deriving from union with the living Christ, that was the driving force behind his thought and research.

The second dispute, between the Lutheran and Reformed parties in Strassburg over the doctrine of grace, involved Martyr through his friend Zanchi, who had remained there after Martyr's departure for Zurich. In the past, Strassburg had lent sympathetic ear to the doctrine of predestination presented by Luther, Bucer and Calvin. But the subsequent "Supper-strife" introduced differences over the nature of grace, as well as personal bitterness. Zanchi inherited the Reformed cause, while Marbach took up leadership of the Lutheran side. These two engaged in a heated controversy involving the doctrine of ubiquity, the doctrine of predestination—and the matter of certain pictures which Peter Martyr had left in the Church!

Zanchi's position emphasised the doctrine that the state of grace of the regenerate cannot be lost, along with the corresponding doctrine that "the individual will know his election better *a posteriori* than *a priori*."[27] Martyr wrote to Peter Sturm in support of Zanchi, saying that he but followed Augustine, Luther and Bucer on this question. Martyr summed up the two views: one, that election, the Holy Spirit and faith may be lost again; the other, that these could be diminished and lie dormant, but not cease. Both could be supported from scripture, he contended, but the latter is "the more probable," and is the teaching of Bucer and Calvin.

Zanchi now visited other centres of theology to confer about the doctrine, and spent eight days with Martyr in Zurich. He proposed fourteen Theses, which Sturm asked the Strassburg Magistrates to have judged. Meanwhile Bullinger suggested that Martyr draw up "the Zurich view." This he did, completing on 29th December 1561, what Hottinger termed the *Zurich Confession on Predestination*, and which Schmidt calls "a remarkable document for the history of the development of Reformed Church teaching, and a proof of Martyr's dominant influence in his Zurich College."[28] The statement agrees substantially with Zanchi's teaching "insofar as it shall be interpreted properly." We will summarize Zanchi's theses, with Martyr's comments. The first three concern eschatological questions then in dispute, the rest concern predestination.

(1) No one can know the time of the End. *Martyr:* "agreed."

(2) Anti-Christ will come, but it is not necessary that the Pope must be he. *Martyr:* "probable" and certainly not heretical.

(3) Regarding Romans 11.25f and Luke 18.8: after the reign of Antichrist a little faith will remain, till Christ conquers all. *Martyr:* here Zanchi has acted as a good teacher, commending rather than condemning in his attempt to resolve two Scriptural passages.

---

27. The material in this paragraph is from Schmidt, *op. cit.*, p. 276.

28. Schmidt, p. 278. I have found this document only in Schmidt (pp. 278-81).

(4) There is a definite number to elect and to reject. *Martyr:* agreed, since without God's will and gifts of grace, faith and the Spirit, no one can be saved. "Then one thinks that he writes a blind and accidental bargain" *(Handeln).*

(5) As the elect unto life cannot be lost, so those not predestinated to life are necessarily damned. *Martyr:* agreed, for none can be saved except Christ draw him. God's decision is always just, but not always revealed. The "necessity" here is blameless, if we exclude a necessity of force and accept only the necessity of results. The result is the blessedness of the elect, therefore one who enjoys this has certainty of salvation.

(6) Someone once elected can never become reprobate. *Martyr:* that God's will is unchangeable requires no discussion, and this is the ground of election. But will Zanchi not allow that he who is seen and judged (as elect) in the Church now can become reprobate?

(7) Two bands are required to join men to Christ and the Church: election and the Holy Spirit with faith: both inward, invisible, inexplicable; also two outward, visible, explicable ones in the Church: confession of doctrine and participation in the sacraments. *Martyr:* agreed, for no one can lose the first bands, although the latter two are prone to loss.

(8-9) In this world the elect are given true faith but once, and are conscious of it. *Martyr:* we say that the unique *(einmalige)* gift is retained, but allow for increase or decrease. Besides such true faith there is a false and temporary kind, which may vanish and return.

(10) Two men struggle in the regenerate, and sin is the victory of the outward man. *Martyr:* agreed, for when the regenerate sins, it is not whole-heartedly but reluctantly *(widerstrebend),* as Romans 7:1 5ff states.

(11-14) The promise of life must be preached to all in general but only the elect are truly reached. *Martyr:* so is it in fact the promise is preached to all, but becomes effective only in the elect, and yet the servant of the Word knows not the divine decision.

Peter Martyr sums up his comments as follows: "In Dr Zanchi's Theses we find no heresies or absurdities; rather we accept part as necessary and part as probable, and none contrary to scripture. We testify also that he affirms what not only the old Church Fathers but also Luther, Capito, Bucer, Brenz and other most noble pioneers of the evangelical doctrine held."

The document was signed by the Zurich clergy, and well received at Strassburg. But Marbach was driven into more serious opposition yet, and the situation became worse, until the call of Zanchi to Chiavenna in 1563 relieved the tension. For our part, this debate further indicates the influence of Peter Martyr, and extends the scope of his doctrine to other moot points of dogma. The deeper question of whether the best insights of his biblical commentaries are modified or even perverted through polemic, is one to which we should return a tentative "No," although further research on this point in his case and in Calvin's is doubtless required.

In conclusion we should note the relationship between the doctrine of predestination and other aspects of Peter Martyr's theology. For instance, a first principle of Martyr's teaching (like that of Calvin's) is that, since the human mind cannot comprehend the infinite, all knowledge of God is the result of a divine "accommodation" or humility. Scriptural language adopts a kind of anthropomorphism when seeking to communicate to our minds the properties of God. Such language "after the condition of men" will therefore be characterized by a certain "impropriety."[29]

This doctrine of the divine accommodation and its consequent impropriety of theological language has special significance for the doctrine of predestination. "The will of God is both hidden and. manifest."[30] When this familiar distinction is ignored it contributes to the error of grounding the doctrine of predestination in the absolute decree of a secret will of God. He continues, "But we must follow the will of God expressed by a common rule and sealed by his law—to that

---

29.   This teaching is found throughout Martyr's OT commentaries, and particularly in the treatise "On Visions," in the *Comm. on Judges* 6.22, translated in *Phil. Works*, 138-54.

30.   Martyr, *Comm. In Iud.* 4:15.

will we must direct both life and manners. For the other will we must not have too much care." The secret will may have separated Jacob from Esau in the womb, but of it we can only "say with Paul, O the depth of the riches. . ." His conclusion is the crucial point: "these two wills are not indeed separated in God, but are one and simple." The will of God revealed in Jesus Christ is neither qualified nor complemented by another, hidden will; and this singular ("simple") revealed will is altogether a will to love.

How then are we to explain the fact of *rejection*? A concept from Aristotle helps Martyr here, the distinction between essence and accidents (*per se, per accidens*). Properly speaking, revelation is single, *simplex*, Gospel. To speak properly, *God's will for man is altogether gracious*. Even his Law is spiritual, no more "an instrument of death" than Gospel.[31] Rejection and death come "accidentally"—the divine will may be final cause, but never efficient cause. In fact, Martyr states, we must speak properly only of an efficient cause within the sinner, or better still of a *"deficient* cause."[32]

Against this background we may sketch the positive doctrine that informs all Peter Martyr's theology: *faith means union with Christ*. The living Christ conjoins men with himself, and this union is a dynamic conjunction of persons: "these members are so completely joined to the Head, that they are called flesh of his flesh and bone of his bones."[33] Predestination, therefore, is in order to this union, and its divine origin as well as its human outworking must be specifically related to this organic miracle. A striking example of this is the way in which Martyr relies upon his doctrine of predestination to expound the doctrine of infant baptism. Since baptism signifies and seals the rebirth that begins union with Christ, its efficacy is related not to human decision but to divine, that is, to election. Or again, Martyr makes much of the fact that by his Incarnation Christ united *all* human beings to himself, and only on the

---

31.   *Comm. in Rom.*, 8:2.

32.   *Comm. in I Sam.*, 16:22.

33.   *Comm. in 1 Cor.*, 1:2.

basis of this universal union with Christ is the inward union of faith possible. [34]

Finally, the question of rejection is not so simple as the opponents of "double" predestination would have us believe. That some word about a positive rejection must follow from a proper exegesis of scripture, especially passages such as 1 Sam. 15 and Rom. 9-11, will doubtless be granted by all. The mystery of rejection, like the mystery of iniquity itself, can be rationalized as much by rescuing God from all contact with it as by assigning it to his will. But what must save the doctrine of predestination from a logic which perverts the Gospel into the half-will of a rationalized Deity is its christological context and content: *in Christ* and *into Christ.* And precisely here the distinctive contribution of Peter Martyr to the theology of the Reformation has ultimate relevance, for he was explicit where others were implicit in referring all theology to this christological touchstone.[35] And in his teaching on predestination he offers to us not only a Reformed view most significant for historical theology, but also a positive guide in our own attempt to work out a scriptural and christological doctrine of divine and human willing.

---

34.   See my *Visible Words of God* (1957), pp. 139ff.

35.   e.g. in a letter to Martyr of 1555, Calvin replied to Martyr's discussion about union with Christ with basic agreement, concluding that "we feel the very same on all points"—*Epist. et Resp., Ep.* 208.

8

EPISCOPACY IN THE REFORMED CHURCH

*Study Paper prepared for the North American
Conference on Faith and Order, 1955.*

When Archbishop Wake wrote, "I know no government older than Calvin's time, but what was episcopal, in the Church of Christ," he was correct only in a certain sense.[1] The medieval tradition had involved king, clergy and people in appointments. The Swiss Reformation before Calvin's part in it had not been truly episcopal, while Martin Bucer had instituted a system of lay curators at Strassburg, by which the Magistrates co-operated in the local Synod.[2] But it was John Calvin who shaped a Church polity in which the ministry is fundamentally "presbyterian" rather than traditionally episcopal. This paper attempts to show that the Reformers understood their doctrine *of* the Ministry to be a genuine form of episcopal government, and indeed that their counterparts in England understood episcopacy in almost identical terms.

---

1. Quoted by Norman Sykes in *Old Priest and New Presbyter* (Cambridge University Press, 1957), p. 122.

2. The question is, what *kind* of episcopacy? The medieval tradition, for example, involved king, clergy and people in appointments. One could mention also groups such as the Waldensians, and within the Roman obedience, special arrangements in monasteries and convents by which the leaders functioned as quasi-bishops. See, e.g., E.G. Jay, fn 6 below, and G. Donaldson, *Scottish Church History* (Edinburgh: Scottish Academic Press, 1985), Ch. 3, "The Appointment of Bishops in the Early Middle Ages."

Calvin begins from the Ministry of Word and Sacraments as "a perpetual mark and characteristic of the church" (*Inst.* 4.2.1). Thus when he expounds the "notes" or marks of the true church as "the Word of God purely preached and heard, and the sacraments administered according to the institution of Christ" (4.1.9), he is really expounding his doctrine of ministry. For his whole struggle in Geneva was with a civil government that refused to acknowledge the church's right of *discipline*. Discipline here meant that aspect of the Ministry of Word and Sacrament which exercised the power of the keys. Now in 1519 the Bishop at Geneva had surrendered his temporal powers to the people; when they later refused to return them, the Town was placed under ban *of* excommunication. The subsequent rebellion of Geneva expelled the Bishop, so that The Council of Two Hundred took over the total episcopal jurisdiction. Calvin's struggle in his warfare with the Council was over the return of episcopal authority to the ministers of Geneva.

Calvin understands the ministry in terms of Cyprian's teaching of a universal episcopacy held corporately by the entire church as Body of Christ. "Cyprian also, after the example of Paul, deduces the origin of all ecclesiastical concord from the supreme bishopric of Christ" (4.2.6). He quotes Cyprian's words from *The Unity of the Church*: "And this unity we ought firmly to hold and assert, especially those of us that are bishops who preside in the Church, that we may also prove the episcopate itself to be one and undivided. The episcopate is one, each part of which is held by each one for the whole."[3]

This is the Patristic basis guiding Calvin's doctrine of ministry, explicitly in the *Institutes*, Book 4. Christ alone is Bishop of the Church, but through the Ascension he has gifted the church with its own ministry, properly a sub-ministry diffused throughout the membership (totam subministrationem per membra diffusam: *Inst.* 4.6.9). Therefore Paul "mentions a unity; but it is in God, and in the faith of Christ. He

---

3.   ut episcopatum quoque ipsum unum, atque indivisum probemus ... Episcopatus unus est, cujus a singulis in solidum pars tenetur. —*De Unitate Ecclesiae* 5 (PL 4, 501).

attributes nothing to men but a common ministry, and to every individual his particular share."

Now Calvin is not hereby suggesting a doctrine of "priesthood of all believers" in a minimalist sense, one that would disorder the Church. On the contrary, he is especially concerned to stress the outward and visible church (*ecclesia externa sive visibilis*) as a real ordering, and not a mere mask (*larva*) in Luther's sense. He contends for a "true and genuine face of the church" that will image the bishopric of its Head—thus its discipline has a positive and not a negative end. Here we should remember that Calvin is striving to restore the pre-Gregorian Church, the Church of the Ecumenical Councils, whose canons he regards most seriously: the church as it "showed its face" in the great creeds. He makes this clear in his *Reply to Sadolet*, while in *The Necessity of Reforming the Church* addressed to Charles V he advances the view that the Reformed Church is an episcopal Church in the sense which the ancient canons imply, namely in terms of the life and doctrine of its ministers, and the presence of a council of presbyters along with the bishop at ordinations. He mentions such examples from the ancient Church and concludes, "they afford an easy means of judging how much consideration is due to this smoke of succession which our bishops emit to blind us."

It is in terms of this fundamental doctrine of the corporate episcopacy of the Church that Calvin enunciates his second principle: that although the ministry is the "fixed form" (*stata forma*) of church order, to lose which is "to unnerve the Church, deface and dissipate it entirely," yet there is a freedom about the hierarchical forms taken by the ministry in various historical times and places. The Ministry of Word and Sacraments belongs to the essence of the Church, but its particular form depends largely upon human factors: "we know that every Church has liberty to frame for itself a form of government that is suitable and profitable for it, because the Lord has not prescribed anything definite."[4]

---

4.   *Comm. on 1 Cor.* 11:3.

There is a most significant application of these two principles in Calvin's *Letter to the King of Poland* (1554): "The ancient church indeed instituted patriarchates, and to different provinces assigned certain primacies, that by this bond of concord, the bishops might remain more closely united among themselves. Exactly as if, at the present day, one archbishop should have a certain pre-eminence in the illustrious kingdom of Poland, not to lord it over the others nor arrogate to himself a right of which they were forcibly deprived, but for the sake of order to occupy the first place in synods, and cherish a holy unity between his colleagues and brethren. Then there might be either provincial or urban bishops, whose functions should be particularly directed to the preservation of order. As nature dictates, one of these should be chosen from each college to whom this care should be specifically confided. But it is one thing to hold a moderate dignity such as is not incompatible with the abilities of a man, and another to comprise the whole world under one overgrown government."[5]

Calvin's argument in the Letter is directed against the claim to supremacy of the Roman See; but it makes clear his attitude towards episcopacy as a form of Church government: where conditions justify it, it is proper and perhaps preferable. Thus a country such as Poland, where both monarch and existing bishops appear favourable to Reformation, should be encouraged to consider episcopacy as its normal polity, whereas in a city-state such as Geneva, whose bishop has been a chief factor in creating reaction, a continuation of the episcopal authority and oversight must needs assume a new form.

At this point we may note that Calvin's view of episcopacy follows the accepted patristic and medieval teaching, that the episcopate was ordered within the presbyterate, but was not a separate (eighth) order: the bishop had a jurisdictional distinction from the presbyter, without a difference in orders. Jerome had stated: "A Bishop is the same as a

---

5.   Peter Martyr Vermigli also wrote letters to Poland, which at the time was near becoming a Reformed church in polity and doctrine: see *Life, Letters and Sermons*, Peter Martyr Library vol. 5, ed. J.P. Donnelly, S.J. (1999) pp. 142-54.

Presbyter ... Let Bishops know that they are greater than Presbyters more by custom than in consequence of our Lord's appointment."[6] The Eucharist is the ordering Sacrament, to which the ordination of priests pertains; but the consecration of a Bishop does not involve such essential order, does not imprint character—indeed, the episcopal power derives from the church rather than from Christ, as Aquinas noted.[7] The *jure humano* authority of bishops and the congruent doctrine of the parity of bishops and priests was of profound influence until Trent. And this was also the attitude of the original Reformers of both Continent and England.

Calvin's correspondence with Anglican Reformers turns chiefly on the necessity for a right doctrine of the eucharist as the key to unity, rather than upon matters of polity. Cranmer's proposed "godly Synod" was intended to deal chiefly with the former; and his delight with Peter Martyr and Martin Bucer, whom he was at last able to procure for Oxford and Cambridge, owed itself primarily to their mastery of the doctrine of the Supper.

Peter Martyr Vermigli exemplifies this history well. For he was, in the years before he was forced to leave Italy, a close friend of those Cardinals (notably Contarini and Pole) who had produced the reforming document *Consilium delectorum Cardinalium ... de emendanda ecclesia* of 1538. Even more significant is the fact that he himself was raised to the office of prior of S. Frediano at Lucca, in which position he shared the episcopal oversight of the City. Thus he is one of the few members of the episcopal hierarchy to accept the Reformation. Let us quickly examine his doctrine of ministry as complementing what we have said of Calvin's.

Martyr's normative principle is this: "God wills that in the Church there should be an Aristocracy; that bishops should have the care of all

---

6. See E.G. Jay, "From Presbyter-Bishop to Presbyter and Bishop," *The Second Century* 1981, vols 1 & 3. Jay argues that the evidence does not support the thesis (e.g. Dom Gregory Dix) of an original monepiscopate.

7. episcopus accipit potestatem ut agat in persona Christi supra corpus eius mysticum, idest super Ecclesiam: *S. Theol.* III, 82.1, ad 4.

these things, and should choose ministers, yet so that the suffrage of the people is not excluded."[8] But he interprets this *Aristocratia* as follows: "If you consider Christ, it shall be called a Monarchy, for he is our king, who with his own blood has purchased the Church to himself. He is now gone into heaven, yet governs this kingdom of his, not indeed with visible presence, but by the Spirit and by the Word of holy scripture. And there are in the Church those that execute the office on his behalf: Bishops, Presbyters, Doctors, and others bearing rule—in relation to these it may properly be called an Aristocracy.... But because in the Church there are matters of very great weight and importance referred to the people, as appears in the Acts of the Apostles, therefore it has a respect of *politia*." Again: "Paul indeed mentions bishops and presbyters, but does not teach that they are diverse orders."[9]

An interesting application of this doctrine is given in the history of Martyr's return from the Colloquy of Poissy, 1561. Bishop Caracciolo of Trois, a former student of Martyr's at Naples, had attended Poissy and through the debates about the nature of ministry had become concerned about his own standing. He therefore took Martyr with him to Trois, where the Reformer advised him to assemble his clergy for a consultation. This resulted in his acceptance as Bishop over the Reformed Churches of the district, with one dissenting vote. This case remained unique, and problematic to Rome. He was deprived of his office, but had already taken the congregation (and income) with him. Ultimately the Queen settled a pension on him, as a Bishop of the French Reformed Church.

Martyr's significance lies chiefly in this, that he introduced some decisive patristic authorities to the eucharistic debates in the Church of England. His influence at Oxford, where the Disputation of 1549 was his victory because of patristic teaching (especially the christological analogy of Theodoret and Gelasius), and his relationship to Cranmer

---

8.   "Whether there may be two heads in the church," *LC* IV.3.

9.   *De Excomm.* (LC IV.5). His teaching here reflects Aristotle's concept of the three proper orders of government, and their deformed counterparts, in *Pol.* III.7.

and Jewel, was on solid ground. Cranmer was a learned patristic scholar, but Martyr brought with him works, particularly of Chrysostom and Theodoret, to which Cranmer now fell heir, in his *Defence* of 1550, for instance. John Jewel, on the other hand, was expelled from Oxford for being a disciple of Peter Martyr, with whom he spent his exile during the Marian persecution. His correspondence during Elizabeth's reign shows the closest ties, as between father and son, while his doctrine in the *Apology* and his teaching on the eucharist is a faithful representation of his mentor's theology.[10]

On the death of Edward and accession of Mary, it was Martyr whom Cranmer singled out to aid him in the defence of the Prayer Book and religion of Edward' s reign; it was the Anglican refugees who financed Martyr's reply to Gardiner on behalf of the late Archbishop (*Defensio ... ss. Eucharistiae ... adv. S. Gardineri*, 1559). And it was to Martyr that Jewel wrote his famous words in 1562: "As to matters of doctrine, we have pared everything away to the very quick, and do not differ from your doctrine by a nail's breadth."[11] At this very time Martyr was Bullinger's chief support at Zurich.

The figure of John Knox presents a like attitude towards episcopacy. During his sojourn in the Church of England, Knox had refused the benefice of All-Hallows in London, not so much because of the problem of episcopal polity as of the eucharistic liturgy, which he felt allowed the unworthy to participate in the Sacrament. Later he was offered a bishopric, which he refused on similar grounds. It is Beza who remarked in this context that Knox censured the episcopal office as destitute of divine authority and not even exercised in England according to the ancient canons. But the Frankfort troubles among the English exiles ought not to mislead us into thinking that Knox was simply a troubler of episcopacy: far from it. The division between Knoxian and Coxian at Frankfort had to do with liturgy rather than polity; and after Knox's

---

10.   See my *Visible Words of God*, "The Affairs of England," pp. 55-60.

11.   *Zurich Letters* I, p. 100; App. 59.

banishment, the English exiles themselves rejected the title Bishop as applicable in their situation, then also rejected the name Superintendent as being "only a bad Latin word instead of a good Greek," finally settling on "Pastor" as a practical compromise.[12]

It seems a fair conclusion to the story of Knox to point out that Scottish scholars today agree that the office of Superintendent (its Latinity notwithstanding!) indicates, in Donaldson's apt summary, "such a bishop as can exist in a Church which knows neither the necessity of episcopal ordination, nor the inviolable parity of ministers."[13] In fact, therefore, the Church of Scotland as reformed by Knox involved an office of an episcopal nature; and indeed, Scotland equally with England apparently began its Reformation with the doctrine of "godly prince and godly bishop" as the chief means for its establishment. The office of Superintedent was clearly ambiguous, with patronage still casting its shadow to make appointments, and oversight itself tendentious.[14]

But if Luther had his Melanchthon, Calvin had his Beza and Knox his Melville. The Court of Presbytery is Melville's distinctive contribution to the history we are sketching. Yet even here we do not have a simple doctrine of the parity of ministers, as with Puritan theology, but a more subtle yet explicit doctrine of *corporate episcopacy* following Calvin. For instance, in T.F. Torrance's valiant effort to relate both historic and corporate episcopacy, we have this statement of the difference between presbyter in the Churches of England and Scotland: "In the Church of England the presbyter is regarded as a delegate of the bishop in that he does not hold the episcopate *in solidum* with the bishop. Consequently in the Church of England the episcopate is given an individualist

---

12.   Seee T. McCrie, *Life of John Knox* and *Story of the Scottish Church* for this paragraph. Bishop Grindal was content to serve as an Elder in Geneva during the exile; Jan Laski's *Forma ac Ratio* had called the Superintendent *episkopos*.

13.   G. Donaldson, *The Scottish Reformation* (London: Cambridge University Press, 1960) Ch. V: "'Godly Bishop' and Superintendent."

14.   See Donaldson, *Scottish Church History* (Edin.: Scottish Academic Press, 1985), Ch. 7, "The Example of Denmark' in the Scottish Reformation," pp. 52-70.

expression in a single bishop. There are, however, relics of an ancient practice in the association of presbyters with the bishop at ordinations, and in the tradition that the pastoral charge of the congregation is shared by the bishop and the presbyter. In the Church of Scotland the presbyter is a presbyter-bishop who along with his fellow presbyters holds and exercises the episcopate *in solidum* in the presbytery; consequently the episcopate is given a corporate or collegiate expression in the presbytery, known therefore as 'The Rev. the Presbytery."[15]

As summary and conclusion, let me submit two theses:

1. The Church is a structured body of Head and members; structure is of its essence, a "vertebrate organism" in the words of Newbigin. "Organization and structure are necessary for the existence and witness of the Church. This does not mean, however, that any particular historical form of these is necessary for salvation."[16] This would be to say that *episcopê* is of the church's essence but not necessarily episcopalian polity. Or in the broader sense of the Reformers' use of the term, church government is by definition "episcopal," but this may vary in form, the "corporate episcopate" being the normal (and probably the historical) form.

2. Presbyterianism is therefore not anti-episcopal but rather emphasizes a different orientation for polity. The great Presbyterian canonists of the 17th century in Scotland, for instance, examining this question of order in the church, stressed the fact that there was an unbroken succession of ordained ministers in Scotland through the Reformation, providing "a *perpetua successio presbyterorum* from before the Reformation." They claimed that the substance of true ordination continued through the Court of Presbytery.[17] Perhaps their point is put most directly by a later scholar, A.R. Macewan of Edinburgh in 1911: "The Presbyter, not the Presbytery, is distinctive of Presbyterianism." Thus ordina-

---

15. Torrance, *Royal Priesthood* (Edin.: Scottish Journal of Theology Occasional Papers, 1955), p. 104 (this usage is followed by The Presbyterian Church in Canada).

16. World Alliance of Reformed Churches, Princeton 1954, *Report* § 111, p. 19.

17. E.g. Lord Balfour of Burleigh in the influential composite volume *Jus Divinum Reg. Eccl,* first published London, 1646.

tion—the central point or test case—is not in the hands of the Court of Presbytery (which includes "Ruling Elders" in its episcopal function) but only and strictly in the ordained ministers of that Court.

9

COVENANT THEOLOGY—
A RE-EVALUATION[1]

A mong the forces that have shaped the pattern of historical theology and have brought us to this ecumenical hour is one that is both strong and persistent, one that is aptly summed up in the term "covenant theology." By this we mean not only the classic Federal Theology of orthodox Calvinism but also that type of biblical theology which sees in the doctrine of the covenant its unifying principle of interpretation. This Covenant Theology demands re-examination today partly because of its historical place in Reformed theology, and partly because it poses the deepest questions for "practical theology." To speak of the doctrine of the covenant, for instance, is to speak of the extent of the atonement, the effectual use of the means of grace, and the nature of evangelism. Perhaps such re-examination is especially demanded by the very fact that our modern theology sees little or no tension at these points. Let us present a brief study of the idea of covenant in historical theology, and then offer a possible solution to the problems raised by our historical investigation.

1.   Published in the *Canadian Journal of Theology* Vol. III (1957) No. 3, pp. 182-88.

Biblical research confirms the insight of the Early Church in naming the two parts of its scriptures "covenants" *(testamenta)*. For the fundamental motif of the scriptures is best summed up in the concept of *berith (diathêkê* in LXX and N.T.). The covenant of Horeb-Sinai was the foundation of Israel, whose knowledge of God and service of God derive from and are judged by that historical act of grace. Thus the Ten Words of covenant were housed in "the ark of berith-Yahweh" (Deut. 10: 8) as the foundation underlying the mercy-place. The other covenants, in the Book of Genesis, probably are best regarded in relation to the Mosaic pact—Adam's is its absolutizing (Gen. 2:16f), Noah's its universalizing (Gen. 9:16), while Abraham's is essentially of the same kind, its evangelical precursor (Gen. 17).

The Hebrews were a covenant-people because theirs was a covenant-making God. This is evident from a study of the "distinctive ideas" of the Old Testament such as Norman Snaith has given us. Consider the two primary words *chesed* and *'ahabah*: *'Ahabah* is "the cause of the covenant: *chesed* is the means of its continuance. Thus *'ahabah* is God's Election-Love, whilst *chesed* is his Covenant-Love."[2] The term *chesed* becomes the distinctive divine attribute of Hebrew theology, God's faithfulness or "real-love" (G. A. Smith), although we may think that the complementary term *chen* (the condescending love of a superior for an inferior) is necessary to express the true nature of the divine grace. Yet the clue to the Old Testament history is the covenant, and therefore "the whole secret of God's continued mercy towards Israel was that they were the people of his choice. Israel ultimately depended upon the Covenant, and her hope of salvation was in God's persistent covenant love."[3] The temptation to legalism and self-righteousness is strong here, and the prophets struggled against it, reaching at last the doctrine of a New Covenant that is truly "the New Testament latent in the Old" as Augustine put it.

---

2.   N. Snaith, *The Distinctive Ideas of the Old Testament* (Epworth, 1944), p. 95.
3.   *Ibid.*, p. 129.

It would seem that Eichrodt's stress on the idea of the Covenant in his *Theologie des alten Testaments* is a valid one: Yahweh is a God who initiates covenants, a *Bundesgott,* and his people are the *Bundesvolk.* But if this is a true and fruitful interpretation of the Old Testament, it is a sad commentary on the Church (on its "hellenization"?) that it virtually lost the doctrine of the covenant, except in terms of an Augustinian predestination. This twist in the association of the covenant-idea shaped the pattern of historical theology so that the doctrine of grace became a question of ecclesiastical authority and ordinance rather than of divine activity of seeking and saving. The Schoolmen could write at length about the divine attributes, but the relationship to the quality of *chesed* is difficult to ascertain. Even the Angelic Doctor's treatment of predestination, for all its merit, fails to notice the evangelical tension in the whole matter.[4] This pattern obtains until the Reformers break through the scholastic method with a renewed understanding of the mighty acts of God in Jesus Christ. Thus Calvin's *Institutes* accepts the approach of the Apostles' Creed rather than the traditional *summae* or *loci.*

Calvin's understanding of the significance of covenant may be summed up from three references. First, the concept of covenant expresses the way God deals with us: "All those persons, from the beginning of the world, whom God has adopted into the society of his people, have been federally connected with him *(fuisse ei foederatos)* by the same law and the same doctrine which are in force among us" *(Inst.* 2.10.1). Second, as this same passage makes clear, his chief concern is to illustrate the *substantial identity* of the old and new covenants: "The covenant of all the fathers is so far from differing substantially from ours, that it is the very same; it varies only in the administration." In terms of its substance and reality *(substantia et re ipsa)* the Old Testament is one with the New, for the substance and reality of both covenants is Jesus Christ. Hence the identity in content of the sacraments of both Testaments, inasmuch as the sacrament is both sign *and seal* (effective as well as cognitive) of

---

4.   Aquinas, *S.T.* Ia, Q. 23.

the covenanted grace: "By the figure metonymy, the name of covenant is transferred to circumcision, which is so conjoined with the word, that it could not be separated from it" *(Comm. on Gen.* 17:9). The third reference unfortunately became central in subsequent Calvinism. This is Calvin's relating the "principle of the gracious covenant" to a supra-lapsarian scheme of double predestination *(Inst.* 3.21.5). That is, he understands the divine activity of covenant-making only as derivative from that of decree-making. The latter has priority, and atonement is subordinately related to its secret mystery. Yet even here we catch a glimpse of that other strain which informs all his thought, and which itself gives the tension and the dynamic to his theology. I mean his doctrine of faith as *union with Christ:*

> In order to maintain the efficacy and stability of election, it is
> necessary to ascend to the head, in whom their heavenly Father
> has bound his elect to each other, and united them to himself by
> an indissoluble bond. Thus the adoption of the family of Abraham
> displayed the favour of God, which he denied to others; but in the
> members of Christ there is a conspicuous exhibition of the superior
> efficacy of grace; because, being united to their head, they never fail
> of salvation *[Inst.* 3.21.7].

To this doctrine we shall return later.

Subsequent Calvinism concentrated on the third reference to the detriment of the first two (e.g. Beza's supralapsarian system) so that a reaction was almost inevitable, and James Arminius bowed to the will of history. The resulting Calvinist-Arminian debate, as underlined by the Synod of Dort, indicates the inner connection between election and atonement in these terms: conditional election means universal atonement, while double predestination implies limited atonement. Thus simplified and hardened, it is little wonder that Protestant church history becomes the story of a new scholasticism. One interest-ing attempt to break the deadlock was made by the French school of Saumur, whose impetus came (of course!) from a Scot, John Cameron, but whose pupil and successor, Amyraut, is chief representative. He taught a doctrine of "hypothetic universal grace," in which the decree of atonement precedes the decree of election, and the reason why the inward light of grace is given to some and not to others remains a mystery, without having to declare the latter to be predestinated to unbelief (a theory much like the later New England theology). Amyraut won his case, proving that he was not speaking contrary to the canons of Dort. Against the Saumur school such men as Turretin and Wetstein sounded the old refrain of the *decretum horribile* (which Turretin varied by asserting the inspiration of the Hebrew O.T. vowel points!). Thus did Calvinism march on from strength to strength, secure in the knowledge that predestination was the first principle of Reformed theology, and that the question of the relation of the cross of Jesus Christ to sinful men was strictly derivative from the prior question of the details of the covenant made between the Father and the Son before the dawn of creation.[5]

In light of this development, Federal Theology appears as a more hopeful sign, although it is basically the child of this debate. The classic utterance of the new system is the *Summa Doctrinae de Foedere et Testamento Dei* (1648) of Johannes Cocceius of Leyden. His basic desire is to interpret history in terms of the nature of the covenant operative at particular times: "Man who comes upon the stage of the world with the image of God, exists under a law and a covenant, and that a covenant of works."[6] The second covenant, of grace, which succeeded after the Fall, is divided by Cocceius according to "a twofold economy," the first "in expectation of Christ," and the second "in faith in Christ revealed." Some theologians made a different analysis, distinguishing a threefold administration of one covenant of grace, from the Protevangelium in Paradise to Moses, the Mosaic law, and the N. T. Gospel. But in general

---

5.   The problem of Reformed Scholasticism has become a hot debate in recent years; see especially the works of Richard Muller, e.g. *Post-Reformation Reformed Dogmatics*, 2 vols. Grand Rapids, MI: Baker Book House, 1987.

6.   Quoted in Heppe, *Reformed Dogmatics* (E.T. by G. T. Thomson, Edinburgh, 1950), p. 281. Heppe's sources are in Ch. XIII, "The Covenant of Works and the Righteousness of the Law," 281-300.

COVENANT THEOLOGY—A RE-EVALUATION

this was rejected, and even those who further subdivided the economy of grace (e.g., Wollebius) make clear that the one ordinance of Christ Jesus operates throughout.

Perhaps the most significant historical aspect of Federal Theology is its acceptance by the Westminster Assembly. The basic idea of covenant had become part of the life of Scotland as early as 1556, when members of the struggling Reformed Church entered into a "Band" at Dun, vowing to "refuse all society with idolatry." The following year at Edinburgh "ane Godlie Band" was established.[7] By 1645 the Federal Theology as such seems to have been fully developed in Britain, when John Ball wrote A *Treatise of the Covenant of Grace,* a book recommended by such Westminster divines as Calamy and Reynolds.[8] But apart from such external evidence, the Westminster Confession adopts the concept of two covenants, one of works and one of grace, with the latter differing in its parts only administratively (VII.5).

The Westminster Confession thus adopts as its frame of reference, its principle of biblical interpretation, the full-orbed Federal Theology involving as its chief points the doctrines of double predestination, limited atonement, covenants of works and of grace, and imputed justification. Its teaching on those points of doctrine which have relevance to evangelism, such as Effectual Calling, is necessarily shaped by this frame of reference. The problem evident at these points received attention historically in the development of American Calvinism. The New England Theology sought to retain the distinctive principle of the sovereignty of God, while also working out homiletic methods of approaching sinners according to the theory that "God has opened a door for all to be saved conditionally" (Bellamy). This school discussed at great length such moot questions as whether one should urge the unregenerate to pray for conversion, and whether the imputation of sin by virtue of the representative nature of Adam is mediate or immediate.

---

7.   J. Kerr, *The Covenants and the Covenanters* (Glasgow, 1895), p. 12.

8.   See Fisher, *History of Christian Doctrine* (Scribners, 1896), p. 348 fn.

In general, New England Theology moved away from the extreme (supralapsarian) position of Jonathan Edwards himself. And in reaction to its development the Hodges of Princeton declared exhaustively the old Calvinism. Charles Hodge accepts the Federal Theology at its basic point: "The Nature of the covenant, therefore, determines the object of his death,"[9] yet in the growing doctrine of "common grace" he indicates one way of solving the evangelical tension of scholastic Calvinism:

> It will of course be admitted that, if efficacious grace is the exercise
> of almighty power it is irresistible. That common grace, or that
> influence of the Spirit which is granted more or less to all men is
> often effectually resisted, is of course admitted.[10]

Finally, what of the contemporary attitude towards the Federal Theology? There would seem to be three main attitudes, the teaching of the Westminster Seminary approaching most closely to the traditional system.[11] In the impressive theology of Dutch theologians, however, we see a more critical attitude. Bavinck, for instance, resolves the tension between supra- and infra-lapsarianism inasmuch as the divine decree is "a system the several elements of which are coordinately related to one another."[12]

It is Karl Barth who seeks a re-orientation of the problem of predestination, and a more personal and dynamic approach to the problem of atonement.[13] It is also significant to consider his appraisal of the Federal Theology, as given incidentally in a comment on the historical theology of Heinrich Heppe:

---

9.   *Systematic Theology* (Nelson, 1873), Vol. II, p. 546.

10.   *Ibid.*, p. 687.

11.   E.g., L. Boettner, *The Reformed Doctrine of Predestination* (Grand Rapids, MI: Eerdmans, 1932).

12.   H. Bavinck, *The Doctrine of God*, trans. W. Hendriksen, (Grand Rapids, MI: Eerdmans, 1951), p. 383.

13.   E.g. *Kirchliche Dogmatik*, II/2, ch. VII: "The Election of God," and IV/1, §57.2, "The Covenant as the Presupposition of Reconciliation."

On Heppe's historical outlook we should note that according to him, wonderful to relate, not Calvin but the later Melanchthon must have been the Father of Reformed theology. And he has paid his tribute to the spirit of the nineteenth century, in that for him the incursion of the covenant-theology of Cocceius and his pupils, proclaimed alongside of Cartesianism, into the line of the older expositors of Reformed dogma seems not to involve any deeper problem; so that we ask in vain how it came about, that, in this particular, Reformed orthodoxy in the eighteenth century can be so marvellously and painlessly "intellectual," i.e., pietistically rationalist.[14]

Here Barth indicates the confusion in our historical attitude: we have approached the Reformers through the orthodoxy of their successors, and have failed to notice the basic disagreement between the two, from dynamic to static and from biblical to philosophical theology. Why should it be taken for granted that Calvin's theology stands or falls with the doctrine of predestination? Because of the caricature so systematically and skilfully drawn for us by the orthodox Calvinism. Yet this orthodoxy failed to assess Calvin aright, failed to balance his Augustinian concept of grace (which emphasis is not necessarily supralapsarian, we should add) with that which informed his doctrines of justification, sacrament and predestination too—that faith means union with Christ. The final sign of the caricature is the fact that Charles Hodge interprets our relation to Christ as "a federal union,"[15] and draws a close parallel between the representative role of Adam and of Christ. But it is highly questionable whether this is a fair reading of Paul's central concept of being *en Christo;* and the relation between Adam and Christ according to Paul (e.g. *Rom.* 5:12ff, *1 Cor.* 15:21ff) is not sufficiently homologous to bear the interpretation which the Federal Theology assumes.

The critical question for Federal Theology was the effective use of the means of grace: how was the Minister of the Word and Sacraments to offer God's grace, and how was the repentant sinner to receive

---

14. Foreword to Heppe, *op. cit.,* p. vii.
15. *Op. cit.,* p. 551.

it?[16] This is the question for which Protestant orthodoxy could find no adequate answer in its covenantal interpretation of Reformed theology. And this is precisely the question to which the doctrine of union with Christ provides the positive answer. Calvin, in company with Peter Martyr (and Martin Bucer), had stressed *the dynamic communication of the new humanity of the Ascended Lord* as the content of faith, given through the means of grace committed to the Church. This union with Christ was to be discerned on three levels. First was a general or absolute union by the Incarnation, which affords the theological basis for anthropology and ethics, since in this prior sense every person *as person* bears the image of God (e.g. *Inst.* 3.7.6). The second kind of union is effected by the Holy Spirit, who unites us to Jesus Christ in justification and new life: "For no other way are we reconciled to God by the sacrifice of His death, except that He is ours and we are one with Him," writes Calvin to Martyr.[17] The third union is the result of this justifying grace, by which the Spirit communicates the properties of Christ's new humanity ("sanctification"), which is perfected in us by Resurrection alone.

The question of whether justification is imputed or imparted, it may be observed, does not arise for the Reformers, but only for a more scholastic generation. Barth puts the case thus:

> In emphasizing this more than mystical and more than speculative statement, that faith means unity with the thing believed in, i.e. with Jesus Christ, Calvin did not in the least lag behind Luther, or either of them behind an Augustine, an Anselm, a Bernard of Clairvaux.

---

16.   Now that the Göttingen Dogmatics is available we have Barth's critique in fuller expression—*Unterricht in der christlichen Religion* (Zurich: Theol. Verlag, 1990) vol.2, §27. Barth agrees that the doctrine of covenant is part of the "family estate" (*Stammgut*) of Reformed theology, but he rejects Cocceius's distinction of covenants of works and grace, the "fatal historical moment" that opened the possibility of a dualistic view of revelation and covenant (27.III). To see stages in revelation is to historicize it. Cf. Michael Horton, *God of Promise: Introducing Covenant Theology* (Grand Rapids, MI: Baker Books, 2006).

17.   Peter Martyr Vermigli, *Epistolae (L. C.* 1094ff.); Ioan. *Calv. Epist. et Resp., Ep.* 208.

Without this statement the Reformed doctrine of justification and faith is impossible to understand.[18]

When we grasp this basic orientation of justifying faith in the Reformed theology, we take a decisive step away from the bent of the Federal system and towards a more positive understanding of the means of grace and the task of evangelism.

Let us be quite clear that Reformed theology is first and last a theology of the Holy Spirit. He is the answer to the problem of the effectiveness of scripture, sacrament and church. He *quickens* us by his use of creaturely means, so that we "lift up the heart" to that communion with Jesus Christ which is our life. In the office of the Holy Spirit, therefore, we have the context in which we are called to seek today's answer for today's problem of communicating the Gospel and evangelizing the world. No doubt a sign that the Spirit uses every theology is the fact that the Federal theologians did not argue from their doctrine of limited atonement to one of limited evangelism! Nevertheless our task today is to seek a more scriptural norm for the doctrine of the covenant. Scripture is less concerned about questions of decrees and limits than about the question of the People of God and its responsibility as his Servant in and to the world. The Covenant means a covenanted people *(laos)*, a Laity, who form the "ordinary" means of God's gracious activity towards his world. The doctrine of the Laity demands that we think again about our dichotomy of clergy/laity, and our restriction of the term "evangelist." Finally, in this People's history and destiny we have the true meaning of "covenant theology," namely the mystery of that divine-human Body which ministers to its generation the grace of God, even Jesus Christ, Head of his Body, King of His People.

---

18.   *C.D.* I/1 (Edin.: T. & T. Clark, 1936), p. 274.

10

CALVIN AND PHILOSOPHY

Presidential address to The Canadian Theological Society,
Kingston, May 1964.[1]

The question of John Calvin's attitude towards philosophy places us in controversy. There seem to be two dominant schools of thought, in the English-speaking world at least. One states that Calvin was completely free from philosophical entanglement, a purely biblical theologian, Semitic rather than Hellenistic, a man of the Word (a picture not unlike that which Karl Barth claims for himself today). The other is the conservative Calvinism usually processed in Dutch packages, boldly proclaiming Calvin as the Christian philosopher, preferring Aristotle and ancient logic to Kant and everyone after him. Thus the American Calvinistic Congress hails the work of B. B. Warfield as the fountainhead of "classical Calvinism." In continental Europe there is a different attitude towards our question, viewing Calvin as stemming from French humanism, although not simply a humanist. In philosophy therefore he is oriented by the Graeco-Latin classicists, more Platonic than Aristotelian, like the Humanists more practical than theoretical, and much less rationalistic and systematic than later Calvinism supposed. Our situation reflects the situation described by John T. McNeill: "Calvin

---

1.   Published in the *Canadian Journal of Theology*, Vol. XI (1965), No. 1, pp. 42-53.

formerly stirred debate because people agreed or disagreed with his teaching. Recently men have been in disagreement with regard to what his teaching was."[2]

1. THE STATE OF PHILOSOPHY IN THE SIXTEENTH CENTURY

We are familiar with the fact of history that medieval theology and philosophy were virtually one and the same discipline, the "Christian philosophy" which Etienne Gilson has made his particular concern. We are also familiar with the fate of this impressive harmony of reason and faith, its collapse in late medieval philosophy, in what has been termed the "weariness with scholasticism."[3] The Renaissance therefore appears not as a philosophical movement, although it involved a recovery of classical learning and a revival of Platonism, in particular at the Academy of Florence. Rather, its humanism seemed to threaten all Christian thought, to be a risky business which glorified the human and relied on reason and good taste. Three groups had emerged: neo-scholastics, nominalists, and humanists. But as early as 1482 the Ancients (Thomists and Scotists) and the Modems (Occamists) at the University of Paris had made common cause against the Humanists.

The sixteenth century was an era of reaction for philosophy, chiefly because the great transition to the modern world-view had begun, to the scientific method and its consequent philosophy of science which would demand a new quality and character for philosophy itself. The humanists were the advance party, and the remnants of the medieval schools were waging a losing battle. The Reformation must be understood against this complex background, in which a pure philosophical issue is not to be discovered. The Reformers therefore are not so directly involved with the subject as we might suppose. Bertrand Russell has

---

2.   John T. McNeill, *The History and Character of Calvinism* (New York: Oxford University Press, 1954), p. 202.

3.   Jaroslav Pelikan, *From Luther to Kierkegaard* (St. Louis: Concordia, 1950), p.5.

stated: "Philosophically, the century following the beginning of the Reformation is a barren one."[4] It is to the credit of Lutheran theologians that they have investigated the question of the relation of medieval philosophy to their sixteenth and seventeenth century forefathers with thoroughness and frankness. To be sure, they have explicit references in Luther himself, for instance, to spur them on—tantalizing references to Occam, Biel, and Nicolas of Lyra among others (and strong antagonism to Aristotle). In Calvin we have more restrained references, more implicit data, more ambiguous material concerning his humanism, for instance, and the effect on it of his "sudden conversion."

One datum exists apart from the foregoing which is most relevant in our study. That is the fact that the development of later Calvinism took the direction of a Reformed Aristotelianism, producing the "classical" form already mentioned. Was this an inevitable direction, given certain things in Calvin's own thought and situation? How does it stand in relation to the humanistic Platonism that attracted Calvin himself? Does it, in short, represent a faithful continuation of Calvin? These are some of the questions posed; and although we cannot detail answers in this paper, they must not be far from our thoughts.[5*]

2. CALVIN AND FRENCH HUMANISM

It is important to notice that John Calvin was a second-generation Reformer. Born in 1509 (as Jean Cauvin), he published his first work, the commentary on Seneca's *De Clementia*, in 1532. Erasmus was then sixty-six and Luther forty-nine: the Reformation was an established

---

4.   *Wisdom of the West* (Garden City, N.Y.: Doubleday, 1959), p. 544.

5.   Since the time of this address, research on Reformed Scholasticism has burgeoned, a hot debate sparked by Brian Armstrong's *Calvinism and the Amyraut Heresy* (Madison, WI: University of Wisconsin Press, 1969). See especially the substantial contribution of Richard Muller (e.g. *Post Reformation Reformed Dogmatics* (Grand Rapids, MI: Baker Book House, 1987), and my summary in Martyr's *Commentary on Aristotle's Nicomachean Ethics* (PM Library vol. 9, 2006), "Reformed Aristotelianism," xxvi-xxx.

reality, and the atmosphere one of change and reconstruction. Without entering on detailed biography, we should note Calvin's environment as his theology developed. Here we must acknowledge the studies of the Strasbourg school, notably Pannier and Wendel, as well as the recent works of Jean Boisset and Joseph Bohatec.[6] Calvin was clearly humanist in his youth. In Paris he studied at the Collège de la Marche, learning from Cordier both Latin and humanism. At the Collège de Montaigu he later studied (perhaps in the company of Ignatius Loyola?) under John Major, the (Scottish) Occamist, began his profound Patristic learning, acquired the art of dialectical reasoning and argumentation from the austere Noël Beda, and meanwhile moved in the circle of his cousin Olivétan, William Cop, and William Budé, the most learned Hellenist in France. His interlude with the study of law at Orléans and Bourges involved also the study of Greek under Wolmar, and attendance at the lectures of the distinguished humanist Alciati from Milan, whom he considered extreme and vain.

By 1532 Calvin was back in Paris, publishing his commentary on Seneca. It is a thoroughly humanist work, although some apologists see an evangelical angle in the treatment of clemency for an age of intolerance. So in his twenty-third year he discusses a classic of Stoicism; in the work he quotes from fifty-six Latin and twenty-two Greek authors. He has begun well in his chosen career: a man of letters. Later he will remark that his chief desire is still to pursue "the enjoyment of literary ease with something of a free and honourable station." But the following year, 1533, was marked by Nicolas Cop's rectorial address to the University on "Christian philosophy." Its evangelical note precipi-

---

6.   J. Pannier, *Recherches sur l'évolution religieuse de Calvin jusqu'à sa conversion* (Strasbourg, 1924), *Calvin à Strasbourg* (Strasbourg, 1925), *Recherches sur la formation intellectuelle de Calvin* (Paris, 1931); F. Wendel, *Calvin: Sources et évolution de la pensée religieuse* (Paris: Presses Universitaires de France, 1950); J. Boisset, *Sagesse et Sainteté dans la pensée de Jean Calvin* (Paris: Presses Universitaires de France, 19'59); J. Bohatec, *Budé und Calvin: Studien zur Gedankenwelt des französischen Frühhumanismus* (Graz: Verlag H. Böhlaus, 1950).

tated the flight of Cop and his young adviser (and co-author?) Calvin. Between this and the first edition of his *Institutes,* Calvin experienced his conversion, and turned his humanist and literary vocation in the service of Reform.

The work on Seneca displays a scholarly and sympathetic approach to Stoicism, but no uncritical or passionate attachment. His authorities are Cicero and Aristotle, but he feels free to correct Stoic ethics in the light of "our religion." I do not understand Boisset's description of "anti-Stoic,"[7] but suggest that he is a critical humanist, judging the classical philosophy by received Christian teaching. He observes that "Human nature is so built that we are more affected by the viewpoint of utility or of pleasure than by these Stoic paradoxes so far removed from ordinary sentiment." The concern for utility is itself humanist—a philosophy must bear fruit in an ethic, theory in practice. Professor Harbison the Princeton historian concludes that Calvin's constant reference to the usefulness of his immense literary output over the years was a means of justifying "this continual yielding to his early zest for scholarship" so that "scholarship could be a Christian vocation of high significance."[8]

In French humanism we have a movement of the human spirit influenced by Florentine Platonism but pursuing its own motif of worldly wisdom and joy in creation. Of course, one can hardly group together Calvin's friend and teacher Budé along with the satirist Rabelais, who ridiculed Calvin in *Pantagruel* (Calvin retorted in a sermon on Deut. 13: 6-11, the command to condemn and kill whoever entices to idolatry!). But what all had in common was a preference for Plato over Aristotle. That is probably too simple a statement, yet even the reform of Aristotelianism proposed by the genius of Lefèvre d'Etaples was really an attempt to harmonize Aristotle with Plato. Calvin may be identified to a great extent with this Platonic humanism. Next to the Fathers, Plato is quoted most by Calvin in the *Institutes,* for instance: once in 1536, eighteen

---

7.   *Sagesse et Sainteté,* pp. 221, 248.

8.   E.H. Harbison, *The Christian Scholar in the Age of the Reformation* (New York: Scribner's, 1956), p. 164.

times by 1559 (Cicero gets nine references, Aristotle eight), and almost all in outright praise. Boisset's careful analysis of the passages and the more general Platonic themes leads him to conclude: "On peut dire que pour Calvin, Platon est, comme philosophe, ce qu' Augustin est comme théologien."[9] Now any theologian influenced by the Fathers is bound to be Platonic, for they were themselves influenced to varying degrees by Middle Platonism, while Augustine remained Neoplatonic in certain respects all his life. Yet Calvin has jumped over this Patristic Platonism thanks to his humanism: *ad fontes!* A purer Plato was now available through the Renaissance research, so that Calvin's Platonic themes—a hint of dualistic anthropology, even of pantheism, and especially the marked resemblance in matters political and moral—should be judged in terms of Plato's own work rather than of the mystagogue of Middle Platonism.

Is Calvin therefore to be described as a Platonist, understandable from within the context of French humanism?[10] A thematic parallelism may be explained on other grounds than direct influence. Besides, Calvin is a critical student of Plato. When faced with the "Nicodemites," the compromisers who wished to effect a Christian Platonist synthesis, he refutes them in strong words: "They change half Christianity into a philosophy. . . . In addition, a section of them have Platonic ideas in their heads and thus excuse most of the superstitions known to the papacy as being matters from which it is not possible to escape. This band consists almost entirely of men of letters. . . . I would prefer that all human knowledge were exterminated from the world rather than it should be the cause of cooling the enthusiasm of Christians in this

---

9.   *Sagesse et Sainteté*, p. 221.

10.   Quirinus Breen tends to overstatement of his thesis, which is nonetheless most important: *John Calvin: A Study in French Humanism* (Grand Rapids: Wm. B. Eerdmans, 1931); cf. Roy Battenhouse, "The Doctrine of Man in Calvin and in Renaissance Platonism," *Journal of the History of Ideas*, IX (Oct. 1948), for Calvin's "subterranean dependence" on the Florentine school, especially Pico della Mirandola.

way and causing them to turn away from God."[11] And although many French humanists regarded him as colleague (Lefèvre gave the young scholar his blessing at Nerac in 1534) yet as time went on they knew that he served another wisdom and authority. Let a modern spokesman have the last word here. In Van Gelder's study of "the two reformations" he wants to show the divergence of the "minor" (Protestant) Reformation from the "major" (Humanist). He notes Calvin's apparent humanism, but concludes that in his adherence to the general orthodox theology, "Calvin is opposite the 'major Reformation,' and close to Catholicism, much as he deviated in the working out of these points of doctrine from what was then orthodox."[12]

3. CALVIN AND SCHOLASTICISM

Did Calvin's positive, if critical, attitude towards Plato mean that he was against Aristotle? He openly repudiates the neo-scholasticism of his age; yet he continued to rely on Aristotelian categories in his theology, and later Calvinism felt justified in its Aristotelianizing trend. If the facts seem confusing, we may yet discern a pattern. At the Collège de Montaigu he had learned the traditional scholastic discipline, couched in the dialectic of argumentation. The method that originated in the *Disputed Questions* of medieval learning, later refined by Thomas Aquinas, had become oracular (witness the oral debates and colloquies of the Reformation itself). It was this scholastic Aristotelianism, with its subtle dialectic and love of verbal exchange, which Calvin rejected. He called it a "frigid philosophy," manufactured chiefly by the *Sorbonnistes* who engaged in mere "sophistry."

Once again we must enter a qualifier for the model, in this case Calvin the anti-Aristotelian. He somewhat resembles Luther here, for Luther once remarked that he knew more of Aristotle than Thomas did, in the

---

11.   *Excusatio ad Pseudonicodemos* (Geneva, 1549).

12.   H. A. Enno Van Gelder, *The Two Reformations in the Sixteenth Century* (The Hague: M. Nijhoff, 1961), p. 268.

sense that he was free of bondage to the philosopher, free to accept only what is agreeable to the gospel.[13] Calvin has a positive appreciation of Aristotle's logic, and follows many of his distinctions to fruitful theological ends. Thus the familiar themes of the mean between extremes, the distinction *per se/per accidens,* the concept of analogy, and fourfold causality, have an essential place in Calvin's theology, especially in key doctrines such as election, sanctification, and eucharist. As a humanist—according to Harbison's thesis—Calvin sat more lightly to scholasticism, retaining much of its value, whereas others like Erasmus and Luther reacted violently against it. Therefore "there is actually more continuity between Aquinas and Calvin than between Aquinas and either Erasmus or Luther."[14] In this respect there is a significant historical question which I simply raise here: Is *Strasbourg* the key to Reformed Aristotelianism? The city of Martin Bucer was heavily coloured by the Aristotelian tradition of the local Dominicans as well as of the educational system of Jacob Sturm. To this city came John Calvin in those critical years 1539-41, during the exile from Geneva. Here he wrote his enlarged second edition of the *Institutes* (1539) as well as the beautiful 1541 French edition, so formative of the modern French language, and the *Short Treatise on the Lord's Supper.* In all of these we see certain signs of Bucer's influence, notably the increasing significance of the concept of faith as union with Christ. Also in the 1539 *Institutes* he first introduces a fourfold causality in his doctrine of election.

After Calvin's sojourn in Strasbourg, Peter Martyr arrived, an Italian already schooled in Aristotle. In this milieu Aristotle and scripture were balanced in alternate days' lecturing, for a time by Bucer himself. In his second sojourn there (1553-57) Martyr lectured on the *Nicomachean Ethics,* and Zanchi on the *Physics;* the latter became even more thoroughly Aristotelian, as seen in his penchant for the syllogism. Probably

---

13.   Pelikan, *From Luther to Kierkegaard,* p. 11.
14.   Harbison, *The Christian Scholar,* p. 145.

in Zanchi and Theodore Beza we have the true origin of Reformed Aristotelianism and therefore of that "classical Calvinism" noted above. But
that is another story.[15]

Calvin's ambivalent attitude to Aristotle may be illustrated by two
examples. One is the concept of *substance*. Here Calvin was very wise,
making a valiant effort to qualify the traditional *quidditas* by a more
dynamic definition (an anticipation of today's theory of matter as
energy?). This is notably evident in his doctrine of the eucharist. The
sixteenth century Supper-Strife, involving Romans, Lutherans, Reformed
and Anabaptist, was hampered and even doomed to failure because
everyone tried to work with the old medieval categories, the school distinctions. I submit that Calvin, like Peter Martyr,[16] launched a twofold
attack, on philosophical and theological levels. Philosophically he tried
to show the logical absurdity of the scholastic teaching, transubstantiation in particular. Theologically he tried to break through into a new
dynamism and personalism more suited to the subject. Central was the
personal union of Christ: the "substance" of this living and lordly Person
demanded a new framework, only tentatively outlined by the Reformers,
especially in their stress on the office of the Holy Spirit.

The second point is opposite: in this regard, Calvin remained too much
the Aristotelian. I refer to the bitter controversy with the Lutherans about
Christ's presence in the eucharist. Here Calvin tended to rely too much
on spatial categories, and some of his disciples more so. This is a complex
subject, whose bitter heritage is only lately moving towards healing in
our time.[17*] Let me summarize by stating that the Calvinist party relied

---

15.   See my Introduction to Vermigli's Commentary (Peter Martyr Library, vol. 9,
2006).

16.   See McLelland, *The Visible Words of God* (Edinburgh: Oliver & Boyd, 1957);
for Calvin, *Inst.*, IV.17.8-10.

17.   Conversation groups in Europe and North America are currently at work
—since this was written, a dialogue group of Lutheran and Reformed theologians
produced the volume *Marburg Revisited: a Reexamination of Lutheran and Reformed
Traditions*, ed. Empie & McCord (Minn: Augsburg, 1966).

on Aristotle's dictum "no place, no body," and tended to locate, and even localize, Christ's personal presence in a "heavenly place." To be sure, they qualified this by denying that it was simply the dimension of height extended to infinity; but the Lutherans recognized the resulting predicament, and (I think) offered a better solution in such concepts as Christ's *multivolens* presence. Probably also, Martin Bucer was even more correct to condemn both sides and to insist on the power of negative thinking here: "not of this world, not of sense, not of reason"; "Let them not make a new article of faith concerning the certain place of heaven in which the body of Christ is contained."[18]

In terms of historical philosophy, therefore, John Calvin stands in reaction to medieval scholasticism on behalf of Platonic humanism, although his use of certain categories of thought indicates his continuity with much of Aristotelian tradition. His critique of human wisdom as such is probably best illustrated from his epistemology.

4. CALVIN AND HUMAN KNOWLEDGE

The basic decision in thinking is that between ontology and epistemology, or at least as to which is determinative (which comes first, *being* or *knowledge*?). If one chooses ontology, being as such is one's concern, and one can pursue what Gilson is fond of calling "the metaphysics of Exodus," the ontological implications of divine revelation, "He Who Is." It is significant that in one of his rare discussions of Reformed theology, Gilson treats not Calvin but Lecerf, and remarks that Calvinism "clearly subjects reason to faith, or more exactly, forbids faith to speak another language than that of faith."[19]

---

18.   Bucer's letter to Calvin in criticism of the Zurich Consensus of 1549: *Corpus Ref.* XLI, *Cal. Op.* XIII, pp. 350ff.

19.   *Christianisme et Philosophie* (Paris: Librairie Philosophique, J. Vrin, 1949), p. 44. Cf. the famous French discussion of "La Notion de philosophie Chrétienne," Séance du 21 mars 1931 (Paris: *Bulletin de la Société française de Philosophie*). Gilson continues: "Sans doute, il s'agit bien encore d'une connaissance, et d'une pensée

Although much depends on definition here, it is surely right to say that Calvin's is not a "Christian philosophy" so much as a theology using philosophical data and method in critical fashion, that is partially. The grounds for so stating the case lie in his attitude towards human reason and so in his epistemology. A brief summary from T. F. Torrance's fine study of Calvin's anthropology illustrates the point:

> As a natural gift, the reason is not totally destroyed, though it is seriously impaired, and totally perverted. The total perversion of the mind or reason means that the whole inclination of the mind is in the direction of alienation from God. The reason has therefore lost its original rectitude, and is indeed alienated from right reason, until it is renewed by the Spirit through the Word.[20]

Now like the other Reformers, Calvin distinguishes reason as applied to "earthly things" and to "heavenly things" (e.g. *Inst.* II.ii.12-17). He allows to the natural man a wisdom and ability in arts and science sufficient to maintain order and to advance civilization. His affection for men like Plato, Cicero, and Seneca reflects this position. God

> fills and makes and invigorates all things by virtue of his Spirit, and that according to the peculiar nature which each class of beings has received by the law of creation. But if the Lord has been pleased to assist us by the work and ministry of the ungodly in physics, dialectics, mathematics, and other similar sciences, let us avail ourselves of it lest by neglecting the gifts of God spontaneously offered to us, we be justly punished for our sloth" (*Inst.* II.ii.16).

On this level, Calvin makes it explicit that arts and sciences manifest "a universal apprehension of reason and understanding" (II.ii.14). "If we regard the Spirit of God as the sole fountain of truth, we shall neither reject the truth itself, nor despise it wherever it shall appear, unless we wish

---

véritable, mais d'une 'connaissance religieuse,' et d'une 'pensée religieuse,' qui presupposent explicitement la fai comme leur fondement et leur point de départ."

20.   T. F. Torrance, *Calvin's Doctrine of Man* (London: Lutterworth, 1949), p. 116.

to dishonour the Spirit of God' (II.ii.15). It is here also that his positive aesthetic appears, as Wencelius has shown, an aesthetic which destroys the caricature of Calvin drawn by the negative mood and puritan spirit of his successors.[21] Again, the "common grace" of which he speaks in this context, as well as the "special grace" granted to men of excellence, is not a question of degrees of salvation: this is not soteriology but epistemology, the validity of reason when it turns to "inferior things." It is when the reason attempts to grasp higher reality that it quickly discovers its limits, or rather tries to deny them and so displays its ability as a factory of idols *(Inst.* II.ii.18-21). Here is the beginning of his discussion:

> We must now analyse what human reason can discern with regard
> to God's Kingdom and to spiritual insight. This spiritual insight
> consists chiefly in three things: (1) knowing God; (2) knowing his
> fatherly favour in our behalf, in which our salvation consists; (3)
> knowing how to frame our life according to the rule of his law. In
> the first two points, and especially the second, the greatest geniuses
> are blinder than moles! Certainly I do not deny that one can read
> competent and apt statements about God here and there in the
> philosophers, but these always show a certain giddy imagination.
> As was stated above, the Lord indeed gave them a slight taste of
> his divinity that they might not hide their impiety under a cloak
> of ignorance. . . . They are like a traveller passing through a field
> at night who in a momentary lightning flash sees far and wide,
> but the sight vanishes so swiftly that he is plunged again into the
> darkness of the night before he can take even a step let alone be
> directed on his way by its help. . . . Human reason, therefore, neither
> approaches, nor strives toward, nor even takes a straight aim at,

---

21.   L. Wencelius, *L'Esthétique de Calvin* (Paris: Presses Universitaires de France, 1937). Calvin's concept of beauty may be gathered from *Inst.* III,x.2: "Did he not, in short, render many things attractive to us, apart from their necessary use?," and from his sermon on 2 Samuel 14 (11 Sept., 1562) on Absalom's beauty, the use and abuse of divine gifts of body and spirit *(Supplementa Calviniana,* Vol. I (Neukirchener Verlag, 1961), No. 46, pp. 399ff.). His humanism appears in his aesthetics; for instance in his evaluation of music in worship and in human life generally, he reflects the musical humanism of the Renaissance *(laus musicae),* e.g. *Preface* to 1543 Psalter.

this truth: to understand who the true God is or what sort of God he wishes to be toward us (II.ii.18).

For Calvin, then, philosophy may indicate the universal desire for truth and the remarkable achievement in human affairs, but it is almost completely unreliable in things divine. In a notable passage he states that the evidence of God in creation does not seem to profit us: "In this regard how volubly has the whole tribe of philosophers shown their stupidity and silliness! For even though we may excuse the others (who act like utter fools), Plato, the most religious of all and the most circumspect, also vanishes in his round globe."[22] And what might not happen to others when the leading minds, "whose task it is to light the pathway for the rest, wander and stumble!" *(Inst.* I.v.11). They "wander and stumble"—the *labyrinth* is a favourite symbol of Calvin's, and even the *abyss*. Reason wanders in an "inextricable" labyrinth, "if the Word does not serve as a thread to guide our path." Only scripture saves us "from wandering up and down as in a labyrinth, in search of some doubtful deity." Again: "All knowledge without Christ is a vast abyss which immediately swallows up all our thoughts"; "All that knowledge of God which men think they have attained out of Christ will be a deadly abyss."[23]

Knowledge of God is knowledge of divine mystery, made actual and therefore possible through the Spirit's enlightenment. Commenting on Paul's idea of mystery, Calvin states: "Let us, however, learn from this, that the gospel can be understood by faith alone—not by reason, nor by the perspicacity of the human understanding, because otherwise it is a thing that is hid from us." This is why knowledge of God apart from Christ means that they "contrive to themselves an idol in the place of God."[24] So there is a profound scepticism about reason when it thinks about God, unless it follows the Word of God, particularly its written

22. Cf. *Timaeus,* 33B.

23. *Inst.* I.vi.1, 3; *Comm.* on 1 Peter 1:21, on John 6:46; cf. Torrance, *Calvin's Doctrine of Man,* Chap. 11: "Natural Theology (1)."

24. *Comm. on Colossians* 2:2.

form of scripture, chief datum in the leading of the Spirit. Scripture teaches "an exclusive definition" of God, which "annihilates all the divinity that men fashion for themselves out of their own opinion" (*Inst.* Lxi.1). In a telling passage Calvin writes:

> Now this power which is peculiar to Scripture is clear from the
> fact that of human writings, however artfully polished, there is
> none capable of affecting us at all comparably. Read Demosthenes
> or Cicero; read Plato, Aristotle, and others of that tribe. They
> will, I admit, allure you, delight you, move you, enrapture you in
> wonderful measure. But betake yourself from them to this sacred
> reading. Then, in spite of yourself, so deeply will it affect you,
> so penetrate your heart, so fix itself in your very marrow, that,
> compared with its deep impression, such vigour as the orators and
> philosophers have will nearly vanish. Consequently, it is easy to see
> that the Sacred Scriptures, which so far surpass all gifts and graces
> of human endeavour, breathe something divine (*Inst.* I.viii.I).

Calvin accepts sense data as the basis of human knowledge—he would belong to the cosmological rather than ontological type of philosophy of religion, for instance, in his acceptance of the argument from design (e.g. *Inst.* I.v.2-9). But faith is interpreted as a higher and discontinuous form of knowing:

> When we call faith "knowledge" we do not mean comprehension
> of the sort that is commonly concerned with those things which
> fall under human sense perception. For faith is so far above sense
> that man's mind has to go beyond and rise above itself in order to
> attain it. Even where the mind has attained, it does not comprehend
> what it feels. But while it is persuaded of what it does not grasp, by
> the very certainty of its persuasion it understands more than if it
> perceived anything human by its own capacity. . . we conclude that
> the knowledge of faith consists in assurance rather than in compre-
> hension (*Inst.* III.ii.14) .

For Calvin, this idea of persuasion (recall the Rhetorical tradition) is the key to the knowledge of God. In this form of communication the mystery involves a new relationship beyond common comprehension. Edward Dowey has stressed "the existential character of all our knowledge of God" according to Calvin.[25] Doumergue termed this theology "une doctrine de pratique," a suggestion which explains Calvin's impatience with "speculation." In a most significant sentence he states:

> Those, therefore, who in considering this question propose to inquire what the essence of God is *(quid sit Deus)* only trifle with frigid speculations, it being much more important for us to know what kind of being *(qualis sit)* God is, and what things are agreeable to his nature *(Inst.* I.ii.2).

Thus he can praise the teachings of the philosophers as "true, not only enjoyable, but also profitable to learn, and skilfully assembled by them. And I do not forbid those who are desirous of learning to study them." But over against their "subtle" teachings, it requires only a "simple definition" for "the upbuilding of godliness" (I.xv.60).

Like Luther's refrain of "for your sake" *(pro te),* this practical-utilitarian bent of Calvin maintains the unity of epistemology with soteriology, so that knowledge of God involves the self in conversion, the fruit of new life. Many large questions are at stake in our brief survey, but perhaps they can be indicated best if we conclude with a final question about Calvin's methodology.

5. CALVIN'S THEOLOGICAL METHOD

Revelation, for Calvin, is itself an accommodation to human creatureliness and sinfulness: their interaction makes the human predicament complex and the divine action correspondingly hidden.[26] The business of theology is the analysis of this accommodated revelation, and its commendation to others. Calvin's method therefore displays two motives, faithfulness to the data of revelation, and apologetic or evangelical fervour. It

---

25.   *The Knowledge of God in Calvin's Theology* (New York: Columbia University Press, 1952), pp. 24ff.

26.   See T. H. L. Parker, *The Doctrine of the Knowledge of God* (Edinburgh: Oliver & Boyd, 1952).

is necessary to appreciate how fully Calvin accepts the theme on which the *Institutes* open:

> true and sound wisdom consists of two parts: the knowledge of God and of ourselves. But, while joined by many bonds, which one precedes and brings forth the other is not easy to discern.

This idea is familiar in Augustine, but it was actually a received definition of philosophy in the classical world, recovered by the Humanists.[27] Thus Book I opens with this ancient philosophical theme of the twofold nature of knowledge, while Book II opens with the motto of the Delphic oracle: "Know thyself."

Now the twofold knowledge is a distinction without separation, as Calvin said; moreover, both aspects depend on the accommodated reve-latory data. Theology will be less systematic than philosophy, therefore, more like an empirical science or a phenomenological discipline. Calvin's method suggests the truth of this conclusion—Doumergue described it as "méthode des contrariétés"; Herman Bauke's interest in the *Formgestaltung* rather than the specific content of Calvin's theology gave evidence of a *compositio oppositorum,* or inharmonious elements; Peter Barth has also stressed the dialectic character of Calvin's thought.[28] McNeill states: "It is a superficial judgment that regards him as a resolute systematizer whose ideas are wholly unambiguous and consistent and set in a mould of flawless logic. In dogmatic exposition, says Henry Strohl, "Calvin did not seek harmonization; he was fond of tracing a middle way between two extreme solutions."[29]

---

27.   E.g. Cicero, *De Finibus.* Cf. Boisset, *Sagesse et Saintété,* pp. 1ff; Bohatec, *Budé und Calvin,* pp. 241ff.

28.   See the excellent article by John Leith, "Calvin's Theological Method and the Ambiguity in His Theology," in *Reformation Studies,* ed. F. H. Littell (Richmond: John Knox Press, 1962); also the opening chapter of W. Niesel's *The Theology of Calvin* (Philadelphia: The Westminster Press, 1956): "The Present State of Critical Studies."

29.   *The History and Character of Calvinism,* p. 202.

It is the grasp of Calvin's motive and method that has led Quirinus Breen to make so much of Calvin as standing within the "rhetorical tradition" of Humanism—a "dynamic Ciceronianism." After his careful analysis of Calvin's relation to the chief elements in rhetorical style and argument, he concludes: "There is a logic in the *Institutes*. In fact, it is full of logic. But the logic is not syllogistic. It is rhetorical logic. Syllogistic logic uses induction and the syllogism; rhetorical logic uses example and the enthymeme." [30] I submit that it is somewhat along this line that we must look far a proper understanding of John Calvin, especially his attitude towards philosophy. He stands against philosophy as metaphysical speculation about ultimate reality, and against a systematic philosophy as preamble to faith. [31] How modern that sounds! For indeed it is characteristic of his theology that it appreciates the "impropriety" of human language about God, that it understands the "suspense" by which revelation holds back ultimate reality so that it is present in signs and symbols, and so often hesitant and careful lest it say too much. Therefore he accepts only a critical philosophy, moving within the idea of *epochê* of his beloved Plato, and of the Stoics. (Hamann once described the thought of Socrates as forming a series of islands, with no bridges between.) Perhaps there is a similar relationship to philosophy evident in Calvin's modern disciple Karl Barth, who has declared: "We must return to the method of the *Loci*, the method of Melanchthon and also of Calvin, which was wrongly set aside as unscholarly by the more progressive of the contemporaries of J. Gerhard and A. Polanus." [32]

Thus we should be wary of those later Calvinists who systematized their "Christian philosophy" with the help of Aristotle. The selection of the doctrine of predestination as the ordering principle of theology is symptomatic of this step. Such an analytic method misses the

---

30. "John Calvin and the Rhetorical Tradition," *Church History*, March 1957, p. 13.

31. Jacques de Senarclens, *Heirs of the Reformation* (trans. by G. W. Bromiley, London: S.C.M., 1963), pp. 85ff., concerning the *praeambula fidei* of scholasticism and its fate in the sixteenth century.

32. *C.D.* 1/2, p. 870.

point of Calvin's style, his theological form. The philosophizing of theology characteristic of "classical Calvinism," in which a philosophical preamble returns, albeit with new content, suggests a shift from Calvin's own style to a different understanding of theology's task.[33] In this sense the last word must concern his positive relationship to the theological datum, the Gospel. Here his humanist conviction—his philosophy of persuasion[34*]—that truth will come not by proof but by invitation, not by rational comprehension but by total commitment to a style of life, comes to the fore. His speech is too broken, his theology too dynamic, to substitute for a philosophy. Philosophy is serious, a preparation for death; theology is gay, a guide for new life.

---

33.   Cf. H. Dooyeweerd's chapters 5-7 on "Philosophy and Theology" in *In The Twilight of Western Thought* (Philadelphia: Presbyterian and Reformed Pub. Co., 1960); also the "established categories" presupposed by Leroy Nixon in *John Calvin's Teachings on Human Reason* (New York: Exposition Press, 1963). A recent book in ecumenical mood attempts to show the common basis of medieval Catholic and seventeenth century Protestant scholasticism, and so brings significant tangential evidence to our subject: Robert P. Scharlemann: *Thomas Aquinas and John Gerhard* (New Haven: Yale University Press, 1964).

34.   The distinction is well made by Aristotle: "it is the mark of an educated man to look for precision in each class of things just so far as the nature of the subject admits; it is evidently equally foolish to accept probable reasoning from a mathematician and to demand from a rhetorician scientific proofs"—*Nic. Eth.* I.2, 1094b24ff.

11

PETER MARTYR: RENAISSANCE
PHILOSOPHY AND REFORM

Paper presented to the Sixteenth Century
Studies Conference, St Louis, 1996.

Peter Martyr Vermigli (1499-1562) is best known these days as one of the founders of what is called "Reformed Scholasticism" or even "Reformed Aristotelianism." Our *Peter Martyr Library* series of English translations hopes to correct this simplistic assessment by showing his stature as Old Testament exegete, apologist for Reformed theology, especially its understanding of the sacramental signs, and colleague of such leading theologians as Martin Bucer, Thomas Cranmer and Henry Bullinger. He represents the truth in the charge that the label "Calvinism" has been applied too narrowly to carry the freight of such contributions as his own.[1]

The subject of this paper concerns the relation between philosophy and theology in Vermigli's thought. It is drawn from my research for the

---

1.   See J.P. Donnelly, *Calvinism and Scholasticism in Vermigli's Doctrine of Man and Grace* (Leiden: E.J. Brill, 1976) 1; R. Muller, *Post-Reformation Reformed Dogmatics* (Grand Rapids: Baker Book House, 1987) I.22.

fourth volume of the *Peter Martyr Library*, an anthology entitled "Philosophical Works."

Our story begins with the youthful Pietro Martire Vermigli in Padua, where he studied for eight years, 1518-1526. Padua exemplified "one of the sixteenth century's most important philosophical characteristics, the development of a revivified Aristotelianism."[2] This has been described as "Paduan Averroism." Paul Oskar Kristeller considered this "a misleading name"[3] although their ideas of a universal intellect and pantheistic determinism inspired Calvin's Libertine adversaries. In Martyr's case, he concentrated on the practical works of Aristotle in line with the pragmatic bent of Renaissance Humanism. He considered the speculation that led to antitrinitarianism, for instance, as a sign of the *hybris* of fallible minds. During his eight years at Padua he also studied theology; the theology faculty featured chairs *in via Thomi* and *in via Scoti*: he much preferred the former. He follows Thomas chiefly in methodology, although his use of *quaestiones disputata*, of *objectum* and *respondeo*, is much looser. Nor does he rest on demonstrative argument, but looks to the Holy Spirit's drawing out our inchoate knowledge of God.[4]

ARISTOTLE AND AQUINAS

Renaissance philosophy involved the revival of three classical systems: Platonism, Aristotelianism and Neoplatonism, along with alchemical and occult ideas.[5] For Vermigli there were three chief authorities: Aristotle, Augustine and Aquinas. It was the Church Father who remained the first love of this Augustinian monk, domi-

2.   *Cambridge History of Renaissance Philosophy*, Chas B. Schmitt & Q. Skinner, eds. (Cambridge University Press, 1988) 69f.

3.   *Renaissance Thought: The Classic, Scholastic and Humanist Strains* (NY: Harper 1961) 37.

4.   e.g. *Comm. in Rom.* 1:19 (*LC* 1.2, §3).

5.   See P.O. Kristeller, *Renaissance Thought and its Sources* (NY: Columbia University Press, 1979).

nating the others. His spirituality, as it were, served as control over his philosophical and theological learning. But I sense a prior question at issue here, namely the relation of Aquinas to Aristotle. Since Vermigli may be labelled a Thomist, with qualifications,[6] and since he pursues his theological agenda much as Thomas did, we must inquire into that Doctor's use of "the Philosopher."

I submit that Aquinas was influenced by Augustine and the Patristic tradition in a positive way that controlled his philosophical axioms in a similar fashion to our Reformer's. For instance, philosophers take the famous--or notorious--"five ways" as the Thomist solution to the problem of divine existence. I consider this a major fallacy in historical philosophy. The few paragraphs Thomas devotes to this topic are far from expressing the heart of his system.[7] After all, he begins his theological *Summa* with a sort of negative theology. To be sure, "Sacred doctrine proceeds by argument," but the motion is from beliefs to their necessary corollaries: "the first principles of this science are the articles of faith ... the whole of a science is virtually contained in its principles."[8] Rational argument is in order insofar as this process of unfolding foundational truth requires reason as apologist and persuader. Even the philosophical *Summa* had not transgressed this rule. Its opening shows Thomas using arguments *a posteriori* only, since the divine essence is unknowable. The argument from motion, i.e. cosmology, leads to remotion: "we cannot apprehend [the divine nature] by knowing what it is. But we have some knowledge thereof by knowing *what it is not.*"[9] Martyr follows suit, treating negations with respect and even privilege in his epistemology and applauding Clement of Alexandria's apophatic notion of God.[10] Thus

6. See J. P Donnelly, S.J. "Calvinist Thomism," *Viator:Medieval and Renaissance Studies*, vol. 7 (Berkeley: University of California Press, 1976) 442-55.

7. *Summa Theol.* Ia, Q2, art. 3: *Utrum deus sit.*

8. *S.T.* Ia, Q 1.1.7, ad 2.

9. *Summa Contra Gentes* I.12ff.

10. "Visions," scholium in *Comm. in Iud.* 6:11 (*LC* 1.4, §12); in McLelland, ed. *Philosophical Works*, (PML Library vol. 4), 138-54.

we have a method quite in line with the Augustinian-Anselmic *fides quaerens intellectum.*

ARISTOTLE AND VERMIGLI

In his introduction to the commentary on the *Nicomachean Ethics*, Martyr states: "After Plato came Aristotle, a man of singular genius, who subjected all the relevant material to methodical analysis and arranged it with the greatest accuracy. ... The school of Peripatetics sprang from Aristotle; it had fewer errors than any other school, and flourishes to this day."[11] His own brand of Aristotelianism was not quite Paduan; it selected the Philosopher's 'dialectics' (i.e. logic) and certain metaphysical categories agreeable to the scriptural and patristic canon of Martyr's Augustinianism. "We don't agree with the sayings of Aristotle because of the author but because we consider some of his axioms true, in the same way Paul quoted certain verses of the poets. But when the Philosopher was mistaken and taught something contrary to religion, we support him least of all and even oppose his errors utterly."[12]

In his second stage of life, as colleague of the Northern Reformers (1542-62), Peter Martyr became famous not for his biblical expertise but for his apologetics or polemics. His contemporary Joseph Scaliger remarked: "The two most excellent theologians of our time are John Calvin and Peter Martyr, the former of whom has dealt with the Holy Scriptures as they ought to be dealt with—with sincerity I mean, and purity and simplicity, without any scholastic subtleties. ... Peter Martyr. because it seemed to fall to him to engage the Sophists, has overcome them sophistically, and struck them down with their own weapons."[13]

---

11.   "Philosophy and Theology" §3 (*Philosophical Works*, p 11).

12.   *Dialogue on the Two Natures in Christ*, trans. and edited by J.P. Donnelly (Kirksville MO: Sixteenth Century Journals Publishers, Inc., 1995--Peter Martyr Library volume 2) 14.

13.   Quoted by B.B. Warfield, *Calvin and Augustine* (Phila: Presbyterian and Reformed Publishing, 1956) 481.

This "sophistical" method opens up the question of Martyr's role in the introduction of "Reformed Scholasticism." Here is yet another label being reexamined these days, not least by Richard Muller.[14] Almost thirty years ago, Brian Armstrong argued that Beza, Zanchi and Martyr introduced a distinct shift from Calvin's own scriptural theology to a scholastic method and content.[15] The debate still continues, with both sides offering more nuanced interpretation of the complex history of late medieval, Renaissance and Reformation methodology.[16] In sum, the concept of a fall from Calvin's "nonscholastic theology" is hardly justified by appealing to the use of school methods or systematizing. There is also the danger of making John Calvin the archetype of Reformed theology, if not its saint. This misses the significance of the original circle of Reformers, including the complementary role of Bullinger's Zurich academy, the *schola tigurina*, which included Vermigli in his final years.

Harking back to Vermigli's formative years at Padua, Philip McNair concludes: "Of the three A's who contended for the mastery of his mind, Aristotle out-rivaled Averroës, but Augustine outclassed them both: in the life of this Augustinian, Augustine was to remain to the end his favorite reading after the Bible."[17] We should note in this regard the influence of the *schola Augustiniana moderna* recently examined by

---

14.   See *Post-Reformation Reformed Dogmatics* (Grand Rapids: Baker Book House, 1987) 2 vols.; *Christ and the Decree: Christology and Predestination in Reformed Theology from Calvin to Perkins* (Grand Rapids: Eerdmans, 1988) and "Calvin and the 'Calvinists': Assessing rhe Continuities and Discontinuities Between the Reformation and Orthodoxy," *Calvin Theological Journal* (Grand Rapids, MI) 30 (1995) 345-75 and 31 (1996) 125-60.

15.   B.A. Armstrong, *Calvinism and the Amyraut Heresy* (Madison: University of Wisconsin Press, 1969).

16.   See J.C. McLelland, "Peter Martyr Vemigli: Scholastic or Humanist?" in *Peter Martyr Vermigli and Italian Reform* (Waterloo ON: Wilfrid Laurier University Press, 1980) ed. McLelland, 141-51.

17.   *Peter Martyr in Italy* (Oxford: Clarendon Press, 1967) 94.

Heiko Oberman, Alister McGrath and Frank A. James.[18] The key figure in this tradition is that of Gregory of Rimini (d. 1358), a famous general of the Augustinian Order and known for his doctrine of predestination. Frank James claims that Vermigli follows Gregory in breaking with "the Thomist inclination to view predestination as *pars providentiae*."[19] The implication is that predestination is a corollary of grace rather than of creation, as we will see in a moment.

A final point of note is that Protestants tend to regard Aristotle as himself the arch-scholastic. But what of that other Aristotle, author of *On Interpretation* and the *Rhetoric* and *Poetics*—the last given modern notoriety through Umberto Eco's *The Name of the Rose*? Aristotle the literary and theatrical critic, the hermeneut and aesthete? We know the thesis that Calvin belongs to the rhetorical tradition, preferring argument as enthymeme to the syllogism. Now Martyr prefers the latter, but after all, "an enthymeme is a syllogism starting from probabilities or signs."[20] In other words, both Calvin and Martyr share in the rhetorical-dialectical tradition that recognizes the priority of *probability* in theological argument, and therefore of *persuasion* in apologetics and homiletics. The necessary principles of mathematics and ordinary science entail strict demonstration or proof, but where those principles are merely probable we resort to persuasive argument to commend their truth. In his commentary on *Romans*, Martyr notes the eloquence of Paul's speech and recommends "the study of good arts" for preachers.[21] He also uses figures of speech and tropes aplenty,

---

18. Seee H.A. Oberman, *The Harvest of Medieval Theology* (Grand Rapids: Eerdmans, 1967) 196ff; H.A. Oberman & Frank A. James III, eds. *Via Augustini: Augustine in the Later Middle Ages, Rennaissance and Reformation* (Leiden: E.J. Brill, 1991); A.E. McGrath, *Reformation Thought: an Introduction* (Oxford: Basil Blackwell, 1988) 55f, 60f.

19. Frank A. James III, "Juan de Valdés before and after Peter Martyr Vermigli: the Reception of *Gemina Praedestinatio* in Valdés' later thought" in *Archiv für Reformationsgechichte* 83 (1992) 180-208.

20. Aristotle, *An. Prior.* 70a10.

21. *In Epistolam ... ad Romanos* (Basel: P.Perna, 1558) Praef.

with references to tragedy and comedy: Christian hope, for instance, must await "the fifth act."

PROVIDENCE AND PREDESTINATION

The key issue in our topic is that of the concept of *causality* in Reformed theology. This shows itself best in the twin doctrines of providence and predestination. I say "twin" deliberately, for they form the horns of our dilemma. In brief, the question (which becomes the formal test of "Reformed Orthodoxy") is whether predestination is "part of providence" as Aquinas put it (*quaedam pars providentiae*). This fateful phrase reappears in Peter Martyr, although only in one of three "Summaries" still disputed as to authorship.[22] Whether this brief text is from Martyr's hand or that of a disciple, I do not think it contradicts his general teaching. In an early locus on the subject from the Strasbourg lectures on *Genesis* (1553-56) Martyr states: "In providence we see predestination, which brings so great a comfort to the godly as to strengthen them greatly;"[23] and in his later treatise *De Providentia* Martyr concludes his analysis of divine governance by saying: "we have in a sense established the roots and foundation of predestination."[24] Thus the question of the soteriological context of the doctrine of predestination in the tradition of Rimini seems threatened by such placing it under the doctrine of providence. Whether the special and salvific divine will should be understood within creation rather than the doctrine of God, for Peter Martyr the emphasis on causal willing does not seem to compromise his biblical criterion.

Richard Muller has noted that we must look not to the "scholastic" tradition but to the "exegetical" to interpret the Reformed doctrine of God and its corollary concept of the divine will. He notes that such

---

22.   Aquinas, *ST* Ia, Q 23, 1c; Martyr, *De providentia et praedestinatione*, App. to *Loci Comm.*, E.T. in *Philosophical Works*, pp. 328-32.

23.   Scholium *De Providentia* in *Comm. in Gen.* 28:16 (*LC* 1.13, §2).

24.   Scholium on 1 Samuel 10:2 (*In Duos Libros Samuelis Prophetae* (Zurich: C. Froschauer, 1564) 59r (§16).

a distinction as that between the antecedent and the consequent divine will "was governed as much by soteriological interest like the priority of grace as by questions concerning the divine essence."[25] Peter Martyr clearly drew his understanding of causation from Aristotle, the complex causality of a fourfold nature (formal, material, efficient, final)[26] to solve the problem of how divine and human willing can coexist, allowing priority to the former but a certain "concurrence" to the latter. Muller concludes: "The issue confronting the study of post-Reformation Protestantism is not Calvin 'against' the Calvinists (or Calvin 'for' the Calvinists), but rather the analysis of continuities and discontinuities in thought in the context of diversity and development in the Reformed tradition."[27]

Now let us take three examples from Martyr's writings that show his understanding of the role of philosophy in theological thinking. They are from the commentary on the *Nicomachean Ethics* of Aristotle, a scholium from the commentary on Samuel, and another on Resurrection from the commentary on Kings. They illustrate the careful way in which Martyr uses philosophy to interpret the biblical narrative when it raises moot questions about divine and human willing.

1. THEOLOGY'S HANDMAID

Martyr lectured on Aristotle's *Nicomachean Ethics* at Strasbourg 1553-56,[28] alternating with Zanchi's on the *Physics*. A preface to this posthumous work was supplied by Martyr's *famulus* Giulio Santeranziano. This remarkable companion throughout Martyr's twenty-year exile from Italy had become quite a scholar. He sums up the role of philosophy in the familiar image of *ancilla theologiae*: "we join phi-

---

25.   *CTJ*, 130ff.

26.   See Aristotle, e.g. *An. Post.* II.11,94a20ff, *Meta.* V.2,1013a24ff.

27.   *CTJ*, 131, 158.

28.   Only the commentary to III.2 was published: *In primum, secundum et tertii libri Ethicorum Aristotelis Nicomachum ...* (Zurich: C. Froschauer, 1563) —PML vol. 9, 2006.

losophy to its queen, theology, not as equal in place and rank but as a modest and submissive handmaiden." Martyr's own introduction begins by distinguishing revealed from acquired knowledge. Such *duplex cognitio* or *notitia* is a common theme of Martyr's, echoing the Pauline natural knowledge sufficient to render sinners (and atheists) inexcusable.

Martyr relates this twofold knowledge to Aristotle's distinction between theoretical and practical knowledge. Theory includes metaphysics, physics and mathematics, and aims at contemplation. Practice issues in action and therefore is superior. Theology is a practical science since it fulfils theory and serves the human goal of happiness (*eudaimonia, felicitas*). A moral philosopher such as Aristotle is helpful because he remains within the limits of a knowledge derived from the works of creation. In this way Martyr meets Paul's warning to beware of philosophy defined as "empty deceit"(Col. 2:8). Here we see the practical Aristotelianism that the young Vermigli learned at Padua, one that makes use of the logic and ethics of The Philosopher rather than the metaphysics.

As is usual with Martyr, he soon relates his subject to biblical criteria: "Now we must see how what we have so far discussed agrees with Holy Scripture." Whereas in philosophy action precedes contemplation, revelation teaches us the opposite: first we believe and then good works follow. The contrast is clear: philosophy's goal is to "reach that beatitude or happiness which can be acquired in this life by human powers," but the goal of Christian devotion is "that the image in which we are created in righteousness and holiness of truth be renewed in us, so that we grow daily in the knowledge of God."[29] Martyr concludes that philosophy is a positive helper to piety, although its concept of virtue needs correction by the role of Holy Spirit in human morality. Yet it teaches us self-knowledge: "What could be more noble than to know oneself?"

---

29.   *Ethicorum* Praef. §6.

2. THE DIVINE WILL AND CAUSALITY

Martyr's typical Reformed stress on the divine will in human affairs both secular and sacred leads him often to ponder whether God is responsible for evil. Among several scholia on the subject, "Whether God is the Author of Sin" from the commentary on 2 Samuel presents his full and mature view of the topic.[30] If God wills all things actively through providence, with special concern for salvation through predestination, not only is human free will jeopardized, but the responsibility even for sin seems to lie with God. The dilemma is common: "the logic of the Reformed doctrine of election left theologians with the obligation to show that God did not cause the fall."[31]

Martyr's solution is twofold. First, in terms of the complex causality of his Aristotelian-Thomist logic, sin entails only a "*deficient*" cause, not an efficient one. God is involved not as agent but simply as final cause. Second, the divine will embraces all human actions, but differently according to whether these are good or evil. His thesis runs: "That God is not *per se* and properly the cause of sin; second, nothing happens in the world, not even sins themselves, outside his will and choice or providence."[32] But he insists that what is at stake is not some possible divine power but its actual effects: not the *posse* but the *velle*. Like Calvin, Martyr rejects the Nominalist distinction between absolute and ordained power (*potentia absoluta et ordinata*). He also condemns this distinction when refuting the Roman concept of transubstantiation and the Lutheran concept of ubiquity.

A theologian can reason only after the fact: he does not have prior knowledge of what God *could* do, only reflection on what God *has*

---

30.   *An Deus Sit Author Peccati*, in *In duos Libros Samuelis Prophetae ... Comm. doct.* on 2 Sam. 16:5ff. (Zurich: C. Froschauer, 1564) fol. 275r-285r (LC 1.14). The lectures were his penultimate series at Zurich, ca 1556-58 —PML vol. 4, pp. 215-62.

31.   J.H. Leith and W.S. Johnson, *Reformed Reader: a Sourcebook in Christian Theology* (Louisville: Westminster/John Knox, 1993) 187.

32.   *An Deus Sit ...* §6.

done—not *a priori* but *a posteriori*. This is why one cannot speculate by beginning from divine potency (the *posse)*, as if sheer omnipotence is God's chief attribute. Although in popular thought the concept of omnipotence tends to function like this (the disjunctive syllogism: All or Nothing), theologians of Classical Theism were usually careful to balance it with a concept of divine *impotence,* what God can*not* do. Most noteworthy is the idea that God cannot do anything that implies contradiction, that is, what is logically absurd, such as calling black white or making two plus two equal anything else than four. Martyr accepts such qualifications in his writings on providence and free will, and whether God is the author of sin.

Thus while acknowledging the final divine will behind all creaturely action, he appeals to secondary (human) causes as accountable for sin. Proximate second causes provide sufficient reason, absolving God of guilt *per se et proprie.* This solution contains the insight that causation is always complex, allowing a dynamic interaction and cooperation between wills that offers a more satisfactory solution than appeal to omnipotence as a completely obscure final cause. I take this to be an advance over Calvin's more rigid reliance on the ambiguity of a divine will that always moves "in accordance with the highest reason" yet whose rationality remains "concealed in the purpose of God."[33]

3. DEMONSTRATION AND PERSUASION

The scholium *De Resurrectione* in the commentary on Kings comes from Martyr's final lecture series at Zurich, about 1560-62.[34] It deals explicitly with the relation between reason and revelation. The question is, can reason *prove* resurrection? Peter Martyr uses Aristotelian categories to relate reason to revelation in two ways. His analysis shows that only probable reasons, not demonstrative (apodictic) ones, can be generated

33. *Inst.* 1.17.1.

34. *Melachim, id est, Regum Libri Duo posteriores ....* (Zurich: C. Froschauer, 1566) fol. 214v-230v (LC 3.15).

by theological reasoning. He draws on Aristotle to discuss the nature of proof.[35] Some arguments resolve problems into self-evident *principia*, while others are reducible to such principles. Still others may rest on necessary principles but cannot be demonstrated in the dependent discipline or "subalternate science" that uses them, only in the higher discipline. For instance, music makes use of mathematical principles which are demonstrable only in mathematics. But to someone versed in both disciplines, the musical principles, although derivative, will be conclusive. Similarly, arguments for resurrection are apodictic for the theologian, who knows their foundation in scripture, whereas they are not so for the philosopher, who cannot trace them back to natural causes.

A second dimension to Martyr's argument draws more on Aristotle's rhetoric, since "persuasion" is a form of argument that is quite reasonable (i.e. "rational") when the causes are probable rather than necessary. The rhetorical tradition is familiar in the case of John Calvin.[36] Yet it is not far from Martyr's kind of reasoning. For instance, as noted earlier, both enthymeme and syllogism are forms of legitimate argument, reflecting the twofold nature of premises as either necessary or probable. Human reason is always at work (i.e. at *play*) in understanding the articles of faith, which function as the first principles of the science of theology.

Thus we see in Peter Martyr one who brings his Aristotelian and Thomistic heritage, in their Renaissance form, to his biblical and apologetic work on behalf of Reform, and for whom the biblical criterion of his Augustinian theology and spirituality remains decisive.

---

35.   E.g., Aristotle, *An. Post.*, I.10, 766b23; Aquinas, *S.T.*, Ia, Q 1.2, resp. a5.

36.   See Q. Breen, *Christianity and Humanism* (Grand Rapids, MI: Eerdmans, 1968) 4: "John Calvin and the Rhetorical Tradition;" C. Vasoli, *"Loci Communes* and the Rhetorical and Dialectical Traditions" in *Peter Martyr and Italian Reform*, ed. J.C. McLelland (Waterloo, ON: Wilfrid Laurier University Press, 1980) 17-28.

12

THE MUNDANE WORK
OF THE SPIRIT

Address to the World Alliance of Reformed
Churches, Frankfurt, 1964.[1]

The Gospel is the good news that God loves the world. In Jesus Christ his re-creation of all things has begun. God himself supplies the faith to discern his presence and power in the world. These elements—God's love, new creation, the vision of faith—are gathered together under the "third article" of Christian doctrine, the Holy Spirit. He relates us to the new creation, he brings the future redemption into the present age. So we live by *hope*, that is, by the knowledge of what tomorrow will bring, despite what today holds. This is why hope breaks forth in joy, at times and in places where it seems folly to have joy. This is why the Christian can see signs of tomorrow in the events of today, and can celebrate the presence and power of the Lord Jesus Christ. As we celebrate we pray: *Come, Creator Spirit!* Not for the triumph of the church, but for the redemption of the world.

---

1. The Conference theme was "Come, Creator Spirit!"

We are asking the Holy Spirit to come for the redemption of a world that no longer wants redemption, or understands what it means. It has reduced all meaning to the human level, all hope to the secular sphere. It is a world that has "come of age." The swift spread of science and technology over our globe marks the end of man's "minority," the advent of his "maturity." As human knowledge races ahead, the various disciplines of thought proceed "as if there were no God." The old supernaturalism no longer convinces people; they have become "one-dimensional."

Christians must interpret this process in light of the Gospel. We must distinguish "secularization" from "secularism." Secularism is a spirit of self-sufficiency, a denial of faith. It puts its hope in the secular structure as the ultimate human good. In the form of "scientific humanism," it draws on a mystique of the human spirit, and rejects the claim of Jesus Christ to be God's true Man. But secularization, on the other hand, is a process of maturation which reflects the work of the Holy Spirit among us. For it is a grasp of the world as an order "on its own." If this were not God's creation, secularism would not be possible. Indeed, must we not claim that the Reformation swept out the spirits from the Western worldview, freeing us for the scientific quest? "Justification by faith" means that we do not rely upon outward proof, a sacred structure of events, observable without faith. The Christian meets God hidden within the true humanity of Jesus Christ, and must not search for some further proof, some naked divinity better than that! We are called to be content with signs, outwardly human, "secular;" but to eyes of faith, signs of the presence of God. If we walked by sight we would not need the Holy Spirit to open our eyes to the signs. If we believe in the Holy Spirit; we believe also in the secular.

At the Reformation, the hiddenness of God within our world was firmly grasped, along with its meaning for the *saeculum*. Luther's attack on the "religious" is based on this theme: "Here now a check is given to those slippery and skipping souls who seek God only in great and glorious things, who thirst after his greatness, who bore through heaven and think that they are serving and loving God by such noble ways, when all the time they are betraying him and pass by him in their

neighbors, here on earth in whom he desires to be loved and honored."
And Calvin's "social humanism" takes shape in the same way: "Since God
is invisible, our piety cannot be seen by men. . . . He therefore presents
himself to us in our brothers and in their person demands of us what
we owe to him." Calvin never tires of this idea, that God has bound all
mankind together in a "holy society," and in Jesus Christ has bound
himself to them so that one's fellowman becomes "as it were, his substitute."[2] Little wonder that his Geneva was a city of refuge, whose people
were engaged in a genuine diaconate!

This was God's way within the world in Jesus Christ. He looked like a
man: "Is this not this the carpenter? . . . and they were offended at him."
(Mk. 6:3) Here was Christ himself, the sign of signs, the essential and
decisive divine-human event. Will his Holy Spirit be unfaithful to his kind
of presence? The Holy Spirit does not correspond to "human spirit" but to
"Spirit of Christ." He does not witness to himself by working on our spirits,
giving ecstatic experiences such as may be found in most religions. Rather,
he witnesses to Jesus Christ by working on our whole humanity, giving
new depth and openness. The kind of "spirituality" which the Holy Spirit
brings to man is not a naked spirituality but one clothed in humanity, a
new creation. To discover God's presence in the world is always an act
of faith. As such it is always a precarious vision, holding together Spirit
and world, accepting the world as the place where the Spirit is busy with
his redemptive work. The "spiritual" man is not non-worldly or even
other-worldly, but *new-worldly.* He does not live by the separation of the
sacred from the secular, but by the recreation of the secular from within.
Therefore he looks for signs of the recreative Spirit at work in the world.

II

The world is a sign for the Christian, and the Christian is a sign for the
world. Now "sign" means that which points to a greater reality than itself,

2.   For Luther, see G. Wingren, *Luther on Vocation,* trans. C. Rasmussen (Phila:
Muhlenberg Press, 1957). Calvin: *Commentary on Gal.* 5: 13; *Inst.* III.7.6.

or that which shows that such a reality is present. Signs are always ambiguous. Therefore they can be misunderstood, unless looked at from a certain point of view. The decision of faith is a decision to look at everything in the light of Christ's transforming activity. Outwardly speaking, our world is a place of dying, of evil, of humanity's lone struggle against the meaningless future. But the Christian sees rather a place of life, of victory over evil, of Christ's gift of the future when his kingdom will fulfill all hopes. We are not to be disheartened by its tragedies nor elevated by its triumphs; we are neither pessimists nor optimists. We do not possess a "philosophy of history," a sort of blueprint to mark the stages in Christ's progressive establishment of the kingdom. That would be neither faith nor hope.

Prayer to the Holy Spirit is itself a sign that we recognize the world not only as creation but also as creation with its meaning lost and its purpose perverted: creation in need of re-creation. "Redemption of the world" indicates this re-creating activity, confirming the world in its worldliness as God's creation, restoring its original purpose as "the theatre of his glory" (Calvin), and changing it into a new order fit to function as the city of God. Redemption is a rich word, formed in the agony of Christ's cross, sweeping towards us out of his new order which will come only in judgment, in the world's own crucifixion. Part of its richness consists in the present reality of new creation, so that even though we acknowledge the mystery that hides its fulfillment from us, yet we rejoice that here and now the living Christ reclaims the created order, and establishes its work and words by his. Redemption is not just a kind of knowing, however, as if faith were chiefly a problem in theory of knowledge. No matter how many barriers to belief one tries to pull down, it is never easy to believe. Faith is allegiance to a Lord, acceptance of his forgiveness, and participation in his battle with evil. We are not saved by right doctrine, necessary as this is for understanding our faith. We are called to act within the world, to such action as is appropriate to the Word of God. The Gospel is word-made-deed, the active presence of Christ the Lord: what human action is suitable to that? Every human action that celebrates Christ! We are not called to *philosophize* the faith but to *dramatize* it. Redemption is a drama now in progress and we are commanded to step on stage and play our part.

The likeness to theatre is more than accidental. Every nation has its mime, its dramatic enactment in which the hero struggles towards redemption, following his vocation, his pilgrimage of faith. The classic drama of Greece was born from the mystery religions, whose ritual cleansing turned on the moments of tragedy and victory. Gradually playwrights like Sophocles and theorists like Aristotle came to emphasize the tragic, man's bondage to fate and to pride, and the catharsis that comes through dramatizing the human situation. Comedy was relegated to an interlude, rustic humour in between the deeper moments of tragic drama. So it is that the artist still takes the extreme case, man at the end of his rope, to disclose our existence in separation, estrangement. So it is that God's Everyman, Jesus Christ, entered into the tragic drama and made its lines his own. He rearranged all human tragedy and every ritual protest around his central act. But if that were all, if crucifixion were all, then tragedy would have the last word. The cross itself is not only part of the human situation (as if God offered us only his sympathy), but is the sign of God's transforming power at work in the human situation. The cross is inseparable from the resurrection, Calvary from Easter. Tragedy does not go far enough, it does not know the surprise ending, the comic finale which Christ effected. For the Gospel is truly good news because it is the disclosure of God's act in which redemption is accomplished and renewal begun. No wonder that Karl Barth has called theology "a peculiarly carefree and, indeed, gay science"![3]

The gaiety of the Gospel will rest on those who live in the Spirit, who pray for his coming. Both tragedy and comedy are present in our world, and both are welcome to the Christian. To weep and to rejoice may be a prelude to witness. To walk with the mourners of the world and point them towards resurrection; to laugh with the comedians of the world and measure their humour against Easter —just so do we pray for his coming.

---

3.   *How I Changed My Mind*, (Richmond VA: John Knox Press, 1966), p. 62.

He comes from the near side of Easter, the Spirit who stormed forth at Pentecost to re-create humanity in the image of God's own Man, Jesus Christ. The stormy career of the church reflects his presence, and indeed "the very turbulence of contemporary life" also is a sign that people are reacting to his work.

The Spirit works God's proper work of new creation, life itself. What some accept and others reject is the power of resurrection. At Pentecost the church learned that the Holy Spirit had become identified in a decisive way with the crucified and risen Man, so that one has to do with Christ in his Spirit. (St. Paul can say simply, "The Lord is the Spirit" (2 Cor. 3:17). Death is still a reality in our world, the sign of our creatureliness as well as of God's judgment on evil; but the greater reality, the ultimate reality, is life through resurrection. We are called to hope in the Easter victory, trusting in God who raises the dead. The Holy Spirit is not a substitute for an absent Christ but the agent of his presence. The Lord is with us! Therefore lift up your hearts, put evil in its place—beneath the feet of its conqueror. Evil is an alien in God's good creation, an intruder whose origin remains shrouded in mystery but whose end is clear. In Christ redemption takes priority as the theme for the whole cosmos. To celebrate this joyful news, to become the "music men" of our world, the men of harmony—that is the way towards reconciliation, unity, peace.

III

The Gospel is a message of harmony, reconciliation, divine-human relationship already accomplished in Jesus Christ. The Holy Spirit is the Spirit "whose chosen milieu is relationship" (M. A. C. Warren). He comes between us in our personal relationships, our life together, for that is where the Lord Christ belongs as mediator. In an age when terms such as communication, encounter, and dialogue are common, the church must recall us all to the creative power behind society, the Spirit of the living God. To do this, the church itself must continually reform its group life, cleansing it of disorder, enmity, and pride. Like salt that is collected for processing, like wheat or grapes gathered to be crushed together into one loaf or one cup, the church is called to hear the Word of God and to offer its sacrifice of thanksgiving. But this particular Word concerns the world's redemption, and the thanksgiving is for new creation. At the heart of the church stands the world, the object of its service, the content of its love. Liturgy and ethics, worship and work, church and world—none of the pairs is to be separated. The church exists for the world, to help it recover its true worldliness, to celebrate the new creation as the future towards which it moves.

The missionary situation has altered radically since 1945. The burgeoning evolution and revolution of new nations thirsting for technology, the drive towards independence and nationalism, the resurgence of ancient religions, all these have ended the traditional age of missionary imperialism. Evangelism no longer means direct preaching to listening and waiting thousands, prepared (in one sense) by want, ignorance, and superstition. A new dynamism is at work, shaped by machines, power politics, economic planning —and resurgent religions. This is a time of testing for the church. For so long it has told itself that it has a right to address the world because others need "our" God! But now the secular world denies need of any God, and the religious world denies its need of the Christian God. We must cultivate a patience and perhaps a reticence in such an age as this. To make room for proclamation we must be content with other forms of service that may prove to be genuine "witness." To identify ourselves with people's hopes, protests, and struggles, for instance, may be our witness. The chief thing is to be present with people in a realistic way. "Christian presence" is the need of this hour.

The church is present within the world not as a piece of holy humanity but as *the true world*. It is that part of the world which celebrates its proper nature as creation and its real destiny in Christ. It reflects God's decision to be for the world. It hopes well of all people, for the mystery of Jesus Christ involves humanity and cosmos, headed up once again in him: "that the universe, all in heaven and on earth, might be brought into a unity in Christ" (Eph. 1:10). Our hope for the future is not a substitute for and denial of hope for the present age, however. If that were so then we should let the world go to hell, that is, let the demons possess it. The Gospel bids us rather rejoice that Christ has cast them out and denied them sovereignty. It calls us to lead the world in its dance of life. Therefore the Christian is able to look for and to identify the present hopes, temporary and partial though they may be. Because we know the resurrection power we can spot its presence within the dying order of our world. By their presence Christians side with such hopes, such power, and direct others towards the centre, where Christ awaits their coming. If we cut ourselves off from human hopes and causes, we make the Gospel a side issue, and do not pray for the redemption of the *world*.

The church may be said to be "in but not of" the world. This means that we are "in" the world completely, even as Jesus Christ was completely human. But we are also not "of" the world, that is, we do not draw our life from the world, even as Jesus Christ's humanity did not have its beginning or end within history. The Spirit was there, at his birth, like the divine midwife assisting at the birth of God's true Human; and there, at his death, helping him offer the eternal sacrifice. True humanity is dependent upon the divine; yet God so acts as to allow and encourage a humanity that has its own human activity to offer, a "partnership in the Gospel." The relationship between Christ's work and ours, Christ's presence and ours, is rather like that of musical counterpoint. His is the melody; ours is a corresponding yet different tune, a counterpoint to his. Not simply "harmony"—that is reserved for the saints already with him (and for the angels!)—but something truly human, a bit of this world already in tune with his "new song." Throughout the world we see such folk with a song, people who are like grains of salt or lumps of yeast or bearers of a light. By their presence they mark the world as God's, and invite mankind to enter into life.

IV

Here is what "redemption" means for the world: a true humanity, dependent upon God and echoing the praise of his Christ. The church exists for the world, as God's mission to the world. Therefore its form—its polity, liturgy, and morality—is dictated by the missionary or "apostolic" nature of its task. It does not exist so that world will become church. It exists so that the world will be renewed, will become God's new creation. When the mission of the church is understood as an essential, then we see that one day the church will come to an end, but not the world. The world will be transformed, created anew in a form suitable for the Kingdom. That will be "world without end." (One need only mention the Book of Revelation, in which the Kingdom is not described as an eternal church but an eternal state—in fact, a metropolis!) Our "church work," therefore, is a means to an end, and functions properly when it expresses itself in "secular" or worldly activity. This should be familiar enough to Calvinists, who have been accused of stressing worldly activity too much, in their understanding of "vocation." The charge is false if it attacks the principle itself; but it has some truth inasmuch as our Reformed churches have tended to accept the bourgeois image of what "true humanity" means. By concentrating on a certain type of individual happily placed in a position of relative freedom and responsibility, we have forgotten how minor and outdated this person is. We still find it difficult to listen to those voices (beginning with Karl Marx?) who warn that the coming of industrial society makes our idea of vocation, our attitude towards work and property, almost irrelevant today. "The idea of duty in one's calling prowls about in our lives like the ghost of dead religious beliefs" (Max Weber). Little wonder that we turn to religion itself, to church work and to the activity associated with an ecclesiastical building, as if this were what "redemption" means!

Our Lord Jesus Christ is the Exemplar in this task of subjecting religion to its proper end, the redemption of the world. Think of his radical reversal of the Jewish religion: "The Sabbath was made for man, not man for the Sabbath." In that sentence the decisive mark of religion, Sabbath observance, was placed under the sign of mission, and humanity was declared to be the end of religion. ("End" is helpfully ambivalent here, for it means both "finish" and "'fulfillment.") It is the temptation of the church—especially the church in North America?—to

156

make religion the end of religion. The institutional church is regarded as an end in itself, and the world becomes merely the place where one recruits church members. So the church is engaged in "church extension" rather than "world redemption." Accordingly, "religious behavior" tends to be narrowed to the private sphere, to inner feelings and personal morality. Certain habits of an older Puritan ethic, which once possessed a public influence, now hang on among us, witnessing only to our despair over the modern age. We wish the world had not come of age. We long for a simpler society, where decision-making was less technically involved, and where everyone knew what "morality" meant. We have not yet met the challenge of this new world, and so we cannot yet rejoice at its maturity. What does vocation mean in an industrial, technological, automated society? What is Christian behaviour in an age when we share the same "style of life" with various others? What different meaning can we give to the words that Marx used: overcoming "estrangement," achieving "reconciliation," producing a "socialized humanity"?

It is the *world* we want redeemed. It is not a mythical world of the past, or a more congenial part of the present, but the real world in which we live. We have said that the world is a sign to the Christian, because the Spirit is already at work in the world. Our task is to identify the signs of that work, and so to celebrate the presence and power of God's Word in the midst of world history. We shall "identify" the signs only as we take our place within the world, in the vanguard of its protest against inhumanity, its struggle for justice and freedom. Thus we may look hopefully for signs in the structure of nations and cultures, remembering that the redemption of the world will not deny the nations but will allow them to "bring in their glory" (Rev. 21: 24). May not the new nations—and certain old ones!—have a "glory" which is strange and unexpected? Can we tell beforehand what the Spirit intends for Russia, Africa, China? May not the very temptations and denials of our modern situation indicate a new awareness of God's grace, for example, in "God's beloved East Zone," as Johannes Hamel has reminded us?[4]

What is the "end" of religion in such a time as ours, then? In the little battlefield created by labor-management encounters (not to mention that actual warfare among nations), in the pressure of warring interests where business and advertising and salesmanship stalk their prey, or in the fantastic world of the arts with its profound influence upon whole cultures and its cinematic imagery of supermen and goddesses? It is in every such power structure that the clash between Christ and the demons continues. Little people find that their choices are largely conditioned by the major decisions issuing from the corporate images that people create, serve, and worship. And wherever someone protests and rebels, toppling an image or revealing its masquerade, wherever someone offers himself in sacrifice to open a new way for others, there the Christian may well discover a sign and may attempt a commentary. Especially in those areas of political economy which form the fabric of international relations should we look for signs that the world is still founded on God's Word. We should work for good order, complex as this has become in the web of human relationship within a great metropolis or across our one world. For the ancient philosopher Plato it was a thing of wonder that the planets are round; for us today the will of God becomes clearer as we learn more about the mystery of life together on a globe. The earth has no corners where one can retreat from one's fellows.[5] In this the world itself is a sign of God's will, of the common calling of humanity, of the unity we seek.

V

When we pray for the coming of the Spirit, we ask for trouble. Do we know whom we are inviting when we pray, "Come Creator Spirit?" This

---

4.   In 1964 the question of the divided Germany was paramout at the Frankfurt Assembly.

5.   A favourite image of Teilhard de Chardin: "Why are you so happy?— Because the earth is round."

is the Spirit who creates anew, killing to make alive, always reforming. He creates an open society, open towards the future redemption and, therefore, open towards every sign of renewal in the present. We have spoken of that; now we must speak of what it means for the Christian to be a sign for the world. Christ's Spirit makes *us* the sign. What kind of sign? A sign like Christ himself: dying and rising, something preposterous and scandalous. We should not lose sight of the little line of laughter that runs through what we have learned of the Spirit. He is riotous, even boisterous; and if one is not careful, exposure to his influence brings great risk. When men expound a systematic doctrine of the Spirit, or develop a complete catalogue of his fruits, what can we do but laugh? For this is the Spirit of whom the early Fathers of the church wisely said, he not only creates love but he *is* love: the mutual love of Father and Son within the Trinity, the love between God and man, and between humans. He is love and He is life. You cannot be doctrinaire about love, nor systematize life. Perhaps this is why the church has never succeeded in developing a doctrine of the third person of the Trinity, as it has of the Father and the Son. Perhaps this itself is a warning sign, lest we today consider this our appointed task, in order to complete something that is lacking. Far better to talk of the Spirit in terms of praise, of doxology (or para-doxology!). Far better to honour the Spirit in sketches, by illustrating our doctrine of the Christian life, especially of its joy.

The church is called to be the open society, the group for other groups, a sign of the new creation. Its life is itself a sign, that is, ambiguous: "hidden with Christ in God" (Col 3:3). Outwardly it shows evidence of similar power structures to those of the world. Yet one thing it must also show—a readiness to experiment with new forms, an openness to surprising things. For the surprises of Christ's grace should be its constant theme. Its very existence is bound up with the restless quest for further signs of that grace, and this is its own peculiar sign. The church celebrates a moveable feast, a joyful march towards tomorrow. Ours is a pilgrimage, "the Church-in-motion." (Do we recognize ourselves in these words, or do we ask, "Where on earth is such a church?") We ought to be on the growing edge of human history, tracing the shape of tomorrow in our readiness to experiment and our cheerfulness about change, both evolution and revolution. Our station is always on the frontier, where the living God stretches us out in the image of the Crucified (Christians as well as churches should have cruciform shape). To be within the world yet not permitted to settle one's ultimate concern on it, to live in the present and draw one's life from the future, this must surely lead either to despair or to humour. The Christian knows that God has rejected all sacred objectivity, and elected instead the way of faith. Therefore he must laugh at all sacred cows, especially doctrine and churchliness when they think they have objectified (i.e. imprisoned) God, whether in dogma or liturgy or ethics. Think of the humour of our situation, we who compose solemn treatises about the good news of the forgiveness of sins!

The light-heartedness of life in the Spirit is one way in which we are a sign to the world. If we want the world to be redeemed, we must enter into its life with good humour, with a lightness of touch that refuses to take the world or the church too seriously. For we should not pray primarily for better doctrine or purer churches or greater faith, that is, for ourselves and not really for the world. To be for the world places us in the position of risk of which St. Paul spoke so movingly in I Corinthians 9. "I am a free man and own no master; but I have made myself every man's servant, to win over as many as possible." Like a Jew to Jews, like a libertine or a weakling or whatever the situation demanded. And the risk lies here: "lest after preaching to others I myself should be rejected." What would Paul say to us today? How can we be like a sign in today's world? Not by rejecting some men, as we in the West tend to do in respect of the other half of the world! Such ideological rejection is the death of evangelism, for you cannot evangelize someone you do not love. Would Paul dare to say, "like a Communist to the Communists"? How far could one carry such identification? For Paul the answer was simple: so far that one's very soul was in jeopardy! The Spirit who is life and love pushes us so far, to give away the substance of our life in "riotous loving," that only the other one's good counts for anything. That is *the* sign, the sign of the *cross*.

"See I am creating a new thing" (Isa. 43: 19). Wherever there is change we should be present, assisting in the breaking up of old patterns of injustice and in the struggle for more humane conditions. Can anything new surprise us, who have tasted the powers of the world that is coming? Indeed, the old balance of traditional ways of doing things and viewing things must be upset if we are truly living in the Spirit. The Spirit thrusts us Christians into the "no man's land" between the warring factions in society, or race, or sex. To be in such an unhappy position, and to be happy, that is the sign the world needs. One could almost suggest a strategy of the Spirit, who reconciles two enemies not by disclosing an underlying harmony, but by creating something new, a third thing, "one new man in place of the two" (Eph. 2:15), upsetting the old tension and introducing a surprising way ahead for both. We are the Holy Spirit's experiment in new humanity, a poor thing offered to the world because we happen to have laughed in response to God's good news. It was not our doing—even this is no cause for pride. Yet it is truly our doing, and it summons us to action, toil, and thought, to vocation and stewardship. By all these means we may witness, if they are a means of praying, "Come, Creator Spirit!"

The Holy Spirit comes to us from the Lord who is risen, reigning, returning. The whole action has a forward look; it moves from the future towards us in the present. Because Christ comes not out of the past but out of the future, must we not be open to the surprises of his grace? If we are not in an expectant condition, how will the new creation be born? For we are "on the way to the world of tomorrow," and our way ahead has been opened from the other side by Christ the Lord of death. Nothing therefore is so modern as he, no power so promising, no vision so clear, no passage so hopeful. For he claims the fruits of his work among us and throughout the whole cosmos. He himself is the new Humanity, and his Spirit bids us pray, "Come, Lord Jesus!"

PART 3

Theology and Canadian Society

13

'BY CIRCUMSTANCE AND GOD'

A Tribute to Walter Bryden (1883–1952)[1]

Scholars, when they cease to be prophets, and thus fail to be theologians, possess a significance little more than that of scribes.[2]

True beliefs are the issues of one's whole being as wrought upon by circumstance and God, and they ripen into great, final confessions.[3]

The author of these words was himself a prophetic scholar, a confessing theologian. In appearance slight, one delicate arm held close, movements denoting energy—and eyes that pierced in eager dialogue. Walter Bryden in his classroom had what is now called "presence." At times it was a burning as he meditated aloud on the wonder of the Gospel, teasing our minds to explore with him its treasures new and old. As students we could not appreciate his worth,

---

1.   Written for *Called to Witness*, vol. 1, ed. W. Stanford Reid (The Presbyterian Church in Canada, 1990) 119-26; reprinted in *The Significance of the Westminster Confession of Faith and other Papers*, ed. R.K. Anderson (private printing, 2005).

2.   *The Christian's Knowledge of God*, 26. (See bibliography at end for Bryden's works.)

3.   Convocation address, The Presbyterian College Montreal, 1929. Published in *Separated unto the Gospel* (SG*).

for we could not reckon the cost of his personal pilgrimage up to and after that fateful year 1925. He was—in retrospect we may say it—the man for that hour, the scholar raised up "'by circumstance and God'" to speak his prophetic theology to a church that had made a grave decision against the Union of 1925, but from mixed motives and without fully understanding the consequences. The facts of his history are easily recounted, for he was not an activist, a conference goer on committee or lecture circuits. For twenty-seven years his energies were devoted to Knox College, Toronto and its task of education for Christian ministry.

Walter Williamson Bryden was born on a farm near Galt, Ontario, in 1883. Matriculating from Galt Grammar School 1901, he took honours Philosophy and Psychology at the University of Toronto, graduating 1906. Despite a physical handicap he was a member of the track team and captained the University soccer team. He entered Knox College to prepare for Ministry, while also completing M. A. in Psychology in 1907. His middler year (1907-08) was spent in Scotland, where G. A. Smith, T. M. Lindsay and especially James Denney showed the young scholar that theology can be done not merely as an academic discipline but as "church dogmatics."[4] He considered Denney "The prince of theologians."[5]

Graduation from Knox college in 1909 was followed by post-graduate studies at Strasbourg, then pastoral ministry in Lethbridge, Alberta, Melfort, Saskatchewan—as he later put it, "in what they call 'spade work' in Western Canada"—and in Woodville, Ontario, "a quiet little village in the heart of Old Ontario."[6] In 1911 he married Violet Bannantyne; their son Kenneth became Associate Professor of Political Science in the University of Toronto.

The year 1925 saw some two-thirds of the Presbyterian membership join with Methodists and Congregationalists to form the United Church of Canada. Leadership in the pulpit and college was the greatest need

---

4. See chapters 15-16 of SG.

5. *Significance of the Westminster Confession of Faith*, 27—(SWCF).

6. SG, 131.

of the "continuing" Presbyterian Church in Canada. Walter Bryden of Woodville was asked to lecture two days weekly at Knox College, in church history. In 1927 the General Assembly elected him to the Chair of Church History, which he was to occupy for the next twenty-six years. He also lectured in History and Philosophy of Religion until 1947, when Donald V. Wade was appointed to that chair.

The quarter century and more during which Bryden taught the theologues at Knox were the most critical in the history of The Presbyterian Church in Canada. Behind lay a mixture of traditions and motives, ahead an uncertain future, no clear theological position emerging, but rather a struggle over the church's relationship to its subordinate standard, the Westminster Confession of Faith. This was Bryden's hour. Occupying one of the highest and most influential educational positions in the church, his considerable intellectual gifts came to bear on the practical issue of theological education—the teaching of the "teaching elders" who must minister to a church undergoing a crisis of identity.

Church politics were much in evidence during the formative years after 1925. Inevitably, parties formed around the strong personalities of the No-sayers, the leaders in the anti-union campaign. The bitter and negative attitudes of that campaign had seemed to many to forebode doctrinal fundamentalism and obscurantism. An influx of conservative Calvinists, chiefly American, to fill Presbyterian pulpits strengthened this tendency toward "rational orthodoxy" as Bryden termed it. He rightly saw that this would constitute the ongoing threat to what he considered the proper Reformed stance. The irony of this little history, however, was that the right wing Presbyterians did not develop a political arm, leaving the opposition to Bryden to a mixed group whose main cohesion was its antipathy to perceived "Barthianism." The scenario reminds us of the more famous encounter between Hamack and Barth in 1923, when the old liberalism and the new revelation-theology parted in a dramatic controversy.

On the retirement of Thomas Eakin as Principal of Knox College, Walter Bryden was appointed his successor, despite the efforts of those who preferred someone more to the right theologically, or oriented towards Scotland ecclesiastically and liturgically. From 1945 until his death on March 23, 1952, it was Principal Bryden of Knox, at the center of theological debate but also at the growing edge of theological education. When he died it was indeed the end of an era, of the direct link with the struggles of 1925 and the need to make theological issues decisive. If that need had been recognized and those issues accepted it was because Knox graduates year after year over that quarter-century had grasped, often against their will, a new vision of God.

The funeral service in Knox College Chapel was conducted by Joseph Wasson, minister of Calvin Church, Toronto, where Bryden had been an Elder, assisted by Norman Kennedy, Moderator of the 1951 General Assembly, and J. B. Paulin.

Certain themes of Walter Bryden's teaching and authorship deserve notice. First must stand his view of the *church*. His entire theology should be seen against the horizon of the People of God—that group visited and redeemed by God's Word and Spirit, called to witness to "the judging-saving Word," constrained to meditate on its belief in the disciplined way called theology. He did not move into theology by way of some other "academic" pursuit such as philosophy; he came through *preaching*, and did not much distinguish it from teaching. He saw himself caught in the net of God's Word, no longer free to dabble in speculative philosophy, but appointed to serve the Gospel. His other key concepts—revelation, faith, theory of knowledge, divine being and human nature—are best approached as items of church doctrine or "articles of faith." It should be emphasized that he came to his own understanding of "church dogmatics" apart from but parallel to the experience of the "early Barth." The latter formed his theological method by meditation on Anselm and so moved from existential to revelational axioms. Bryden's dialogue with church history showed him the perilous options, and how the way chosen by Athanasius and Augustine and especially Luther and Calvin, demanded acceptance of the biblical revelation as starting-point for reasoning out the faith. He stressed the "constraint" under which people confessed their faith in God, and pointed to that "strange ... raw material"—the biblical witness—which forms the presupposition of theology and then, in turn, of creeds.[7]

Bryden's impact on his denomination may be measured by the rise of self-consciousness about its doctrinal position. When in 1942 a committee of General Assembly on "Articles of Faith" was formed, it was that same coincidence of "circumstance and God" at work. The immediate issue was the role of Church and State in light of the War, but those who pressed for formal study and who later worked to produce the "Declaration of Faith Concerning Church and Nation" of 1954—now part of the subordinate standards of The Presbyterian Church in Canada—were led by students of Bryden. From him they had learned the lesson that confessing the faith is the muscle by which the church operates. They also learned that "creeds are not *made,* they are always *born,* often born in blood."[8] His favourite example was the Barmen Declaration of 1934, the rallying cry of the German Confessing Church with its bold witness to the supreme lordship of Jesus Christ and its explicit rejection of errors and heresies on both sides of this Truth. His thesis about confessing the faith was that genuine confession springs from "a vision of God"—the framers of the Westminster Confession, for instance, "had *seen* God anew."[9] Thus there can be no merely denominational confession or creed, as if there is a relative vision of God. "A Church, if it is to justify itself as a true Church of God in Jesus Christ, must be conscious of possessing *the* Gospel."[10]

These quotations are from the book that served as his *apologia* for remaining in the Presbyterian Church. He did not remain for reasons of "denominationalism and ecclesiasticism" which he calls "insufficient reasons for rejecting the union proposals."[11] Rather, among his "personal reasons for refusing to enter the proposed union" he notes

---

7.   SG 96ff.
8.   *Why I am a Presbyterian,* 80 (WP).
9.   WP 82.
10.   WP 162.
11.   WP 23ff.

the emergence of vaunted "new methods" in Christian education, a growing officialdom at head office, and an exaltation of bigness, trends he thought the new United Church might accentuate, while "The Presbyterian Church, through a new dependence upon God because of its difficulties and weakness, might return to a simpler, stronger and more evangelical preaching." His test is the office of preaching, or "the Church's peculiar witness to Christ; its faith and doctrine." Thus he lamented the Doctrinal Basis of Union because it lacked any "compelling vision of God" or "that vital unity which such a vision inevitably creates."[12] He belonged to that small group of theologians who were dismayed by the lack of theological strength on *both* sides of the 1925 debate, and who rejected the Union proposals as lacking that radical vision characteristic of the historic creeds (including the Westminster Confession) and who hoped that a continuing Presbyterian Church might rise to those former heights of confessional teaching, preaching and life.

It is within this context of the need for a confessing church to stand against religious and ecclesiastical errors, that his high regard for Karl Barth should be placed. It was an unpopular attitude, costing him much enmity and misunderstanding. Philosophers and theologians, his enemies within his Church on right and left, as well as many of his own students, could see only what smacked of the irrational, of paradox, of an existential extremism. Now these charges are not to be dismissed lightly. Like the early Barth, Bryden was indeed fond of the negative pole in the rhythm of what he liked to call "the judging-saving Word."[13] He distrusted every analogy that suggested a natural relationship between human and divine for fear that it might deny God's grace which is sheer *gift*.[14] His jealousy for the divine sovereignty tended to underplay the

---

12. WP 118, 75, 80.

13. See *The Christian's Knowledge of God* 131, 135ff (CKG.)

14. Like Barth, he rejected natural theology based on a relationship of being (*analogia entis*), but accepting the relational implications of the divine-human encounter, (*analogia relationis*).

human role in the divine-human encounter. In this sense he stands in the classic tradition of Protestantism, making one point over and over, taking it as the crucial and decisive point and hedging it on all sides against every attempt to qualify it: "by faith alone, by grace alone, to the glory of God alone."

Waiter Bryden's major book, the essential statement of his theology, is undoubtedly *The Christian's Knowledge of God* (1940).[15] He develops the familiar Reformation theme: a biblical revelation which "belongs strictly to the apocalyptic, eschatological category of thinking" and calls for a theology "concerned alone with a *thinking* which arises out of the most radical of all self-negating human experiences, namely, repentance and confession."[16] His forte is theological epistemology—a theory of knowledge that accepts as primary datum the novelty of a Word from God. This new occurrence calls in question every theory of knowledge that assumes a merely human horizon or which describes human "openness" to revelation without taking seriously the self-giving nature of that revelation itself. This last point explains why the book's title concerns the *Christian's* knowledge of God.

Bryden's polemic with "natural theology" looms large in the book. He regards it as an extension of the pride of "natural man," thus turning away from the impact of revelation to explore human potentialities. Even *religion* (or *especially* religion!) becomes a pretence reducible to a human word. He sees two chief enemies facing the church of his day: "modernism" and "rational orthodoxy."[17] *Modernism* relies heavily on a monistic theory that has no room for any Other, plus a strong dose of optimistic progressivism. Its reliance on history and "the factual alone" also constitutes the "grand fallacy" of the critical-historical

---

15.   This is the work that led Fulton Anderson, then Chairman of the Philosophy Department, University of Toronto, to term Bryden "an irrational enthusiast" in his review, "On a certain Revival of Enthusiasm," *The University of Toronto Quarterly* 10.2 (1941), 194—see Vissers, *The Neo-Orthodox Theology*, 150-51.

16.   *CKG*, 40, 31.

17.   E.g., SG 80ff, 188ff.

method in theology. It reduces everything to an impersonal level, and misses the presence of the Holy Spirit. Lacking the radical knowledge of God's presence through the miracle and mystery of Incarnation, we seek "points of contact" and various kinds of synthesis.[18] *Rational orthodoxy* is especially familiar to Bryden since it constitutes a distinct challenge within his own denomination. It is significant that his quarrel with it is cast in similar terms to that with Modernism, for he sees the two as "antithetic products of the same rationalistic process ... both have been intent on finding revelation, in two quite different ways it is true, in the letter of Scripture."[19] (He sees that the "Barthian" challenge hits right wing as well as left on the issue of trust in one's reason.) By "rational" orthodoxy he indicates that "intellectual assent to propositions" which is characteristic of its theory of knowledge. Indeed, despite its strengths, the *Westminster Confession of Faith* is "not so much a true 'confession' as a rational explanation of what it deemed to be Reformed theology" and therefore it "inevitably rationalizes the Christian Gospel." For Bryden such rationalizing tendency compromises the nature of Word of God as event, historical but more than past history, and something other than can be summed up in a series of propositions.[20]

Against these twin expressions of man's trust in the powers of his reason, Bryden set his face despite misunderstanding and unpopularity. In his inaugural lecture on installation as Principal, October 1945, he referred to the fact that "much resentment has been aroused because a certain challenging theology of our day has been addressing the Church, Christians and people in general, in terms similar to the text of Isaiah 41:14, 'Thou worm Jacob'." Noting the complaint over this apparent demeaning of the human, he asks why the prophets, apostles and saints were so little concerned about "such things as human dignity and human personality." And he concludes that nothing is more needed today than that the church might become humble enough "that God

---

18.   CKG 24, 143.

19.   CKG 110.

20.   SWCF 22,28; WP 42ff.

might be permitted to put teeth in her mouth, that having been made Servant of all men, she might be servile to none."[21]

Like every prophet with a single burden, Walter Bryden's harping on this note becomes tiresome. Its presupposition is the positive *Yes!* of Gospel, but because he cannot discern clearly signs of its acceptance, he continues to sound his *No!* Who can deny that the church always needs such a prophet? Who can measure the weight of his burden, the inward pain of the loneliness and alienation which his utterance brought? And who can say that even his own little church has answered his plea for purification and devotion to this supreme Lord who is jealous of every other loyalty? His single-minded articulation of this theme marks him as one who conveys a spirit or *style*, a way of doing theology, rather than a particular content or system of doctrine. He is not the one to solve intricate problems of historical theology, nor the modern question of methodology—even though his pages show evidence aplenty of his reading in church history, and his wrestling with issues of method, especially in religious education and mission.[22]

His earliest book *The Spirit of Jesus in St. Paul* (1925) deserves a word in this brief outline, not least because it presents an aspect of Bryden's thought necessary to recall the mighty positive from which he uttered his prophetic theology. This is a book about experience, about presence, about mysticism. It seems strange to hear Walter Bryden speak so positively about "the mystical," knowing his worry over Schleiermacher's experiential theology, or his rejection of Radhakrishnan's mystical monism. Indeed, he sees (as few besides Karl Barth have) the inner connection between mysticism and rationalism.[23] But in St. Paul he finds a Christ-mysticism, a case of Christ's

---

21. SG 46f.

22. On a personal note, I was introduced to the Church Fathers by him. Once I complained to him that we were not hearing much about the Enlightenment and theological responses to the Age of Reason; he gave me a set of his own notes on the subject, part of the unpublished manuscript *After Modernism – What?*

23. See SG 217.

being formed in us by the energy of the Holy Spirit, and he reckons that this is authentic mysticism, and the "proper mystery."[24]

By the time of his death in 1952 Waiter Bryden had not, like the mature Karl Barth, come to emphasize the positive over the negative, and to talk of "the humanity of God," looking back to the early polemics with a measure of embarrassment.[25] Rather, he maintained his witness to the judgement of God on every human pretension, especially in ecclesiastical and theological dress. He was no systematic or scientific theologian, but a zealot for God's glory. His zeal was tempered and directed by intelligence and insight; and his lifelong struggle to find words to express the strange raw material of faith (like Calvin's insistence that all theology is "improper speech") reflects an authentic mysticism.

In 1934 he wrote of his hope for a spiritual awakening for his beloved Presbyterian Church, but concluded, "I am not at all certain as yet if that hope is to be realized."[26] Perhaps the hope remains unrealized still, as we continue the old debates over Bible and Confession, and fail to develop a common theological agenda. Yet his heritage remains, God's thorn in our side especially during Centennial celebrations: a heritage, a *project*.

One of his favourite poems is apposite, a portrait of the man: "Surely the obscure pastor of Hessen discerned what is the need of the Church today, when he penned the following lines:

God needs men, not creatures
Full of noisy, catchy phrases.
Dogs he asks for, who their noses
Deeply thrust into—To-day,
And there scent Eternity.
Should it lie too deeply buried,
Then go on, and fiercely burrow,
Excavate until To-morrow."[27]

24.　E.g. *Spirit of Jesus*, 77, 244.

25.　Barth recognizes that the youthful enthusiasm for the *diastasis*, the No! (his reply to Brunner's natural theology was entitled simply *Nein!*) should be left behind in favour of the positive of the Gospel's Yes! (*The Humanity of God*, Richmond VA: John Knox Press, 1960), esp. 41-43.

26.　WP 118.

27.　CKG xi.

BIBLIOGRAPHY:
THE WRITINGS OF WALTER BRYDEN.

The Spirit of Jesus in St. Paul: A Study in the Soul of St. Paul Based Upon the Corinthian Correspondence. London: James Clarke, 1925. 256 pp.

(WP) *Why I am a Presbyterian.* Toronto: Presbyterian Publications, 1934; Thorn Press, 1945. 176pp.

(CKG) *The Christian's Knowledge of God.* Toronto: Thorn Press, 1940; London: James Clarke, 1960.

(SWCF) *The Significance of the Westminster Confession of Faith.* Toronto: University of Toronto Press, 1943. Private reprinting by R.K. Anderson, Toronto, 2006. 43 pp.

(SG) *Separated unto the Gospel* (Collected Works), ed. D.V. Wade: Toronto, Burns and MacEachern, 1956. 218pp.

After Modernism, What? Unpublished manuscript. The Presbyterian Church in Canada Archives, Bryden Files.

[A full Bibliography of articles and book reviews appears in John Vissers, *The Neo-Orthodox Theology of W.W. Bryden* (Pickwick Publications, 2006), 271-74].

14

RELIGION IN CANADA:
A STUDY IN POLARITIES[1]

*Written for the special Canadian Centen-
nial edition of* Theology Today, *Princeton.*

Canada is a geographer's dream and a politician's nigrhtmare. Across
four thousand miles of the most varied terrain imaginable—from
peach orchards to frozen tundra, from the world's most ancient rock
formation to prairies only lately tamed into wheatfields—a mere twenty
million or so people share a land of plenty and of latent natural resources.
Yet the sheer size of its space makes communication a problem, and
regionalism of state and church is the price of unity. Canada's story
concerns two "founding nations" (itself a moot theory), French and
English, and their subsequent attempts to work out a viable relationship.
Novelist Hugh Maclennan termed them "two solitudes," and only
recently has genuine dialogue begun. This basic polarity is crossed by
a third force, consisting of immigrants from other than French and
English lands ("allophones"). Notably central European, these groups
have not adopted the American "melting pot" philosophy, but have

---

1.   From *Theology Today* (Princeton), October 1967, pp. 295-305.

created a mosaic of ethnic groups, an old-world style which adds to the complexity of the new search for a Canadian identity.

A famous student revue at McGill University once described what it means to be a Canadian. You spend half your time telling the British you aren't an American, and the other half telling Americans you aren't British; there's no time left for being "Canadian." The truth in that statement has now been swallowed up by a new reality: the "French fact" has asserted itself in an explosive way. The bold challenge hurled at Confederation ("one hundred years of injustice") by Quebec *separatistes* has sharpened the issue of Canada's ties with Europe and the U.S.A. If many *Québecois* see in their English-speaking country-men only a pale imitation of the Yankee stereotype, many English-Canadians see Quebec as the bulwark against American imperialism. What is distinctive about Canada seems destined to stand or fall with the future of Quebec.

The traditional image of the Canadian as a diffident gentleman, ambivalent in orientation, suffering from an inferiority complex as little brother to his southern neighbor—this is now at issue. One hundred years after Confederation, the corpse of colonialism and dependency is being interred and a nation is struggling to be born.

I

Religion in Canada must be approached in terms of the foregoing analysis. Colonialism was not altogether a bad thing for the church. At first it was a case of zealous pioneers bringing their faith with their culture: early missionaries, military chaplains, circuit riders. Then it was schooling, for the history of higher education in Canada is insepa-rable from the story of Christian concern for a literate laity. Most Canadian universities were established by churchmen with some form of evangelical intention. Much later, the colonial spirit still lingered in the custom of church leaders and theologians from abroad who spent considerable time and effort in the service of the young Dominion before returning to France or England or Scotland to continue their careers. Early in the present century a British publishing house launched a series of volumes, "The Canadian Library of Religious Literature," to honour the work of these and other theologians in Canada. Names such as T. R. Glover, A. R. Gordon, John Baillie and Nathaniel Micklem belong to Canada through such theological colonialism.

It was in part owing to the presence of such men that the great debate arising from critical scholarship in the last century was resolved more or less amicably. There was the usual bitterness and heat, the simplistic dichotomy of orthodoxy/heresy, and some cases of professors leaving their posts by choice or compulsion. But in general the continuing effects of the debate polarized within the churches; no distinct sectarian spirit was institutionalized. Today the "conservative evangelical" is to be found within all denominations, nor is any leading Canadian theological seminary (as distinct from Bible college) sectarian in this sense. Of course, proximity to the U.S.A. is an advantage in this regard, since its conservative seminaries offer haven to our more demanding fundamentalists.

The Canadian experience of ecumenism reflects in part this early harmony, and in part the hard facts of the churches' social context. The question of harmony and unity has been raised by the pressures of ministering to a population distributed thinly along thousands of miles of railway lines in the prairie provinces, to lumbermen and miners working in frontier situations where manpower of every kind is at a premium, and to a people in general unwilling to carry the burden of old-world divisions into the twentieth century. Such sociological factors made for comity arrangements, cooperative ministries, and ecumenism by contract. The movement for organic union, initiated by Presbyterians in the late nineteenth century, gained momentum in the early decades of this century. It won unanimous acceptance among the Methodists and Congregationalists, but the Presbyterians themselves created a new division. When the United Church of Canada was formed in 1925, about one-third of The Presbyterian Church in Canada voted against union and continued their denomination. The ecumenical spirit had blossomed early in Canada, however, and despite recurring bitterness, especially on the part of continuing Presbyterians,[2] it has fertilized new fruit in the current Anglican-United conversations looking toward organic union. The working document for these conversations, *Principles of Church Union,* seeks "a new embodiment" of the church. It envisages a new distribution of power and an amalgam of Anglican and United (Reformed) polities. Critics charge that this is a weakness, that it is content to realign old forms and is reluctant to seek genuine newness. The crucial issue of "constitutional episcopacy" is, however, being tackled with openness, and promises to prove helpful to ecumenism in general. Even the Presbyterians have now agreed to send observers to the conversation group.[3] The significance of the proposal may be measured by the statistics of Canadian church life. Over 45% of Canadians are Roman Catholic; of Protestants, 20% are United Church and 13% Anglican, followed by Presbyterians and Lutherans, roughly 3.5% each.

It is obvious that the most important factor in describing religion in Canada is the francophone Roman Catholic presence. Canada was discovered, explored, and settled by Frenchmen. The fact that some originals were Huguenot and that other pioneers, chiefly Scots, opened up the West does not alter the primary significance of Quebec's claim to special status as the embodiment of the founding nation. British by conquest, Canada inherits its distinctive genius and its *problématique* from its earlier roots. The contemporary search for a viable "biculturalism and bilingualism" operates against the background of the basic polarity.

French-Canadian culture is traditionally conservative, geared to the rural, simple needs and tastes of the *habitant* who looked to his *curé* for guidance in things both spiritual and political. Paternalism has flourished under charismatic personalities, notably Premier Maurice

---

2. An anti-ecumenical spirit that challenged the Canadian Council of Churches obtained until General Assembly debates in the late '40s established the Presbyterian presence in interchurch activities.

3. The conversations did not lead to anything more than a formal agreement to seek closer informal fellowship.

Duplessis, *le chef.* The Roman Catholic Church followed the conservative line, a good child of the puritan spirit of the Counter-Reformation. Few recognized the signs of reformation present in theologians informed by contacts with France, the journalists and writers, or the politicians of more liberal bent. When the death of Duplessis offered opportunity for change, no half measures could contain the explosive forces in political economy, the arts, education, and the church. Violence, terrorism, fatalities followed; but out of the brief courtship of separatist theory has emerged a more stable quest for more realistic forms of confederation.[4]

During this unsettling period, Vatican Council II was exerting its own distinctive influence for change. Cardinal Paul-Emile Léger, once typical of the traditional French-Canadian *curé,* became a convert to Pope John's *aggiornamento* and blessed the avant-garde of his diocese in their efforts to interpret and apply it to Quebec. A popular symbol of the new mood is found in the radical departure in church architecture, challenging and controversial; even rural Quebec is spotted with such unusual edifices. Education was bound to be a battleground between old guard and new, as the process of laicization sought to wrest it from the church and create at last a proper Ministry of Education in the government: from clerical to lay to secular education. And through it all, theology moved as a midwife assisting at new birth.

II

A new kind of polarity, however, cuts across all former divisions. No longer is the old liberal-fundamentalist debate our concern, or even the Roman Catholic-Protestant separation, but another sort of engagement, the conflict between conservative and radical responses to the demand for new forms in churchly life, worship, and theology. The

---

4.   This optimistic reading of the facts proved unrealistic. Separatism maintains itself as a viable option for many, embodied in both a provincial party (the Parti Québecois) and a federal (Bloc Québecois); referenda have been held on the issue, the latest (1995) voted down by a narrow majority. But the recent (March 2007) election reduced the Péquistes to third party status, receiving their lowest vote since 1970.

vitality of ecumenism in Canada has been caught up in this phenom-enon; the Christian Pavilion at Expo '67, the International Exhibition at Montréal, is a bold annunciation of what's happening. Truly ecu-menical—the fruit of eight cooperating churches including the Roman Catholic—the controversial building attempts to meet the challenge and need of our electronic age by opting for contemporary symbols of faith rather than historical and traditional ones. Critics aplenty, mostly within the churches, are charging that it is a surrender to the theories of Marshall McLuhan, Canada's prophet of technological environment. The lack of familiar and identifiable Christian symbols and the use of modern photographs showing the variety of human life and problems offend popular piety and theological conservatism.

The Christian Pavilion uses architecture and design to create an atmosphere of contrasts: height and depth, gloom and light, despair and hope, are the stuff of existence. Its interior design moves through the human potential as steward of a good creation, the fall into inhuman-ity and *hubris*, with faith witnessing to a presence here and now that offers hope. The theme of "The Eighth Day" was chosen to suggest what Christian theology can and must say about the general Expo theme of "Man and His World." After the six days of divine work followed by rest, man enters his heritage; it is *his* world, but a world without hope unless he responds to the light that is in it. The difficulty of saying this without relapsing into pious phrases is obvious.

Compounding the difficulty, however, is the fact that so many Canadian pulpiteers have failed to get the message. Preaching glibly about "Man and *God's* World," they sneer at the "humanism" of Antoine de Saint-Exupéry's idea of *terre des hommes*. Their corrective, however, does not do justice either to the profound understanding of the Expo theme (they are usually anglophone, ignorant of French-Canada's appreciation of Saint-Exupéry) or to the intention of the com-mentary offered by the Pavilion. The latter is not so much wounded by humanism as labouring under the ambiguity of the gospel itself. How does one communicate this kind of truth? Kierkegaard or McLuhan, electronic age or hellenistic culture, are there holy words which convey divine truth in themselves? Not far from the Christian Pavilion at Expo is another building in which "Sermons from Science" pursues the hard sell, complete with (cosmological-teleological) arguments for God's existence, the smooth patter of Moody Bible Institute professionals, and elaborately trained counsellors in an after-room. Two solitudes?

The most significant thing about the Christian Pavilion is not its decision to communicate in contemporary modes but the ecumenical nature of its decision. For it is the result of a lengthy and agonizing dialogue among the sponsoring churches, representing some 95% of Canada's Christians, and displays another kind of decision more basic than the first, namely, to witness not to the churches, not even to ecumenism, but to *God*. Whatever one's judgment concerning the success or failure of that witness, it is necessary to measure this self-transcendence of Canadian ecumenism. It reflects a large step forward in a very short time; it augurs well for the coming years. In the committee discussions leading up to Expo, for example, it became clear that the new polarity had little relevance to the old. It was as if the old battle-lines had not shifted, but that the action had; one was constantly surprised to discover who were one's new friends, and enemies. This lesson is only beginning to be learned by the participating churches. Their younger people caught on quite soon, for in part the new polarity corresponds to the difference between generations. Whether our youth sing *go-go* or *yé-yé*, they are one in their demand for relevant worship, morality, and theology.

III

How does one measure theological activity? The traditional yardstick of literary output may prove deceptive. The profound influence of Bernard Lonergan, for instance, on generations of Canadian Roman Catholics studying in Rome, is not to be evaluated in terms of his written works, which have been published only recently *(Insight* and *Collection)*. In fact the international flavour of theology is familiar to Canadians, so that it is difficult to describe what "Canadian" theology is like. In the

Canadian Journal of Theology, founded in 1955 as the successor to the *Canadian Journal of Religious Thought*, 1924-1932, one finds closely similar themes and opinions to those expressed in American journals.[5] There are also similar societies: for biblical literature (related to the American S.B.L), theology, and church history. A striking difference from the U. S. is that our small population makes a single society adequate for a discipline!

Centres of theological study in Canada are few, and geographically far apart. The two largest cities, Montreal and Toronto, have long been distinguished locations for graduate work and authorship. McGill University's interdenominational Faculty of Divinity, combined with the Roman Catholic resources of Montreal, including the philosophical and theological faculties of the *Université de Montréal,* promises increasing stimulus for research and ecumenical teaching. The University of Toronto has five theological colleges, including St. Michael's Roman Catholic, all of which now cooperate at the graduate (post-BD) level. These are signs of our time; closer cooperation is to be expected, according to the recent AATS. report on theological education headed by a Canadian, Charles Feilding of Trinity College, Toronto.

Certain special institutions are noteworthy on the Canadian scene. The Pontifical Institute of Medieval Studies in Toronto, with which Gerald Phelan was long associated, has included as visiting lecturers Jacques Maritain and Etienne Gilson. Toronto's Roman Catholic theological community, where R. A. F. McKenzie once taught biblical studies, continues to flourish: Gregory Baum and Leslie Dewart are well-known examples. At McGill University the Institute of Islamic Studies, presently chaired by Charles Adams, was founded by Wilfred Cantwell Smith, now of Harvard. As a centre for intensive research in Islamic culture and theology, it provides both opportunity for academic study and stimulus for wider dialogue. Interest in 'comparative'

---

5.   Now replaced by Studies in Religion/Sciences Religeuses, reflecting the new reality of Religious Studies depatrtments.

religious studies (or better, "world religions") remains largely inchoate in Canadian theological circles but has received sudden encouragement from the developing departments of religion in a number of our universities.[6]

It may be another sign of changing times that we seem to be moving from "theology" back to "religion." For example, the original *Journal of Religion* was succeeded by the *Journal of Theology*; today the new Society for the Study of Religion is pressing for some journal to recognize the broader interests of the departments of religious studies. Might the *Journal of Theology* therefore revert to its old name and style?[7] More than words is at stake here. Religion as an academic subject is burgeoning in Canada, and theological education has not yet taken account of it. How it will affect the traditional Bachelor of Divinity courses, and especially whether it is best done by theologians or phenomenologists (for want of a better term), remain open questions.[8] Three new religious studies departments are worth noting. McMaster University in Hamilton, Ontario, calls its department, headed by philosopher George Grant, "Religious Sciences"; at the University of British Columbia, the department is chaired by William Nicholls who has begun an optimistic program which specializes in Buddhism; at Sir George Williams University in Montreal, a vigorous department may help bridge the gulf between the old YMCA-style religious enthusiasm and the new mood of objective yet stimulating concern.[9]

---

6.   These two paragraphs would be radically different if written today. Departments of Religion now flourish, attracting a significant number of undergraduates to Religion courses. In Montreal McGill's Faculty is now "Religious Studies" rather than "Divinity," while a new reality is UQAM (l'Université de Québec à Montréal).

7.   In fact the CSSR and the Canadian Theological Society combined interests to launch *Studies in Religion/Sciences Religieuses*, both inclusive and bilingual.

8.   The Association of Theological Schools (North America) has now emphasized "professionalization" and so the Bachelor of Divinity has been renamed Master of Divinity.

9.   This institution merged with Loyola to form Concordia University.

Like Americans, Canadians do not usually follow the European style of "schools," disciples imitating a master. Thus the Death-of-God theology is of widespread influence in Canada, but only two distinctive voices can be said to have emerged. An erstwhile Anglican Church administrator, Ernest Harrison, has championed the cause (e.g., *Church Without God)* but lacks sufficient depth to engage the theological community. At the other extreme stands Kenneth Hamilton of Winnipeg's United College. Thanks to a conservative American publishing house, he has quickly risen to literary fame through his critiques *(Revolt Against Heaven; God is Dead: The Anatomy of a Slogan).* Others who provide helpful commentaries on contemporary movements are William Hordern of Saskatoon and William Fennel of Toronto. Also in Toronto are Eugene Fairweather, editor of the *Canadian Journal of Theology,* David Hay, active in the Faith and Order Commission of the W.C.C., and Stanley Glen, whose books on pastoral psychology (e.g., *Erich Fromm: A Protestant Critique)* represent a small but growing group of Canadians competent in that field.

Another area of obvious significance is that of Canadian church history. The Centennial year is encouraging deeper concern with this as with other aspects of Canadiana. A team of noted specialists is producing a three-volume work: John Webster Grant, John Moir, and H. H. Walsh. Dr. Walsh's earlier book, *The Christian Church in Canada* (1956), remains the only complete church history in a single volume. One of his colleagues at McGill, James S. Thomson, now Professor Emeritus, continues to provide mature commentary on the Canadian theological enterprise; his chapter in the 1965 *Literary History of Canada* is the best survey to date, despite its neglect of Roman Catholic sources.

IV

The polarities of Canadian life and times make "dialogue" a word pregnant with meaning and hope. Our current political unrest and ambivalence turns on moving from uneasy coexistence between French and English to a positive federalism coupling these peoples without denying the distinction. While politicians worry and youth protest, philosophers and theologians begin to mount their own commentary and to experiment in their own dialogical relationships. Patterned after the British model, the Canadian Broadcasting Corporation (long regarded with envy by many Americans), provides an open forum for both monologue and dialogue. Its "University of the Air" has produced slim but important volumes, such as the symposia *Makers of Modern Thought* and W. C. Smith's *The Faith of Other Men*. Television personality Pierre Berton, a professional controversialist, initiated popular debate with his provocative book, *The Comfortable Pew,* which was commissioned by the Anglican Church with the considerable and controversial support of Ernest Harrison.

The mood of change and open discussion encourages our younger thinkers. Hitherto the "brain drain" has included a steady stream of recent graduates and mature teachers to the more stimulating and lucrative academies to the south. Canada is proud of such children: R. B. Y. Scott, J. D. Smart, A. C. Cochrane, Gerald Cragg, Donald MacLeod, to give a few familiar names. Now that Canadian universities are expanding, greater opportunity presents itself for work on larger faculties with better library and research facilities. Donald D. Evans of Toronto's philosophy department is one hopeful sign: his *The Logic of Self-Involvement* (1963) represents a creative move toward fruitful dialogue between analytic philosophy and theology. Leslie Dewart's *The Future of Belief* (1966) calls for a radical restatement of Christian theism. Interpreters of Rahner, such as Charles Henkey of Loyola College, Montreal, and disciples of Paul Ricoeur, a regular visitor to Montreal, may be expected to introduce European elements into the Oxbridge atmosphere of professional philosophy in most Canadian centers.

Canada has not been noted for historical theology, except for individual scholars such as Raymond Klibansky and Eric Jay of McGill, Paul Vignaux of Université de Montréal, or Eugene Fairweather of Toronto. It is to be expected that greater influence in the fields of ethics and practical theology should be forthcoming. For one thing, Canadians have been spared, partly because of history and partly because a small nation escapes the responsibility and engagement of larger ones, the typical American horror of communism with its consequent reaction of belligerence. The Social Gospel took positive root in Canadian political life, and in our country Norman Thomas would probably have been a founding member of the Canadian Commonwealth Federation Party and its successor, the New Democratic Party. Both have nurtured significant Christian social concern. A symposium edited by R. B. Y. Scott and Gregory Vlastos in 1936, *Towards the Christian Revolution,* summed up the radical nature of this widespread mood. In more recent years, a monthly journal, *Christian Outlook,* was published in Montreal (1960-1966) to express New Left thinking. Its editor was J. A. Boorman, pupil and critic of Reinhold Niebuhr. *Maintenant* (Montreal) is a lively Roman Catholic journal of protest and renewal.

The new breed of socio-theologian is becoming prominent in Canada as elsewhere. W. E. Mann, S. Crysdale, and others are pioneering in this none too popular approach. The Board of Evangelism and Social Service of The United Church of Canada has long been an outspoken source of stimulation for all the churches in the area of social action. The Canadian Council of Churches conducted an experimental analysis of the suburban community of Burlington, Ontario, last year under the caption "Satellite City by the Skyway." The Council also runs an Urban Training Project in Toronto, so that inner city workers now add their voice to exponents of renewal. A much earlier attempt to grapple with the social context of religion was the Antigonish Movement sponsored by St. Francis Xavier College in Nova Scotia. It and the related Credit Union movement among Roman Catholics stem largely from the social teaching of Leo XIII.

Theology and the arts is a final polarity to be mentioned. Expo '67 is the catalyst in providing an environment where artist and academic, esthete and theologian, may combine resources to experiment with designs for living. Numerous theatrical projects, moreover, without attempting to rival the prestigious Stratford (Ontario) Festival, present opportunity for new dialogue. Cinema festivals, psychedelic happenings, protest rallies may revolve around youth subculture, but they all force questions that traditional theologies could not foresee. In this respect Canada differs little from the U.S. in problem-solving: demands for new forms and expressions of religion, shortage of candidates for ministry, uncertainty created by new morality and new theology.

A more positive and significant role for Canada, it would seem, blends religion and politics. The critique being mounted against U.S. foreign policy, particularly in southeast Asia, unites students, political leftists, pacifists, and many kinds of concerned Christians. If Canada has a distinctive place in the sun because of its peculiar heritage, it will be as peacemaker, prophet of "convergence"—that harmony of opposites destined to be Canada's cross and crown. Jacques Maritain's option for a logic which does not separate but unites *(distinguer pour unir)* is one element in such a philosophy.[1] If pluralism set the stage in Canada, secularism has now supplied the lines, even in Quebec. At such a time as this, theology needs to move along lines of hope, toward a future which it cannot describe with any precision but whose power it traces already in places of peace, signs of renewal, and people of good will.

---

1.   Maritain, *Distinguer pour Unir: ou, Les dégres du Savoir* (Paris: Desclée, De Brouwer, 1963).

15

THE TEACHER OF RELIGION: PROFESSOR OR GURU?

Paper read to The Society for the Study of Religion, York University, June 1969.[2]

Consider the irony of the present age. On campus the new activism demands involvement, measures faculty by the degree of commitment to "political" positions, and recommends a shrewd balance of teachers from left and right wings of such engagement. And this in political science, English, social studies—and sometimes apparently in engineering! Meanwhile our neophyte departments of religion are often self-consciously intoning the creed of no-creed, denying the academic relevance of personal commitment, and attempting a phenomenological approach which is supposed to assure "objectivity" and to avoid "theology."

Various factors suggest why this situation is upon us. For one thing, we have suffered from an often exclusivist, dogmatic, and proselytizing "theology" both in our official Theology and in our western religious culture in general. The image of the theologian among us tends to be

---

2.   Published in *Studies in Religion* II,3 (1972), pp 226-34.

one of a hot gospeller possessed of the Truth and anxious to act the missionary toward the poor benighted "heathen." But to redress the balance by adopting a contradictory stance is not reasonable, particularly when theology itself has won through to a nobler position. Indeed, a recent book in the Harper Forum series reminds us that within Christian theology some ten "attitudes towards other religions" can be detected.[3] Our popular image misses this diversity, so that our debate is usually wide of the mark. We are in danger of a definition of the study of religion that suffers from an anti-theological bias, refusing to discuss transcendence, involvement, commitment as anything but epiphenomena. Yet at the same time we discover that departments of religion themselves may develop distinctive patterns of religiosity, a sort of surrogate "religious exercise" as Willard Oxtoby has described it.[4]

Two theses may be formulated:

> *First,* the separation of 'religion' from 'theology' is an artificial device that fails to meet the actual situation. We require a frank appraisal of theological questions in which the personal commitment of the 'religious data' will be acknowledged, *and* that of the teacher or student of the data. *Second,* the danger to which such study is exposed comes not from theology or commitment as such but from the *kind* of theology or commitment: from what is 'closed' (the popular sense of 'dogmatic') as against what is 'open.'

THE COMMUNICATION OF KNOWLEDGE

The complexity of the learning process has been familiar at least since Pythagoras initiated his disciples by demanding two years' silence as a sign of the mystery of Truth. Without entering into discussion of this large subject we may call attention to certain relevant issues. One is

---

3.   Owen C. Thomas (ed) *Attitudes Toward Other Religions: some Christian interpretations* (Harper Forum Books 1969).

4.   Oxtoby, *Religionswissenschaft Revisited* (Religions in Antiquity, supplement to *Numen* XIV, 1968).

that teaching inevitably involves a certain ordering of values. Among French sociologists this was an important point. C. Bouglé's important work *The Evolution of Values*, for instance, states: "Whoever offers to humanity a system of thought aims also at influencing the order of our preferences. Even though he should consistently wear the impassive mask of science, a teacher is always the servant and, therefore, the apostle of an ideal."[5] Recall that Bouglé is greatly influenced by Durkheim's work on primitive society and the development of values; both see the evolution of values as reflecting group interest, but nonetheless forming an objective imperative: values "are facts. Values present themselves to me as given realities, as things."

Educational theory now stresses the mutuality of communication in the learning process, the personal presence of the teacher as part of the stimulus to which the student responds. The old tag was *"docere* governs two accusatives"—you don't teach maths, you teach Johnny maths. Today we might add: *"docere* has two subjects also"—not only maths but the teacher himself getting across (or not getting across). This seems to hold true regardless of the subject. Consider the case of the teacher of natural science. Here would appear to be a thoroughly "objective" discipline, where the problem of the teacher's subjective orientation or commitment or whatever is totally irrelevant to the process by which he communicates the truth of his "subject." But even here—in a certain sense, precisely here—the stance of the teacher proves a primary factor, an unavoidable variable in the total learning experience. Many philosophers of science have taken pains to examine this phenomenon—Werner Heisenberg, C.F. von Weizsäcker, Max Planck, Michael Polanyi. They have learned to live with the odd situation in which the subject's own presence must be reckoned within the scientific event. This means not only the distorting focus of the observer but his mind-set, his presuppositions, his world-view. Polanyi has pressed the argument most controversially, claiming that scientists suffer from

---

5.   C. Bouglé, *The Evolution of Values* (NY: A.M. Kelley, 1970).

as great a distortion and dogmatism as any other group of humans, requiring a sort of "conversion" to convince them of new truth.[6]

This situation in the sciences suggests a significant change in definition. The old criterion of induction with its empirical verification has been swallowed up by a complex process in which hypothetico-deductive models operate heuristically, matched by "circuits of verification" (Margenau). Moreover, since scientific *data* are ever more subtle and elusive (most noticeably in quantum theory but correspondingly elsewhere) they are described metaphorically: as "stubborn" or "hard" for instance. This raises the question of whether theology must not be reinstated as a legitimate science, in view of its irreducible data, appropriate method of study and theory building, and experimental verification. Such is the contention of otherwise divergent scholars—for instance, Austin Farrer, Kenneth Cauthen, T. F. Torrance.[7] Still others versed in both fields of science and theology (C. S. Coulson, William Pollard, Ian Barbour for example) agree that there are parallel methods which make for fruitful dialogue and complementary activity. The concept of a "science of God" was discussed in depth by Thomas Aquinas, who concluded that theology functions primarily as a "contemplative science" (as distinct from "practical" science which "studies things we can work"). My point in raising the issue here is to remind us that to speak of a "science of religion" in phenomenological terms does not preclude the proper asking of another question: is there a genuine *theological* science? If we agree with those who answer in the affirmative, we must conclude that this is a sister discipline, with its own rightful place in the university, a special place alongside the study of religion. In that case, the tension between religion and theology should be faced boldly and allowed to become creative through deliberate dialogue. I shall return to this point in the next section.

---

6.   Michael Polanyi, *Personal Knowledge* (Harper 1964) 6: "Intellectual Passions"

7.   A. Farrer, *A Science of God?* (Geoffrey Bles 1966); K. Cauthen, *Science, Secularization and God* (Abingdon 1969); T.F. Torrance, *Theological Science* (Oxford 1969).

Again, consider the contemporary state of literary criticism, which offers a striking parallel to our situation. The vaunted New Criticism restricted itself to a formalistic approach to the text, developing canons of meaning related strictly to aesthetic quality and inner consistency. It was an obvious reaction to traditional rapacious methods that sought literature's moral use or social value or psychological meaning. In the 'thirties it was a new broom ridding us of much academic dust. But it suffered from its own restrictions, its new dogmatism. It is now being challenged to learn to appreciate the values which older approaches rightly saw implicit in literature. Walter Ong[8] has noted the personal pilgrimage of I.A. Richards, one of its apostolic founders, who had begun by hoping for man's salvation through literature. Accepting Coleridge's famous dictum about the "willing suspension of disbelief," Richards wrestled with the problem of sharing someone's beliefs "emotionally" but not "intellectually." (This kind of distinction suggests its own problem, but we should note an irony in the study of religion: our problematic is set by a "willing suspension of *belief*"). Nathan Scott of Chicago, for instance, insists that since its "object" involves matters of ultimate concern, valid criticism must become not just "evaluative" but even "theological."[9] Another approach, from the side of classical studies, makes a similar point: literature reflects an archetypal or ritualistic theme. Here is what James Joyce, much influenced by this approach, termed the "monomyth": the human being is a Daedalus-Ulysses, whose quest takes shape as the ritual conflict expressed in great literature.[10]

---

8.   *The Barbarian Within* (Macmillan 1962), 49ff.

9.   For example, *The New Orpheus* (Sheed and Ward 1964), *The Broken Center* (Yale 1966); cf Cleanth Brooks,*The Hidden God* (Yale 1963); M.H. Abrams (ed) *Literature and Belief* (Columbia 1958) for helpful typology.

10.   I have argued this in *The Clown and the Crocodile* (Richmond: John Knox Press, 1970). Indeed the Joyce corpus yields a more complex figure: Stephen Hero through Daedalus and Ulysses to the wake of all Finnegans.

It is this dilemma of rival approaches to data that has raised with a new acuteness the problem of *interpretation*. Susan Sontag has spoken "against interpretation" but in fact calls for a kind that will honour the form of art rather than reduce it to content alone, "an erotics of art."[11] And Paul Ricoeur is devoting himself to a grand program of analysis on this theme, recently given new direction by his study of Freud's hermeneutic.[12] The point remains true across disciplines: the study of every subject involves the investigator's presence as a prime factor in the interpretive process, so that canons of meaning must undergo a constant scrutiny, to discover the observer's point of view and to seek a balance with other points of view.

Therefore, the recent incidents on campus in which political science departments were being challenged by activists to come clean concerning the political commitment of faculty members are other instances of the same thing. It is significant that the plea was not to ignore such commitment but to meet it head-on by seeking a balance of points of view. The irony of which we spoke in beginning was evident also when the rhetoric of orthodoxy/heresy became familiar jargon in those Humanities departments where Marxist commitment raised this problem. By contrast, "religion" seemed a discipline located in the highest of ivory towers, examining data so free from questions of commitment that the problem need not arise.

THE DATA OF THE STUDY OF RELIGION

I doubt that the introduction of the term "scientific" as a qualifier of the discipline called "study of religion" has proved helpful. In both German and French the term is understood differently, with a breadth of meaning that is lost in our English usage. Even in German, of course, the turn from *Wissenschaft* to *Geisteswissenschaft* provoked no little discussion, for example, with Dilthey. He noted that all science proceeds from

---

11.   *Against Interpretation* (Dell Books, 1969).

12.   *De l'interprétation: essai sur Freud* (Editions du Seuil, 1965)

description to evaluation, and that when human data are under discussion the evaluation involves an intuitive element, a living through *(erleben)* which affords a reconstruction *(Nachbild)*.[13] The question remains whether *Religionswissenschaft* appreciated Dilthey's point, or rather took its model from "natural science" as opposed to "human studies."

Though the issue is crucial, the topic is too large to be answered by mere definitions, for we find little agreement, especially among experts. For example, it seems easy to distinguish "history of religions" from "philosophy of religion"; but there are historians who expand history to include the evaluative-normative enterprise, and philosophers who restrict their pursuit to the descriptive-analytic. And then, of course, Mircea Eliade has recently been called a philosopher of religion.[14] It would seem that method is not the sole criterion at stake, but something that governs one's attitude toward methodology, that which indicates the choice of where to begin to play within the hermeneutical circle.

The point at issue concerns those value-laden implications of our method of interpreting religious data—our selection, criteria, comparison, and so on that constitute a revealing profile of our personal attitude toward this aspect of human behaviour. The teacher of religion may suggest, for instance, that atheism (or at least antitheism) constitutes a more serious response to religious behaviour than theism; as in the new "science" of exobiology, he may feel forced to admit that he is not sure there is a fit subject for study at all! The contrary problem is raised by the teacher who develops something called Religion as substitute for the old Theology. That is, he may play the new guru for those North American students who are typically anti-institutional and who, through a combination of youthful verve and environmental

---

13.　　e.g. *Essays: The formation of the historical world in the human sciences* (Princeton, NJ: Princeton U.P., 1985).

14.　　By Vintila Horia in *Myths and Symbols: Studies in Honor of Mircea Eliade,* Kitagawa & Long, eds. (Chicago, 1969), 387.

malaise, reckon the familiar to be the false, and the exotic the true. We are all tempted to bewitch our students by the esoteric, to play *Magister ludi* to their questing spirits. The temptation is especially great when we suffer from an undue concern for method and a quasi-democratic urge to give all "religions" equal time in curricula. The latter approach is one that looks academically impeccable but on closer inspection suggests a retreat from the more basic issue. If the experience of the discipline of comparative philosophy is relevant, we may conclude that comparative study involves decision about criteria of selectivity which already rely on philosophical aprioristic judgments; and more importantly, that we betray the truth unless we accept the actual living tradition in which we stand and from which we begin, assigning it priority, including priority in critique.[15]

To be self-critical of one's own tradition and personal stance provides the key to our question. Neither "professor" nor "guru" is to be ignored, or allowed to shift the balance unduly. Perhaps the example of Roman Catholic theology will help. Vatican II called theologians to develop a truly ecumenical approach to the teaching of theology:

> Instructions in sacred theology and other branches of knowledge, especially those of a historical nature, must also be presented from an ecumenical point of view... not polemically, especially in what concerns the relations of separated brethren with the Catholic Church.[16]

Is not this the formal principle to be adopted and encouraged among us? That is, does it not face the hard fact that most scholars have chosen within a polemical polarization, and that *all* need to examine their pre-suppositions—in our case, "secular" as well as "theological"—in light of the new situation of open dialogue and reassessment among religions themselves? In other words, "theology" cannot be taken as simplistically

---

15.   See *The Concept of Man: A Study in Comparative Philosophy*, Radhakrishnan and Raju, eds. (Allen & Unwin, 1966), Prologue, 18ff.

16.   *Documents of Vatican II*, Abbott, ed., Decree on Ecumenism, §10.

as heretofore. There are theologians and theologians. Nor can "secular presuppositions" (like Anthony Flew's "presumption of atheism") be assumed as good and proper in the study of religion. Gogarten and others have shown how subtle is the relation (the likeness as well as the difference) between the process of secularization and the ideology of secularism. Secular presuppositions which pretend a viable neutrality about personal orientation and commitment to values are highly suspect among philosophers of value (e.g. Stephen Pepper's idea of "root metaphor" behind one's world hypothesis). Charles Davis has warned the university:

> When [theology] is excluded the other sciences try to play its part
> as well as their own—with results that vary from the clumsy to the
> ludicrous. Where good theology is excluded, bad theology flour-
> ishes. Men will raise theological issues; theology might as well be
> there to tackle them.'[17]

Is there a method in studying religion which avoids the partisanship and apologetics of traditional "theology," and yet honours the new insight into the evaluative enterprise demanded by religious data? Is this what "phenomenology" means? It is significant that Willard Oxtoby concludes that both phenomenology and Wilfred C. Smith's "dialogic" approach represent a "religious sympathy and theological motivation" in departure from the parent *Religionswissenschaft*.[18] I should maintain that this represents a positive gain over a questionable objectivity which missed the decisive datum. It is this latter point that Smith has been making so persuasively. His initial distinction between "cumulative tradition" and "faith," while most significant in itself, is not so interesting for our present purposes as his further distinction

---

17.   Quoted in Harry Smith, *Secularization and the University* (Richmond: John Knox Press 1968), 143.

18.   Oxtoby, *Religionswissenschaft Revisited, op. cit.*

between "open" and "closed" commitment.[19] By this, I believe, Smith intends a critique of attitudes consistent with his claim that the study of religion must advance beyond the level of reified and conceptualized data to that which is given in and with religious phenomena themselves: a human self-understanding through relation to transcendence. How beautifully simple to observe of our western "scholar": "He has conceptualized what for the man of faith does not exist, namely a context for his life shorn of its most significant dimension."[20] And therefore how profound to persevere with his thesis: religion is not "a valid object of inquiry or of concern either for the scholar or the man of faith."

For Smith this is not the end but the beginning: it poses the right question, the *theological* question. His *Questions of Religious Truth* illustrates a method that is theological in the proper sense, a discipline imposed by its subject matter, both dialectical and dialogical as befits an 'object' that is both personal and, in its referential claim, Personal. Here the parallel to contemporary philosophy is striking. For to deny the referential status of religious behaviour and statements is to make an ontological decision, to opt for a metaphysical reductionism. This happened in philosophy, and logical positivism has only recently corrected its ways, although many of its practitioners are still pulling themselves up by their logical pigtails. Paul Tillich's comment is relevant:

> If the restriction of philosophy to the logic of the sciences is a matter
> of taste, it need not be taken seriously. If it is based on an analysis of
> the limits of human knowledge, it is based, like every epistemology,
> on ontological assumptions.[21]

One cannot escape the ontological circle; one can but move along it openly and critically (a "*virtuous* circle?").

---

19.   In his address to the CSSR annual meeting, June 1967, Ottawa. Cf., "Christian—Noun, Or Adjective?" in *Questions of Religious Truth* (Scribner 1967).

20.   *The Meaning and End of Religion* (Macmillan 1962), 137.

21.   *Systematic Theology* I, p. 20.

Suppose one overhears a telephone conversation; that is, *one end* of the conversation. One could take as data the words, tones, etc, of the speaker and develop an appropriate method of analysis. But one would be wrong to consider this a sufficient and true analysis. For the words are, in part at least, a response to another voice, another set of words. A genuine analytic of the conversation would have to develop an appropriate method for describing that as well as this, those unheard words as well as these audible ones. Now the religious person claims that his words, deeds, and attitudes are, in part at least, responsive to a presence and a voice that is Other. Whether and how this may be so (the possibility of this actuality) constitutes a sort of "science of God": *theology* (or, as Karl Barth has observed, a "the-anthropology" that acknowledges the divine-human engagement). An astute observer of the contemporary philosophical scene, James Collins, has noted "the common theme that the problem of God is best treated today within the living context of the problem of religion."[22] To rescue this "problem" from the abstraction of traditional philosophy of religion is a gain indeed; to develop a theological science that opens itself to the wealth of religious data now available to the scholar, and in terms of the data's own claim as referential and responsive, is a task indeed.

Such is the kind of "theology" which is needed in the study of religion—not a theology dictated by partisan dogmatics but one that derives from the subject matter under discussion. R. H. L. Slater has argued cogently for such a dimension of study, philosophical or theological, which may be more honest because it admits to assumptions that are "in the open for all to see." His collaborator in this particular work, the philosopher H. D. Lewis, makes the same point in a different context, speaking of "the prominent part played by philosophy in the life of the great religions." He judges those who divorce philosophy from the study of religions to be "seriously hindered in their work by

---

22.   *Cross Currents* (Spring 1968), 188.

failure to have sufficiently subtle grasp of the philosophical issues in the material they study."[23]

If by "phenomenology" therefore we intend some cult of objectivity that denies the humanity of both subject and object, it would seem an inappropriate discipline for the study of religion. But of course whether this is what phenomenology really is or should be is a moot question. Phenomenology seeks to isolate structures, and its technique of *epoché* is not necessarily wed to suspension of judgment *per se*. After all, one decides to adopt such and such a technique, to see the reality in patterned ways, and to accept canons of selectivity. There are phenomenologists and phenomenologists. Brede Kristensen repudiates the name "comparative religion" as implying judgments of value, and assigns all work on "essences" to philosophy of religion; yet he acknowledges that historical, phenomenological and philosophical studies of religion are interrelated and that one's philosophical presuppositions help formulate the questions for all three.[24]

THE TEACHER OF RELIGION

The teacher of religion need not have a "religious" commitment; but he must acknowledge that everyone does indeed have some personal commitment, some "root metaphor" by which one orients one's life and establishes priorities among values. Our task is to be honest with ourselves, our students and colleagues in allowing such self-understanding to be visible where the pursuit of the data demands it. More important, we must be self-critical enough to develop an *open* commitment, one that does not deny our supreme value-centre (to follow H. Richard Niebuhr's analysis) but which can supply brackets when necessary, and which maintains an

---

23.   H.D. Lewis and R.H.L. Slater, *The Study of Religions* (Pelican, 1969; pub. as *World Religions* 1966), 19, 136.

24.   See J.D. Bettis, ed., *Phenomenology of Religion* (Harper Forum Books, 1969), 35.

openness to persons and to truth. Ninian Smart has commented on this problem:

> The good teacher is not the Christian one or the humanist one. The good teacher is the open one ... For good teaching is hostile to hostility, it is closed to a closed mentality, it is prejudiced against prejudice, it is against narrowness, it is opposed to indifference, it is in dialogue with the real world from which young people spring. The problem, after all, is not the problem of what the teacher believes; it is not *this* problem of belief. It is the problem of insight.'[25]

The "open" commitment is not less serious about personal faith, but more critical. In this sense suspension of judgment (*epochê*) is not an academic device but a constant factor in commitment. Moreover, since open commitment is genuine commitment to *truth* it suggests a potential of empathy toward other persons that is necessary to pursue the religious data to the limits of disciplined study. Without this factor how can one "appreciate" what religion is all about? How can one grasp the data without succumbing to a method of reductionism (reducing personal faith to a thing, or ritual behaviour to verbal rubrics, or conditions to causes)? In short, openness means a critical attitude toward one's own commitment so that one moves between the poles of subjectivity and objectivity, or theology and religion, or passion and apathy, or however we indicate the tension aroused by *thinking* about *living.*

The terms of our title, "professor or guru," therefore stand as two modes of one vocation. The scholarly world demands professors, who profess competence rather than commitment. But scholars now know that commitment is a constant the ignoring of which leads to distortion and deceit. Moreover, religious data, as we have contended, involve the scholar in an empathetic enterprise that puts him on a spot both like and unlike that of related disciplines. The question is whether the teacher of religion will succumb to the temptation to indulge in a quasi-religious enterprise, safe from the tests and challenges to which

---

25.   *The Teacher and Christian Belief* (Edin.: Jas. Clarke, 1966), 15.

theologians are heir from the religious community, or will accept the theological work appropriate to his study. In the latter case he will play the role not of a guru of some abstract neo-religion but of a teacher at one with his students in seeking an honest and full assessment of data that imply transcendent reality. Surely today, when the crisis on campus concerns the very "nature of the university," we must acknowledge how "political" is every stance, including that of a supposed neutrality; how can we escape what Noam Chomsky has called "the responsibility of Intellectuals"?[26]

Let Kierkegaard have the last word. He has been badly misunderstood, because his attack on objectivism (by which he meant Hegelian reification and reduction) and his principle that "truth is subjectivity" are taken to imply a thoroughgoing subjectivism. On the contrary, he was attempting a sort of phenomenology of the subject's encounter with *transcendent objectivity*. He saw that in this case above all, the subject's relation to truth is itself a matter of truth. His demand for the subject's conformity with the object of faith is a move beyond the presumptive polarity of objectivism/subjectivism. It is objectivity which enables subjectivity, and which prevents a false ("existential") subjectivism.[27] It is harder than the short way which "academic scholars" are prone to take. But it has its rewards. Seeking the measure of "good faith" it may avoid bad faith; and in acknowledging a proper subjectivity it may hit on the proper objectivity. And that is the end of this essay.

---

26.   In the symposium *The Dissenting Academy*, T. Roszak, ed. (Random House, 1968).

27.   See *Concluding Unscientific Postscript*, 267ff. It is significant that Karl Barth developed his Anselmic method through this Kierkegaardian problematic. Torrance refers to Barth and to Martin Buber in this light in *Theological Science, op.cit.*, 5.

16

RALPH & STEPHEN & HUGH & MARGARET:
Canlit's View of Presbyterians[1]

An alternative title for this somewhat irreverent look at Canadian Presbyterians might be "The Quest for the Historical Presbyterian, from Irving to Trevor." Thus one might cite literary imagery in Irving Layton, "a man learning to forgive God," through to our own Trevor Ferguson, who enjoys both God and Presbyterians.[2] Layton laments effete Christianity, particularly Puritan ethos:

What luck, what luck to be loved
by the one girl
in this Presbyterian country
who knows how to give
a man pleasure.[3]

---

1.   From *The Burning Bush and a Few Acres of Snow: The Presbyterian Contribution to Canadian Life and Culture*, ed. Wm Klempa (Ottawa: Carleton U.P., 1984), pp. 109-22.

2.   For example, *Onyx John* (Toronto: McClelland & Stewart, 1986).

3.   "Look, The Lambs Are All Around Us!" in *The Love Poems of Irving Layton* (Toronto: McClelland & Stewart, 1980).

Similarly, novelist M. T. Kelly states: "Everything felt like the worst Presbyterian Sunday."[4] American critic Edmund Wilson writes that Louis Dudek and Irving Layton perform "a very useful function by getting rid of Presbyterian inhibitions."[5] (If you prefer the obverse of this popular coinage, remember that the sweet heroine of the Mary Tyler Moore Show was a Presbyterian.)

Besides research on the Reformers and on intellectual history, we need to listen to what Northrop Frye calls the *social* imagination. This explores and expresses "cultural history" which "has its own rhythms."[6] The literary artist plays many parts: entertainer (whether trivial or profound), lie-detector (to unmask hypocrisy, Tartuffery of all sorts), and seismograph (to record the fault in human beings, our weaknesses and convulsions). Religion is not only fair game but stands in constant need of such participant observers. "The corruption of the best is the worst."

WHERE WERE WE?

Literary Criticism, like sociology of knowledge, has helped us, in Robert Burns's words, "to see ourselves as others see us." Northrop Frye in particular—both leading literary critic and erstwhile Reformed theologian—focuses the quest for context with the question "Where is here?" Our "here" is Canada, from colonial outpost to industrial nation, or from Arcadian haunt to urban horror. In this light we can appreciate the beginnings of our literary story, epitomized in Susanna Moodie's *Roughing it in the Bush* and the homely practicality of Thomas McCulloch (founder of Pictou Academy) in his *Letters of Mephibosheth Stepsure*. Poems abound with titles like Snow, Frost, Bushed, Winter's Evening, Canoetrip, Wilderness Gothic. In Grove's "Snow" a man is frozen to death in a blizzard; in Raddall's "Winter's Tale" the Halifax Explosion occurs

---

4.   Kelly, *A Dream Like Mine* (Don Mills: Stoddard, 1987).

5.   Wilson, *O Canada: An American's Notes on Canadian Culture* (NY: Noonday Press, 1984), p. 91.

6.   Frye, "Conclusion" to *A Literary History of Canada*, ed. Carl Klinck (Toronto: University of Toronto Press, 1965), pp. 215ff.

on a winter's day. Ours is "an iron land" (Ralph Gustafson), "north of summer" (Al Purdy), thirty acres of snow. Gilles Vigneault's song has become a symbol:

Mon pays,
ce n'est pas un pays
c'est l'hiver.

Is Canadian *theology* by and large a winter theology? Does it, for instance, evidence the irony and satire of that seasonal modality? And is this wintry character the result of northern environment or of Scots Calvinist heredity, or both? D. G. Jones hears our poetry describing humans "burdened by a sense of guilt," and God, "if he appears, becomes a God of Vengeance rather than a God of Love."[7] (The beautiful and positive poetry of Margaret Avison may be the exception that proves the rule).

One thesis to bear in mind is what Ronald Sutherland of Sherbrooke calls "the Calvinist-Jansenist Pantomime."[8] This is the notion that Quebec suffers from a seventeenth-century hangover, when Louis XIV saw fit to yield what Voltaire dubbed "quelques arpents de neige." Canada (Frye again) began as an obstacle to the treasures of the East, continued as a colony (with garrison mentality), and then was cut adrift in quest of nationhood. The point is that we retain as a sort of frozen section much of that original context, including its language. This is the intellectual dimension of the "auld alliance" between France and Scotland, chief evidence for which lies in their sharing what is called "Common Sense philosophy." The influence of this on both Nova Scotia

---

7.   George Woodcock, ed., *A Choice of Critics* (New York: Oxford University Press, 1966), p. 4.

8.   Ronald Sutherland, *Second Image: Comparative Studies in Quebec/Canadian Literature* (Toronto: New Press, 1971), 60ff. Cf. Sutherland, *The New Hero: Essays in Comparative Quebec/Canadian Literature* (Toronto: New Press, 1971), p. 4 on Jonathan Edwards "harmonizing dark Calvinism with enlightened rationalism."

and Quebec in their formative years goes far to explain the common attitude to life, to work and to death.

Who are we? I submit that this should be changed to read, Where *were* we? Are we not, as the old joke says, displaced Scots who would rather have their debts forgiven than their trespasses? Over a period of some two hundred years they came, mostly forced by rapid social change, bringing their Scots dourness and pawky humour, as well as the Calvinist ethic. The likeness between *Canadien* and Scot turns on a common attitude to the world as a vale of soulmaking, hard and demanding: "purgatoire sur la terre." The epic voice of E. J. Pratt, in what Frye calls "the greatest Canadian poem," shows the tension between the almighty deity of classical theology, the "great Panjandrum," and weak but stubborn human rebels.[9] The thesis of Margaret Atwood, that Canadians in general tend to assume the position of "victim" in face of their challenge to survive, is relevant, and her documentation reinforces that of Sutherland.[10] Also helpful is Atwood's distinction among the locations of coming of age in Europe ("what goes on in the bedroom"), the U.S.A. (the forest), and Canada (the coffin).

If the real question for Canadian Presbyterians is, "Where were we?" then Canlit helps us see how far our religion and theology have been a sort of threnody, a lament for lost homeland, its simple and stem ways, its heroic preachers and scholars. We suffer from what Herbert Butterfield calls the Whig interpretation of history. We are afflicted by hero worship, with Calvin and Knox as supersaints. Hugh MacLennan insists that "there is no group of people anywhere on the earth's surface that think more highly of their collective selves than the Scotch do." Margaret Laurence agrees: "the Scots knew how to be almightier than anyone but God." (You know our favourite toast: "Here's tae us—wha's like us?")

This first point, concerning locale or geographical context, helps explain the emphasis on nature in early Canadian theology. It led James

---

9. E.J. Pratt, "The Truant" (1943). *Selected Poems of E.J. Pratt* (Toronto: Macmillan, 1968).

10. Margaret Atwood, *Survival* (Toronto: Anansi, 1972), 36ff., 222. 10.

S. Thomson to say that natural theology seems indigenous to us, a point Armour and Trott reinforce in their book on philosophy in Canada.[11] Let me phrase it like this: *the natural theology of Canadians is natural theology.* This includes both a theology of nature and a doctrine of natural knowledge that adapted Scottish Common Sense philosophy and later British Idealism to our Canadian universities. But that is another story.[12]

SCENES OF CLERICAL LIFE

If locale was our first point, the role of the clergy is second. It is not surprising that the social imagination should take the clergy as archetypes of the religious life. This is as old as Chaucer and Boccaccio, as new as John Updike for the Lutherans and Peter De Vries for the Reformed. One thinks of the gentle irony of Trollope and Eliot concerning parsons, their foibles, intrigues, and pride. The drollery of the Barchester Chronicles is matched by Eliot's "Scenes of Clerical Life," where we find that most clergy are vain and bumbling innocents. They are "too high learnt to have much common-sense."[13] But turn to Scots literature and a sea-change occurs: a sentimental romanticism on the one hand, and on the other a dark sense of guilt and doom. A thesis has emerged in my research for this paper. The social imagination sees Presbyterians not so much as defenders of a classic theology stressing the sovereignty of God and the vocation of his people, but as burdened with an insoluble problem of evil; afflicted by the obvious injustice of things, yet stubbornly clinging to belief in a beneficent and all-powerful deity, they are

---

11.   Thomson in Klinck, *Literary History,* 554; Armour and Trott, *The Faces of Reason* (Waterloo: Wilfred Laurier University Press, 1981). See Donald Cameron, *Conversations with Canadian Novelists* (Toronto: Macmillan, 1973), p. 134.

12.   I develop this thesis in "The Natural Theology of Canada: Philosophy of Religion in Canadian Theological Education" in *Theological Education in Canada,* ed. G. Brown (United Church Publishing House, 1998) pp. 115-28.

13.   "The Sad Fortunes of the Rev. Amos Barton," in *Scenes of Clerical Life,*1856 (London: Macmillan, 1906), p. 59.

restless and grieving. In search of a viable justification of God, a *theodicy*, they raise their lamentation, a *threnody*. I find this twin theme of theodicy and threnody the most telling in the material before us. My thesis is: Calvinism was a grand attempt at justifying God—theodicy; it proved a glorious failure, and so we lament our unjustifiable God—threnody.

Gavin Dishart of Thrums is James M. Barrie's "little minister"; for an Auld Licht preacher Dishart is incredibly naive. The plays of James M. Bridie are better, while the writings of Ian MacLaren are worse. This genre belongs to the "Kailyard school," embodying that quality of "moral sentiment" characteristic of the Scottish Renaissance. We have been influenced by three waves from the old country. First was what Elizabeth Waterston calls a "cult of Burns," resulting in much Canadian poetry written in Braid Scots. Next came Walter Scott, imitated by John Galt. Robert Louis Stevenson was next, along with the Kailyard school. [14]

The influence of Robert Bums did contribute to a critical appreciation of Presbyterianism. But "the orthodox, wha' believe in John Knox" should be more disturbed by his fellow poet James Hogg, the Ettrick Shepherd. His novel *The Memoirs and Confessions of a Justified Sinner* explores the psychopathology of hyper-Calvinist ideas of predestination and perseverance. (Its antinomian hero provided the model for André Gide's *The Immoralist,* and perhaps for John Buchan's similar indictment of high Calvinism, *Witch Wood.)* Apologists will call this a caricature; and in part they are correct. But unless we listen to the voices of imagination, we become mere stooges in a comedy of errors. That is, we may think that we should be taken seriously, that it is self-evident how important to society is religion. To adapt the words of Mr. Thwackum, Tom Jones's tutor, by religion I mean Christianity, by that I mean Protestantism, and by that Presbyterianism, in fact the continuing Presbyterians in Canada, all 144,000 of them. But only a more detached opinion can verify or falsify such a claim. So let's listen.

---

14.   "The Lowland Tradition in Canadian Literature," in W. Stanford Reid, ed., *The Scottish Tradition in Canada* (Toronto: McClelland and Stewart, 1976), pp. 203-31.

CASE STUDIES, OR WHO ARE WE, REALLY?

Muscular Christians—Ralph Connor

Charles W. Gordon is the G. A. Henty of Presbyterianism. Born in Glengarry, Ontario, in 1860, he suffers from two problems. One is a kind of posthumous excommunication by Presbyterians, since despite his lineage—Scottish minister for father, Knox College for alma mater—he played a notorious role as church union supporter. It was he who, at the stroke of midnight on June 10, 1925, instructed the General Assembly organist to play louder and still louder to drown out the summons to loyal Presbyterians to continue in sederunt even as the new United Church was being born.

More important is the other problem: he is too good to be true. He joined the Kailyard tradition with moral idealism. His villains wore black, his heroes pure white; his thirty books sold three million copies. His theme was the heroics of, and the manly deeds on, the outposts of empire. Charles Sheldon's question, "What would Jesus do?"[15] symbolized the evangelical moralism of the time. Connor's experience as ordained missionary in Banff provided material for books featuring a courageous and visionary saver of souls, whose athletic ability (baseball or rugger or wrestling) turns the sceptical crowd his way.

Connor's first two books *(Black Rock: A Tale of the Selkirks* and *The Sky Pilot: A Tale of the Foothills)*[16] were written, he later said, "to awaken my church in eastern Canada to the splendour of the mighty religious adventure being attempted by the missionary pioneers in Canada beyond the Great Lakes." His preface to the second states that the pilot "came to them with firm purpose to play a brother's part, and by sheer love of them and by faith in them, win them to believe that life is priceless, and that it is good to be a man."

---

15.   Charles M. Sheldon, *In His Steps* (New York: Grosset, 1896).

16.   Ralph Connor, *Black Rock: A Tale of the Se/kirks* (Toronto: Westminster, 1899), and *The Sky Pilot: A Tale of the Foothills* (Toronto: Westminster, 1899).

If this sounds thin as an evangelical creed, it was somewhat developed in the other pair of familiar works: *The Man from Glengarry*, 1901, and *Glengarry School Days*, 1902. Here the Christian virtues are clearly those of the Protestant or Puritan ethic. *The Man from Glengarry* has been called "his first real novel;" its hero is not a member of the clergy, indeed the inspiration for goodness comes from the minister's wife. Gordon's own mother, Margaret Robertson, was his model in this and other works. If his concept of "virtue" (literally "manliness") requires the feminine touch for its strength, is his doctrine of God more complex than it seems? The novel's treatment of the Communion season suggests so, with its delicate balance of law and gospel. Connor grasped the Presbyterian thesis, the dialectic of light and darkness. We look at each in turn.

Religious Romp—Stephen Leacock and Robertson Davies

Canadian letters may have begun with wintry poetry, but they soon found a summer voice. Stephen Leacock deserves a paragraph here. What teasing pen portraits he gives us! Remember "the Awful Fate of Melpomenus Jones," the curate with a pathological shyness, who couldn't say goodbye while on a pastoral visit, became delirious, ill, and at last died?[17] My favourite sketch concerns "The rival churches of St. Asaph and St. Osoph."[18] These Montreal Episcopal and Presbyterian congregations are shown in a dreadfully honest light. St. Osoph's, we are told, was so Presbyterian that it was no longer connected with any other church. "It seceded some forty years ago ... and later on, with three other churches, it seceded from the group of seceding congregations. Still later it fell into a difference with the three other churches on the question of eternal punishment, the word 'eternal' not appearing to the elders of St. Osoph's to designate a sufficiently long period." If this seems like exaggeration, remember that the subject of the duration of heaven and hell was a topic

---

17.   Leacock, *Literary Lapses* (Toronto: McClelland & Stewart, 1957), pp. 12ff.

18.   Leacock, *Arcadian Adventures With the Idle Rich* (Crowell, 1914; Toronto: McClelland & Stewart, 1959), pp. 101ff.

much discussed in Leacock's generation. For example, a symposium edited by William Cochrane of Montreal was entitled "Future Punishment: Or Does Death end Probation?" (1886), while the closest to a heresy trial our church has come concerned D. J. Macdonnell of St. Andrew's, Toronto whose sermon on universal salvation suggested that the "aeon" of punishment could bear a finite interpretation.[19]

St. Osoph's minister, Dr. McTeague, also taught philosophy at the university, having spent fifty years trying to reconcile Hegel with St. Paul. His sermons were three parts Paul and one part Hegel, while his lectures were one part Paul to three Hegel. A reader of his book *McTeague's exposition of the Kantian Hypothesis* declared that "a man who could write that was capable of anything." His successor, the Reverend Uttermust Dumfarthing, provides stark contrast. His first sermon to St. Osoph's was on eternal punishment. He told them he was convinced that seventy per cent of them were destined for hell. "The congregation was so swelled next Sunday that the minister raised the percentage to eighty-five, and everybody went away delighted."[20]

We might add that such sketches of stern seceders are reinforced by Robertson Davies's profiles of "brass-bowelled Presbyterians." Davies is the serious person's Leacock, using his own world of theatre, along with mythology, Jungian psychology, and even the occult to develop a wondrous typology of characters. He too sees us as guilt-ridden. In *Fifth Business,* first of the Deptford trilogy, Ramsay recalls that as a child "I was alone with my guilt, and it tortured me. I was a Presbyterian child and I knew a good deal about damnation." He meets a fitting partner in Liesl: "Calvinism? I am Swiss, Ramsay, and I know Calvinism as well as you do. It is a cruel way of life, even if you forget the religion and call it ethics or decent behavior or something else that pushes God out of it ... they want to show they can be Christians without Christ.

19.   See McLelland, "The Macdonnell Heresy trial," in *The Canadian Journal of Theology,* vol.111/2 (1957) pp. 273-84.

20.   "The Ministrations of the Rev. Uttermust Dumfarthing," in Stephen Leacock, *Arcadian Adventures,* 118ff.

Those are the worst; they have the cruelty of doctrine without the poetic grace of myth." [21]

Davies's eclectic "world of wonders" is donnish and elitist. His own perspective allows gnostic wisdom and mythology to mellow the hard dogma. Still, in a *Saturday Night* article he speaks well of our church: "The Presbyterians knew exactly where they stood; it was narrow ground, but it was firm. ... They did not enter the union and are a strong, if small, denomination commonly called Continuing Presbyterians." And he is grateful that his own Presbyterian upbringing serves him well: "I have found the Shorter Catechism a rock at my back and a sword in my hand."[22]

A Dark Lord – Hugh MacLennan

From light to darkness—Apollo succumbs to Dionysos as we face the underside of our Reformed tradition: "Whenever I stop to think about it, the knowledge that I am three-quarters Scotch, and Highland at that, seems like a kind of doom from which I am too Scotch even to think of praying for deliverance." Again: the exiled Scots brought with them "that nameless haunting guilt they never understood, and the feeling of failure, and the loneliness."[23] It is this tragic sense of life that haunts MacLennan's Nova Scotia characters. His novel *Each Man's Son* (1951) provides the strongest case study.

The novel's protagonist, Dr. Dan Ainslie, is a childless man who seeks surrogate fatherhood by caring for the son of another. The title means that he remains his own father's son, as does the boy. Ainslie's father was a Presbyterian minister. As he wrestles with his sense of guilt, his

21.   Robertson Davies, *Fifth Business* (Toronto: Macmillan, 1970), 226; cf. Brian Thorpe, "Discerning the Contemporary Gnostic Spirit in the Novels of Robertson Davies," unpublished Ph.D. dissertation, McGill University, 1989.

22.   Robertson Davies, "Keeping the Faith" in *Saturday Night* 102 (January, 1987), 187ff.

23.   MacLennan,. *Scotchman's Return and other Essays*, vol. 1 (Toronto: Macmillan, 1960), p. 9.

friend MacKenzie observes: "'You may think you've rejected religion with your mind, but your personality has no more rejected it than dyed cloth rejects its original colour.' His voice became sonorous with irony as he tried to remember Calvin: 'Man, having through Adam's fall lost communion with God, abideth evermore under His wrath and curse except such as He hath, out of His loving-kindness and tender mercy, elected to eternal life through Jesus Christ—I'm a Christian, Dan, but Calvin wasn't one and neither was your father. It may sound ridiculous to say, in cold words, that you feel guilty merely because you are alive, but that's what you were taught to believe until you grew up.'" He pursues the point: "can you name any type in history more ridiculous than a Scotch Presbyterian? If you can't laugh at him, you'll be tempted to murder him." MacKenzie believes that the Highlanders enjoyed a simple, poetic faith; then "the Lowlanders with their Calvinism made us ashamed of living."[24]

MacLennan's preface to the book tells of the coming of the Highlanders to Cape Breton, bringing with them "an ancient curse, intensified by John Calvin and branded upon their souls by John Knox and his successors—the belief that man has inherited from Adam a nature so sinful there is no hope for him and that, furthermore, he lives and dies under the wrath of an arbitrary God who will forgive only a handful of His elect on the Day of Judgment." This prefatory note has its own a significance, recounted by Edmund Wilson. In a footnote he records a letter from MacLennan informing him that the novel "was not written to attack or even to emphasize Calvinism," while its preface was composed at the insistence of his Boston publishers, because "without it the underlying motivation would be incomprehensible to an American audience;" the preface is omitted in subsequent editions. Wilson remarks how curious it is that "any such explanation should have been thought to be necessary—and, of all things, an explanation

---

24. Hugh MacLennan, *Each Man's Son* (Toronto: McClelland & Stewart, 1951), pp. 67, 69.

of Calvinism in of all places, Boston."[25] Compare Herman Melville's comment on Nathanael Hawthorne's "touch of Puritanic gloom": "This great power of blackness in him derives its force from its appeal to that Calvinistic sense of Innate Depravity and Original Sin."[26]

MacLennan's most famous book, *Two Solitudes* (1945), scores the puritan ethic, translated into a means of power in the hands of Scots-Canadian Presbyterians. The familiar laws of Manchester School economics provide a mask of charity to hide self-serving. Huntly McQueen, for instance, makes a will (the year is 1934) leaving his entire fortune "to found and maintain a new Presbyterian theological college. It was to be located in the heart of the Ontario countryside, to have ample scholarships, and the chairs were to be so heavily endowed the trustees would be able to fill them with the ablest theologians they could import from Edinburgh and Aberdeen."[27] Here, then, is a strong statement of the dark side of predestinarian Calvinism. If today we have mellowed, by reinterpreting or even ignoring the doctrine of election, this insider's conscience insists that we face the tragic or pessimistic results in individual and societal instances.

Divine Jester—Margaret Laurence

After visiting Glengarry and Mariposa, Deptford and Cape Breton, we turn to Manawaka, Manitoba. This is Margaret Laurence country, as personalized as William Faulkner's Yoknapatawpha County, Mississippi. Her most memorable characters are women, often with biblical names (Old Testament, of course), who are caught in social repression and inherited guilt. They rebel against injustice; they sacrifice, suffer, endure: here are our two themes of theodicy and threnody. And since the test of a theodicy is whether it can justify not only God's ways but God himself,

---

25. Edmund Wilson, *O Canada*, op. cit., p. 71.

26. Cited by Philip Lee, *Against the Protestant Gnostics* (New York: Oxford University Press, 1987), p. 90.

27. MacLennan, *Two Solitudes* (Toronto: Collins, 1945), p. 353.

Laurence probes this wound of our faith most deeply. In the end God is a jester, a joker. What else can you say in face of the world's injustice, if you accept Calvinism's stress on divine will as almighty and incorrigible? In an interview Laurence had this to say about Puritanism: "You just absorb it through the pores. I come from a people who feel guilty at the drop of a hat, who reproach themselves for the slightest thing, and for whom virtue arises from work; if you're not working twenty-six hours a day, you just aren't virtuous."[28]

Manawaka is peopled with MacLeods and Camerons and fringe dwellers named Tonnerre. Besides her African books, Laurence has given us short stories featuring Vanessa MacLeod, who remembers "pictures of Jesus wearing a white sheet and surrounded by a whole lot of well-dressed kids whose mothers obviously had not suffered them to come unto Him until every face and ear was properly scrubbed." Her maternal grandmother lives by the MacInnes motto, "Pleasure Arises from Work." This means strict order and stern retribution. Her women, especially Stacey and Rachel Cameron, daughters of Manawaka's undertaker (a fitting symbol for the wages of living), endure the same bittersweet taste of hard grace. Stacey is the protagonist in *The Fire-Dwellers* (1969), meaning all of us who dwell in these purgatorial fires or are destined for hell—the novel opens with an epigraph from Carl Sandburg's poem "Losers." Stacey sees through the false fronts people wear to hide their fear, as she does herself. She keeps remembering the song:

Ladybird, ladybird,
Flyaway home;
Your house is on fire,
Your children are gone.

28. Quoted by Donald Cameron, *Conversations with Canadian Novelists* (Toronto: Macmillan, 1973), p. 100.

Stacey's sister Rachel (*A Jest of God,* 1966) is obsessed with the injustice of things. "If I believed, I would have to detest God for the brutal joker He would be if He existed. ... My trouble, perhaps, is that I have expected justice." Here also is a reference to our Protestant iconography, a stained-glass window depicting "a pretty and clean-cut Jesus expiring gently and with absolutely no inconvenience, no gore, no pain, just this nice and slightly effeminate insurance salesman who, somewhat incongruously, happens to be clad in a toga." At the end she hopes for "God's mercy on reluctant jesters. God's grace on fools. God's pity on God."[29]

Hagar Shipley, in *The Stone Angel* (1964) resembles her biblical namesake. She is in bondage and seeks her identity, her separate peace. The book opens with Dylan Thomas's lines, "Do not go gentle into that good night / Rage, rage against the dying of the light." She is meditating; these are her last days. She has "often wondered why one discovers so many things too late. The jokes of God." In a moving and ironic passage we read of her being visited by Mr. Troy, the young minister, awkward before this stern old woman. She regards "God's little man" and tries to be gentle with him. He wants to pray (she lets him). She asks him to sing (he finally does, reluctantly but well). Her request is the Hundredth Psalm. All people that on earth and all that. She wonders why she has never been able to serve him with mirth, to find the Psalmist's joy. Nearing her end, she thinks: "If I could, I'd like to have a piper play a pibroch over my grave. *Flowers of the Forest.*"[30]

The pibroch is sometimes martial, often a dirge. The lament for Flodden, "Flowers of the Forest," turns up again in Margaret Laurence's last book, *The Diviners* (1975). Morag Gunn learns of her family heritage from her stepfather, Christie Logan. The Logan warcry is "The Ridge of Tears!" *(Druim-nan deur).* "A sad cry it is, for the sadness of my people. A cry heard at Culloden." And the Logan badge bears the sign of "a passion nail piercing a human heart, proper." Christie tells of the famous Piper

29.   Laurence, *A Jest of God* (Toronto: McClelland & Stewart, 1966), pp. 41f., 209.
30.   Laurence, *The Stone Angel* (Toronto: McClelland & Stewart, 1982), pp. 40ff.

Gunn, who led his clansmen on to the ship bound for the Red River during the Highland Clearances. He played "there on the shore, all the pibrochs he knew, 'Flowers of the Forest' and all them. And it would wrench the heart of any person whose heart was not dead as stone, to hear him. "[31]

From theodicy to threnody: if you cannot explain Morag's experience of "the chaos of the outer world and the confusions of the inner," your rebellion becomes a lament for a lost meaning and a lost grace. Margaret Laurence was an honest and articulate voice on behalf of better answers, of openness between humans, and of a reformed religion.

CONCLUSION

Canadian Presbyterians, as CanLit sees us, stand under the long shadow of a strict sociotheology symbolized by the names Calvin and Knox. Its archetypal idea is the doctrine of election, understood in its strict sense of "double predestination"—God "Sends ane to Heaven an' ten to Hell, / A' for Thy glory!" according to Burns's hypocritical Holy Willie. In its ethos such a creed includes a life of labour and thrift paced by a humour both melancholic and ironic, in short, pessimism about humanity wedded to optimism about God's future. Provided, that is, we are among the elect (and we are!). I submitted that theodicy and threnody are the two chief themes literature sees in Calvinism. Like all theology (I speak as philosopher), it offers little light on the problem of evil; perhaps it even signifies a darkening of the issue, or a celestial copout.[32] But Calvinism does provide the keening lament of the Celts,

---

31.   Laurence, *The Diviners* (Toronto: McClelland & Stewart, 1976), pp. 47-50.

32.   Like the conclusion to The Book of Job, in which the divine answer to Job's questions is a snowjob, challenging Job to explain the universe. But the socalled "problem of evil" will not be solved by such confrontation politics, only by weighing the *divine* cost of creation and the human experiment: "only a suffering God will help," as Bonhoeffer stated.

afflicting us at last with a frightful demand and a profound protest: *Is it nothing to you, who pass by?*

17

DOXOLOGY AS SUSPENSION
OF THE TRAGIC[1]

P eople gather together for all sorts of reasons—trivial or profound, good or evil. But one group at least gathers for a strange ritual that provides a perspective of irony on our human "reasons"; indeed, it offers a kind of news bulletin, a happy announcement, to be answered only with cheers, and drinks all round. This bit of good news involves a Story or tradition that discloses a surprising presence right here and now: a tradition and a presence, making for a perspective of joy which we may call *doxology*. The word refers to that "praise and thanksgiving" offered by the People of God as they remember the tradition and celebrate the presence.

Our title is a play on an idea from Kierkegaard, or rather, from his pseudonym, *Johannes de silentio*.[2] Expounding those "stages on life's way" which make up the aesthetic, ethical, and religious lifestyles in the Kierkegaardian scenario, Johannes examines the "fear and trembling" with which the ethical style breaks out of the aesthetic. Beyond the

---

1.   From *Theology Today* (Princeton) vol. XXXI, No. 2 (July, 1974).

2.   *Fear and Trembling* (Copenhagen, 1843), "Problem I: Is there such a thing as a teleological suspension of the ethical?"

naive immediacy of the latter, ethics turns one inward to reflect on every relationship. Ethical thought "mediates" every moment as occasion for decision. The question is no longer, "Am I lucky?" but "Am I guilty?"

Ethics is burdened with this question. Nor was anyone more burdened than father Abraham, moving so heavily toward Mount Moriah with his sacrificial son, Isaac. (Don't miss the final irony, that the son was a special favour done by God in the old age of Abraham and Sarah, a foretaste of gospel. *Isaac* means "laughter": it is this good news that is to be slain). Here is the Kierkegaardian vignette: the perfectly ethical man who obeys the divine command, submitting gospel itself to the test of law. Abraham looks like a tragic hero. But he is not, for ethically speaking he is a murderer. Or better, "either a murderer or a believer."

Our concern is not to explore this problem in the *de silentio* mode but to press a different case—the mode *de risu* or *de umore* as it were, the modality of humour. As Abraham stood with knife poised, he heard another word which suspended his moral act—*and changed the rules.* Hitherto he was villain or hero, cast within a tragic view of things. Now he accepts a different lifestyle which unveils a higher end (*telos*), "the teleological suspension of the ethical"

Kierkegaard sees the Knight of Faith as actor in a quasi-tragic drama. His moves correspond to the expectations which tragedy allows. But at the critical moment something new breaks in, unexpected and traumatic. It offers an alternative script, an ending beyond his reckoning. Kierkegaard cannot pursue his theme through Johannes because he has Hegel in mind and is using only the categories of Idealism, universal/particular; other pseudonyms will serve him better, until at last a direct witness suspends them too.[3] Let me suggest that he does not make the most of his vignette, for it stands as a type of every breakout, and pointer to the ultimate end, the presence which suspends every penultimate perspec-

---

3.   I refer to the three kinds of writing S.K. uses to develop his complex philosophy, culminating in his properly "religious" works (the *Discourses*, etc).

tive. Not *telos* but *eschatos,* the sort of end that might be termed "the doxological suspension of the tragic."

The word *doxa* deserves study. It had a bad press in Plato's day, when it signified mere opinion or appearance. "It appears to me . . .," "it is my opinion that. . ." Such usage led to the contrast between mere opinion *(doxa),* and reality or truth *(logos)* and its knowledge *(epistêmê).* Both Jew and Christian, however, gave it more positive life. The Greek translation of the Old Testament used *doxa* to translate *kabodh,* that radiance or glory which attaches to a person of honour, which measures ("weighs") worth. Like the *shekinah,* it comes to mean the very "glory" of God, the radiant sign of presence. The New Testament continues this use, linking it to the risen Lord whose glory signifies divine presence in a unique mode.[4]

The divine glory continues to carry this hidden meaning of weight, hence Paul's reference to "the weight of glory" (2 Cor. 4:17) as a hope that outbalances present afflictions. God's worth not only makes him worthy of worship; it gives weight to his being and to his word. Thus the Old Testament prophets are not always sure exactly what God is like, but they never doubt that when he speaks, we'd better listen. And the inside story of both Testaments, namely *Gospel,* points to the unexpected pleasure in listening since God speaks what is best for us. God has accepted us, appreciated us, weighted us in his favour. Such "praise from God" addressed to us is no longer in style; if it were, we should be more child-like, free, clownish. C.S. Lewis has grasped this subtle point well, in his Narnia chronicles for children as well as in his sermon "The Weight of Glory," where he speaks of the "divine *accolade"* and of the child's "pleasure in being praised."[5] Glory carries this peculiar imbalance, weighting us with grace. (This is the point to the conjunction of "gravity and grace," although this needs to be further joined to the paradox of lightness, levity). Such a grace note to the melody of

---

4.   See Kittel, *Theological Dictionary* of the N.T. (Eerdmans, 1964), Vol. II, pp. 232-55.

5.   C. S. Lewis, *Transposition and Other Addresses* (London, 1949), p. 27.

human existence would later be called justification by grace; or better, sanctification by grace. But that is another story.

A final aspect of glory is the extra sense given in the term *paradoxa*, those "strange things" that surround the presence like a halo of near-transparent signs (Luke 5:26). Whoever has eyes to see what's happening in this "penumbra of mystery" (H.T. Kerr) will glorify God, will acknowledge his singular *doxa*. Perhaps theology has to develop this branch of its science, this para-doxology, as one way of showing how faith arises. As Kierkegaard well knew, like any passion, faith's rise is as sudden as a leap; but its object is not therefore a "logical" paradox. When God is on the scene, so to say, our ordinary language and normal explanations prove too light for the occasion; they are outweighed and outshone by a more substantial and more luminous event that brings an alternative explanation. Thus something "paradoxical" is not necessarily "irrational," in the sense of logical contradiction. Kierkegaard has been defended as entirely "logical" (rational) on this score, since he made it clear that belief in the Paradox (as he called the Christian revelation) appears "absurd" only *before* one chooses one's way into it; after the choice, one sees its non-absurdity, its logic.[6]

"Suspense" is the name of the liturgical game. Christian ritual took its shape from the new rhythm that entered the scene with the Christ-event. It was Jesus who took the older patterns of divine-human presence (how God is present for us and we for God), hammered out through Israel's pilgrimage, and recapitulated them in the short compass of his own. Briefly put, the old Passover-to-Pentecost cycle of festive remembrance and celebration became identified with the personal pilgrimage of Jesus of Nazareth to and through crucifixion. Once he had made it, this breakthrough was recognized as significant for all of us, decisive and absolute. The gospel claim is that our destiny is unveiled at centre stage once-and-for-all. The human drama is far from over, but now it is played

---

6.   See S.K.'s *Journals* (Dru ed.), p. 1084; A. T. McKinnon. "Kierkegaard: Paradox and Irrationalism," *Journal of Existentialism*, Spring, 1967 and "Believing the *Paradoks*: a Contradiction in Kierkegaard?" *Harvard Theological Review*, Vo!. 61{1968). pp. 633-6.

out in relation to this central character and his decisive action. Liturgy is a kind of theatrical event, staged deliberately to let this action show through. It suspends our normal behavior patterns with its invitation to act out an eccentric (that is, weighted in the direction of the Other) and therefore comic set of *rites de passage.*

One of Kierkegaard's few heroes was J. G. Hamann, whom he called "the Magus of the North." Hamann had been the contemporary and friendly enemy of Immanuel Kant, criticizing the latter socratically with his playful needling. He answered Kant's ponderous (that is, having the opposite kind of weight from glory) tome, *The Critique of Pure Reason,* by sending him a slight essay, "The Metacritique of the Purism of Reason." An accompanying letter stated, "I write in epic style, because you cannot yet read lyric language."[7] He described his work as unsystematic, humorous, a laxative. He admired Socrates' style for its sustained irony which rejected the security of systems and the betrayal of living beings into dead truths. Hamann's own lifestyle was consistent, a casual and childlike adventure, preferring customs inspection to professorship, and disdaining formal marriage to his "wife" because they were justified by faith.

Kierkegaard was able to share some of these insights but not others. Like Hamann, he wrote "crumbs," refuting the mighty Hegel with his little book *Philosophical Fragments,* followed (with humorous logic) by the large *Concluding Unscientific Postscript to the Philosophical Fragments.* He played with the Hegelian system, teasing and testing its claim to have summed up human thought in a tidy shelf of books. There is a significant parallel with that other rebellious Hegelian, Karl Marx. In the latter's eleventh *Thesis on Feuerbach* we read: "The philosophers have only *interpreted* the world, in various ways; the point, however, is to *change* it." Kierkegaard states the point in more appropriate form (Christians are more humorous than Marxists): "What the philoso-

---

7.   Quoted in R. G. Smith, *J. G. Hamann* (Harper, 1960), p. 238; cf. p. 110 for Kierkegaard's estimate of Hamann.

phers say about Reality is often as disappointing as a sign you see in a shop window, which reads: Pressing Done Here. If you brought your clothes to be pressed, you would be fooled; for only the sign is for sale."[8]

Kierkegaard's pseudonymous man of humour, Johannes Climacus (one approaching the climax of faith) took religion to be the critic of the ethical, an incognito under which the religious lifestyle masquerades in order to administer its laxative. There are ethical as well as philosophical binds, and purging by humour is the best way to prepare for the gift which religion has waiting. It is this critical/therapeutic role of humour which Kierkegaard seizes on, even though—in contrast with Hamann—he could not support it to the end. Unlike Hamann, he could not sustain a permanent covenant of love, with or without legal contract or benefit of clergy. He broke off his engagement to Régine, lamenting later that he lacked sufficient faith for marriage. Thus he remarked that Hamann's humour "contains a much deeper skepticism than irony."

Irony has a skepticism that destroys the facile optimism of the aesthetic mode of life; Socrates is the ironic hero for both Hamann and Kierkegaard. But a weightier critique exposes even the ethical-ironic to still deeper skepticism. Ethics uses the negation of irony, but religion has access to a *positive* humour that sees even moral striving as a bad joke when it tries to *earn* what is finally a *gift*. (I take what S. K. says about "Religiousness B" as his decisive understanding of religion as gospel).[9] The religious person is humorous not because funny things happen, but because such a person stands on ground that affords a comic perspective on both good and ill; to the religious person *everything* looks nontragic. The comedian always has mother-in-law troubles; the religious humorist

---

8.   In "Diapsalmata," *Either/Or.* Vol. I, p. 31.

9.   See Gregor Malantschuk's *Kierkegaard's Thought* (Princeton, 1971) for evidence against taking "Religiousness B" too seriously for S. K. himself. But I would argue that one must follow the logic of Kierkegaardian humour beyond the point the master was able to reach. Truly to go beyond Socrates S. K. must follow gospel into the divine suffering itself, and its comic issue.

sees that human relations tend to fall into legalism. He breaks up with the funniest of all situation comedies: trying to live with a God-in-law.

Karl Marx saw the root of alienation in property relations, by which someone becomes *Unmensch*, dehumanized. Kierkegaard probed deeper and asked why human relations are liable to such ambiguity that dehumanization is possible. He found an answer in the peculiar makeup of the human being, "a self related to itself," and in the self-centred refusal to allow God-relatedness to relax the terrible tension of human relations. Humorously put, instead of a God-in-law he wished a God-in-love, what Jesus intended by saying "Abba, Father."

Aristotle once demonstrated how drama involves a discovery of identity, a revelation leading to a surprising change in circumstances *(peripêteia, anagnôrisis)*. Such discovery of presence is the key to gospel, to both irony and humour in the appearance of Jesus. The suspension of tragedy is accomplished by what appears in our midst as a presence of more significance, a "weight of glory" that shifts the balance in the human drama. The "comic sense of life," as we may term it, sees things as caught up in a wider horizon, weighted toward gospel. Just as in classical drama the moment of recognition provides a shift in orientation, so the gospel story tells of a hidden Other and the surprising joy this One proves to be when recognized. This sort of (re)cognition contributes to a kind of "comic epistemology," sadly missing from classical theism. The latter presumes that we (as subject) take knowledge of "objects," bestowing existence; to take knowledge of transcendent Being we rise above the subject-object relationship to negation or ecstasy. But comedy *descends* as it follows the logic of incarnation. Infinity is not above but below. It has happened, it's *here*.[10]

Humans do not take knowledge of God but *acknowledge* that God is active in knowing *us* and that this divine knowledge is a kind of loving

---

10. See William F. Lynch, *Christ and Apollo: the Dimensions of the Literary Imagination* (Sheed & Ward, 1960), regarding "the definite" and the analogical direction of the Christian imagination. Cf. Bernard of Clairvaux's thesis that the way to divine reality is downwards, through twelve steps of humility.

—a loving that wills us into Being. It is not the subject-object dichotomy that serves as analogue here, but the male-female coupling which love involves. The "incarnate logos" reveals that the logic of love is at the heart of things, so that one must speak only of God-and-humans, of the *fact* of the divine-human unity, or "the-anthropology," as Barth put it (i.e. both "theology" and "anthropology" as independent disciplines are false).

Gospel is a courting dance which woos us into being-there with this stormy Lover . . . many fall away, considering the dance eccentric and irrational. But to persevere, by looking at your partner and not at your feet, is to learn the secret of be-ing. For such dance of life is the opposite of that deadening spirit which dominates modernity, this dreadful worldwide Necropolis. One separates "humanity" and "God," asking lewd questions about how they got together. Isolation is the stuff of tragedy, but comedy cuts us down to size and acknowledges the unity of being through God's decision to be one with us. Gospel demands a cynicism about the nobility of tragic heroes, a skepticism about the scientific denial of "man" and the philosophical denial of "God." Reinhold Niebuhr once described himself as a "tamed cynic." It is time we suspended the tragic virtues, the heroic stoicism of our do-it-yourself philosophies and religions.[11] That is still the old pessimism, the untamed cynicism. Bertold Brecht, for instance: "The man who laughs has not yet been told the terrible news"; or Eugene Ionesco writing of *l'humoir noir:* "what possible reaction is there left, when everything has ceased to matter, but to laugh at it all?"

Gospel offers a deeper skepticism that suspends gallows humour, denying the validity of this denial. To doubt the doubters is the perspective of faith. Faith contains doubt, but always in suspense, as part of the game (a sort of "willing suspension of *dis*belief"). For Kierkegaard, the religious game turned back on the old modes of aesthetic and ethic, so that one receives back—in "repetition"—both immediacy and mediacy,

---

11. Today the "me generation" has given way to the general "self-esteem" or preoccupation (in the West at least) with one's self-image: self-worth comes from one's own estimation rather than some Other's.

but without the seriousness which made them tragic.[12] Thus comedy learns to live with tragedy, but not to give it the last word.

Theological humour is the guardian of the origins of faith. Without the ode to joy with which faith begins, theology would have nothing to say. Creeds are meant for singing (not signing), so that theology is a joyful meditation on songs of praise and thanksgiving. Theology's temptation is to exchange this lyrical language for a more prosaic one, and even to substitute itself (The System) for the Song. The rhythm of doxology and theology, therefore, is the rhythm of Christian faith. Even theology dare not "use" God-and-man as food for thought. Persons are rather to be "enjoyed" as partners in the Dance—this contrast of *use* and *enjoyment* is as old as Augustine (*uti, frui*). If persons are for our enjoyment and not our use, then the absolute Person must be absolutely enjoyable – and *absolutely useless!* When the Partner is also the best of all Lovers, one may conclude that one has to do with the Irresistible.

"Irresistible grace," as an historic doctrine, probably intended something like that. The present lack of self-confidence on the part of Christian theologians is in large part a failure to appreciate the evangelical *intention* of their inherited subject-matter. As comedy is to tragedy, so is gospel to law, and doxology to theology. By assimilating our forebears' intention to honour gospel in its suspensive state, we may yet learn the art of doxology. There is a theology of humour prowling among us right now (even Moltmann has learned that—from our continent?); but that is a secondary affair. The primary thing is doxology, a "humorous theology"—light, tentative, suspense-full. Its attributes, in short, ought to mirror gospel, that good news of the surprising and joyful presence that started things moving. And since the motion—Christ's *career*—burst through the tragic into the comic (i.e. a nontragic End), theology and doxology must follow the same course. Otherwise ours would not be a "reasonable" service or a "logical" repeti-

---

12.   *Repetition*, by "Constantin Constantius," was published at the same time as *Fear and Trembling*, 1843.

tion of the story. Doxology suspends tragedy: such an *end* provides comic masks for the faithful, as they follow this Way through the world.

18

A SERIOUS PLAYFULNESS

Once there was a child named Laughter.[1] This odd name was given him by his astonished parents, since he was born when they were in their 'nineties. His birth was the result of a promise given by divine messengers. They announced some good news: God cares for humankind and desires a special People to serve as channels of blessing and peace. This covenant would come through the special child given to an ageing couple as a sign of Life. The story of their argument with the messengers—they considered the whole thing a huge joke—is the heart of gospel, "good news." For God had the last laugh: when the human pair learned to share *that* joke they learned what grace is. So they laughed twice; the difference and distance between their laughter *at* God and their laughter *with* God is what we intend to mean by "serious playfulness." If we are only playful we will miss what is decisive in life; if we are merely serious we will miss God's punch line.

The point was that Abraham and Sarah knew they were impotent to provide the line of descendants necessary to carry the divine promise. At first they thought their servant Eliezer might be the heir of the

---

1.　Written for the British quarterly *The Way: Contemporary Christian Spirituality* (July, 1991) 196–205.

covenant as he would be of their goods. But God vetoed that plan. So they made further provision, according to the social etiquette of their time: Abraham fathered Ishmael through his concubine Hagar; that should do the trick! But God had still other plans. The real "provision" (Providence) did not stick at the problem of ageing, or barrenness. It provided a solution that seemed miraculous to the couple themselves. The absurdity of a pair of impotents having a child struck them as so funny that they laughed in the face of the messengers. Abraham in fact felt called to offer apologies for Sarah, doubled over inside the tent.

Nine months later Sarah got the joke. She named her son Laughter (*Isaac* in their Hebrew language) saying: "All who hear will laugh with me." You can read all about it in the book called *Genesis*, chapters 16 to 25. But do you really *hear* it?—if you call yourself Christian, do you chuckle along with Sarah every day?

The humour of the situation turns on the fact that Laughter's mother was post-menopausal, as we say today. That is, having children was an impossibility. This human powerlessness will become a constant in the story of God's covenant with Israel. It is a kind of litany: Sarah was barren . . . Rebekah was barren . . . and Rachel . . . also Manoah's wife (anonymous) . . . Hannah (apparently) . . . and at last Elizabeth and her virgin cousin Mary. So their children, spiritual brothers of Isaac, are a sort of lineage of Providence: Esau and Jacob, Joseph, Samson, Samuel, and at last John the Baptist and Jesus. It forms a pattern, as if our own arrangements for the future fall short. If there are promises to be kept, gods to honour, a future to raise hopes, we are not up to it. Only if God is faithful to his word, only if he can provide alternatives, will there be more to come. It is as if human deadness is the opportunity for divine presence: *resurrection*. If there is "God," there must be Easter, the joy of spring after winter, the comic born from the tragic.

Now the humour became serious through an uncanny event. This same Abraham and his special son Isaac had a little drama of their own to act out. When the boy was older, Abraham was put to a test, commanded to offer Isaac in sacrifice. Up the mountain they went: father, son, donkey, knife, wood and fire for the fatal ritual. What mixed emotions seethed in the bosom of Abraham! This was not only his son but the special child of divine promise. Not his idea or his doing, like Ishmael. Isaac was the child born out of season so that the promise could be fulfilled, the great hosts of the future could be born and live out the divine covenant. Everything depended on him, on his survival: no Isaac, no covenant People. Or so God himself had said—had the all-knowing One forgotten?

In fact Isaac was spared, a lamb was provided (pro-vision again) at the last moment. This cliffhanger occurred on a mountain fittingly named Vision (*Moriah*). What Abraham saw was that God's sense of humour is incorrigible: how can you kill the Laughter bestowed by grace? But at first the commandment seemed as serious as every law. What Abraham learned was that to take it seriously has deadly results; but that a surprise may come to turn law into gospel. And when good news breaks into our tragic affairs, laughter is born again. God taught Abraham that faith is as fragile as the flesh and blood of our children, that we are always one generation away from losing everything.

The Danish philosopher Kierkegaard bids us picture the same little group *descending* the mountain. Outwardly nothing has changed, but inwardly Abraham knows that Isaac will always be a gifted child, offspring of grace. God will always come between them, like a mediator, or a host presenting them to each other all the days of their lives.[2] Here is the very model of Christian *vocation*: your life is a calling from God, giving you a place in his good creation; and of *stewardship*: all that you have is a gift, not possession (ownership) but loan (accountability).

And something more, much more decisive: all the generations must negotiate this narrow gate, this helpless infant, this youth standing submissively on the mountain-top. Our own provision and expectation

---

2.   Kierkegaard, *Fear and trembling* (Doubleday Anchor, 1954). "The ethical expression for what Abraham did is, that he would *murder* Isaac; the religious expression is, that he would *sacrifice* Isaac—the contradiction spells 'dread' for Abraham' (p. 41). Hence 'irony and humour' are 'essentially different from the passion of faith" (p 62).

prove powerless. In this regard, we are all impotent, laughing at God's promise. Hope can displace scepticism only if God will do something special. *Not our Ishmaels but his Isaacs.* Abraham learned this in his encounter with the messengers. (A further irony is that the one who talked was the Logos or Word of God, according to former theologians. Whenever and wherever God speaks it is God's *Word.* So Abraham was talking with his descendant the Christ, as it were!) Anyway, when Abraham heard the absurd proposal he quickly reminded them that he had already thought of how the covenant could be guaranteed. "0 that Ishmael might live in your sight!" As if to say: Don't worry God, I've thought of everything!

Isaac's thirteen-year-old stepbrother Ishmael, however, was not part of this arrangement, even though he had been circumcised. He was sent away, chiefly at Sarah's insistence (how short was her laughter!). But another promise was made to him, for Hagar's children also have their Word from God: "I will make him a great nation" (Gen. 21,18). The Ishmaelites remind us of God's other children and other covenants, in this case the peoples of Arabia, the religion of Islam. For Abraham is father to three religions: Judaism, Christianity and Islam.

Divine Images

The Story so well begun did not continue smoothly. The covenant people kept mistaking God's *care* for *indulgence.* They thought they had it made, as it were, instead of having to make history by faithful loving, that is, taking care for others, for creation, for what the divine Word commended and commanded as the right way of being human (of human be-ing). It is not easy to distinguish "care," that is, whether we should be careful or careless or carefree. "Take no care for tomorrow" said Jesus, "live like birds or flowers." Some of his followers have tried just that, and sometimes it has even worked. Mostly, however, we take this strong saying to be Jesus's way of warning against Abraham' s original sin of thinking that everything depended on him. For Jesus it was more like trusting God's Word to be right about the sort of carefree care or playful seriousness which being human ought to mean.

The deepest of questions for both believers and unbelievers is "what is God *like*?" Most unbelievers reject "God" because they cannot accept what believers say about deity. Often what they say is wrong, and therefore unbelievers are right to reject their bad theology. Theology's first question is always this: what is *appropriate* to God?[3] What qualities may we properly ascribe to divinity? In what sense do we mean that God is all-powerful, or wills everything, or is able to love – and even perhaps to *suffer*? Great controversies always attend theology from age to age as we try to cleanse our human speech about God. The Bible is not so clear or so consistent that we can merely quote its words as self-evident to everyone. As critics point out, it tells us that God is both wrathful and loving, all-powerful yet allowing and even causing evil (Isa. 45:7), both high above history yet becoming human, and so on. Even if we were to call these "paradoxes" we must acknowledge the difficulty in grasping their meaning. Grave mis-takes have resulted from taking them seriously but not playfully, most notably taking God as a celestial tyrant moving us about like pawns.[4]

So let us pursue the Story which casts God as one of the actors in a drama. He is not the deity of ancient Greek drama, the "God from the machine" who is larger than life, raised on the godwalk (and on high heels at that) above the stage. Zeus sounds out his final decree when the human story gets too entangled for anyone to solve. Nor is he a voice offstage whispering lines to forgetful actors. Sometimes, to be sure, the scriptures talk like that. Abraham and Sarah thought that God Almighty was intervening in human affairs. (So God was, but She's no Zeus.) God prefers to act through intermediaries, human agents and

---

3.   The technical term for this appropriateness is *theoprepês*. Coined by Stoic philosophers, it was taken over by Church Fathers—see my *God the Anonymous* (Philadelphia: Patristic Foundation, 1970), "What is Appropriate to God?" pp. 138-40.

4.   See Chas. Hartshorne, *Omnipotence and Other Theological Mistakes* (Albany: SUNY, 1984).

historical events. Opening barren wombs is a sign that another Actor is with us on stage, but it is the kind of sign that tells us God will not overthrow human ways entirely. Means of grace may be abnormal but they are not anti-normal. Or perhaps it shows that the "norm" is broader, more complex, than we think.[5]

To imagine what God is like demands energy and openness. If the Bible is so complex and deep in meaning, we cannot expect to understand it easily. In a remarkable last will and testimony, Martin Luther noted how hard it is to understand nature, the world and scripture. For the first you have to be "a shepherd or farmer for five years." For the second, you must spend twenty-five years in politics. For the third, even guiding the Church for a hundred years will not suffice. "Do not try to follow this divine Aeneid journey, but kneel down in worship with bowed heads over the imprint where He has stepped. We are beggars. That is true."[6]

Luther thought that one must accept a "calling," a vocation to pursue the mysteries of nature or of history. Even greater is the demand when one follows the biblical Story. This good news is won only as a prize for those willing to run and strive. But you get the prize at the start of the race, you become as a child again, you discover that your running and striving, your work and accomplishments are the *result* of faith and not its *cause.* That is, by accepting the covenant as Abraham and Sarah did, as a gift beyond your deserving or your power or your reckoning, you are set free from concern for paying your way or demanding your rights. It is called "justification by faith" and it means that justice comes from a loving God: all is right with God, including *you.* And therefore—this *therefore* signals the punch line in the divine humour—therefore we are

5.   Think of the idea of causation: the Reformers followed the medieval acceptance of Aristotle's doctrine of fourfold causality (material, formal, efficient, final) to solve the thorny problem of how God can will something which we freely accept. If God is Final Cause, the three "second causes" allow human freedom. But today science has taught us to reduce causation to one simple factor, missing the need for complexity in human affairs, and divine-human affairs even more.

6.   See A. Kooiman, *The Mature Luther* (Luther College Press, 1959), pp 106ff.

freed from lifestyles of merit and pride, we are free to enjoy creation, make history, love one another, tell funny stories and baptize our children after the one named Laughter. "Call me Isaac!"

God justifies humans according to his own logic of love, taking their burdens, healing their wounds, co-operating with their efforts. This sets us free from false burdens of pride and merit. You get everything when you know you don't deserve anything. This sounds simplistic; sometimes it is, but there are always saints and holy fools around to show how it works. The logic of love goes like this: if you truly love someone, you do not care what rewards there are, how useful the other can be to you. Indeed, the joy of love comes from the *uselessness* of the beloved: love him just because he is there; let her *be*. It's as if utility and enjoyment are opposites: the more usefulness, the less joy. You would sacrifice everything for the sake of your beloved. It is something like this with us and God. We seek a Power that will prove useful in our lives: health, wealth, happiness. But we encounter a Love that offers nothing but itself; in fact it promises suffering and loss rather than pleasure and goods. It is worse than useless, it is counter-productive. In this case we find ourselves caught by the ultimate Lover. Can it be that God is absolutely useless, and *therefore* absolutely enjoyable?

Great theologians have explored this royal game of divine love. Two of the greatest, Thomas Aquinas (Doctor of Light) and John of the Cross (Doctor of Night), witness in different ways to the supreme Joy who crowns all our striving with perfections beyond our imagining. The magnificent theological system erected by Thomas is a kind of game played for the sheer joy of following the concepts and categories which human minds throw at the moving target named "God." But near the end of his life Thomas gave up his writing after a vision of the living Christ one day at Mass. He wrote only one more thing, a commentary on the Song of Songs. That love poetry between God and Israel was the trademark of Christian mystics. John of the Cross was one of the greatest, as was Teresa of Avila, whose confessor he was. They learned from experience that encountering God is like falling in love. Ecstasy it may be, but every lover knows also the pain. Pain of desire, of doubt, of absence. Teresa put it simply: *divina pati,* "to suffer divine things."

Pain and pleasure, suffering and joy: we are talking the language of *drama* here. Are saints and mystics correct to join the two kinds of human experience so closely? Are both tragedy and comedy forms of one "live theatre"? Which one has the last word to say on stage: the tragic or the comic?

Comedy and tragedy

In theatre, protagonist and antagonist share an *agon,* a testing or suffering. The Bible also is like a script for the human drama, a guidebook for the tours of hell and sideshows of purgatory which make up our history. Sometimes glimpses of heaven are included to relieve the pain. That is what the great poet Dante grasped when he called his sweeping epic of purgatory, hell and heaven "Comedy" (*Commedia*). When we mistakenly call it "Divine comedy" we miss his point. It's *our* story, the human comedy.

Comedy and tragedy spring from different views of life, of reality. Tragedy is considered the nobler of the two, since it deals with heroes, larger-than-life characters whom we praise and try to imitate. Or we learn from their fate as they reach too high and fall to their doom. Comedy, on the other hand, deals with clowns, fools and buffoons. They are lower characters and we laugh at them and learn from their mistakes. So far, the classical analysis of Aristotle's *Poetics* seems adequate. But what if something more is going on in comedy? Could it be that the resilience of the clown, falling and rising again, holds the truth, and not the fall of the hero? The one lies still as death; his body is raised on shoulders and slowly borne offstage (drumbeat, slowly). But the other jumps back on his feet, scars and all, *and laughs*; and so do we.

The Bible belongs to a certain kind of literature, which a leading literary critic has called "romantic comedy."[7] Its romance lies in its

---

7.   Northrop Frye, "Pistis and Mythos," address to The Canadian Society for the Study of Religion, Montreal, June 1972; cf., *The Great Code: The Bible and Lit-*

narrative of the hero's journey into the far country, a lonely and disputed passage, to slay the dragon, to receive a mortal wound, to fall in death. But the romance turns into comedy through a wondrous reversal of fortune (the distinctive mark of comedy) by which our hero is revived, rescues the princess from her doom, and makes the return journey to marry her. This last part is found in the book fittingly called *Revelation*; here are the stock characters of tragi-comedy: hero, beast, princess (the Church!), marriage feast with the toast *L'Chaim*, "To Life!"

We find ourselves in a world of contradictions, of struggle: life against death, light against darkness, good against evil. Tragedy traces the conflict to its bitter end, but comedy unveils a further Act, a finale in which things are set right, justified. But it is a justification by "grace," by the surprising recovery and recognition of the wounded warrior whose renewal adds grace notes to the story. One artist who saw the parallel with his creation of possible worlds was J. R. R. Tolkien. His fantasies of Middle Earth, embattled and imperilled, contain a decisive turning point or crux, which he called "eucatastrophe"—*Frodo lives!* Speaking about "the Consolation of the Happy Ending" he notes that the opposite of tragedy, and its answering reality, is "the good catastrophe, the sudden joyous 'turn'." This means deliverance from tragic doom or final defeat. It is *"evangelium,* giving a fleeting glimpse of Joy, Joy beyond the walls of the world, poignant as grief."[8] The tragic hero is a loner, but in comedy it is *society* that counts. Comic heroes are spurred to action on behalf of their neighbours, or of an innocent victim. (Charlie Chaplin never could resist a face of innocence. Or beauty.) And if there is treasure to be won (dragons always hoard jewels) then it will be for the good of all, for the common wealth. The

---

erature (New York: Harcourt Brace Jovanovich, 1981), pp 156, 169. Also *The secular scripture: a study of the structure of romance* (Harvard V.P., 1976), P 171: "Comedy ends with a festive society. . . . belief is also primarily social in reference, which is why the Christian myth is a comedy rather than a romance."

8.   "On fairy-stories," in C.S. Lewis, ed: *Essays presented to Charles Williams* (Grand Rapids: Eerdmans, 1966), 81.

final scene must therefore be a wedding, signifying the creation of an extended family and the renewal of the race. Even Gilbert and Sullivan knew that, in their farcical endings: the uglies marry the uglies and the beautiful people each other. They also knew the value of the "recognition scene"—Frederick, for instance, was supposed to have been apprenticed in Penzance to pilots not pirates, so he is really a hero in disguise. There is a certain hidden logic at work, a fitting conclusion to our social life. Tragedy moves us with its heroics, but comedy invites us to a wedding and makes jokes about having babies.[9]

Jubilee and Utopia

A serious playfulness teaches us that we are all in the same boat, and it is a ship of fools. But by unmasking the pretensions of those who think too highly of themselves, the clown dis-orders society and unveils the truth of human relationships: on our own we are nothing; what is good must be received from another. ("What have you that you did not receive? If then you received it, why do you boast as if it were not a gift?"—1 Cor 4:7). So these 'others' who share the human condition and adventure may be nuisances or even enemies, but our salvation is tied up with their destiny. Clowns are marginal figures, living on the edge of polite society: missionaries of the extraordinary. Only on the edge can they reveal the truth about our life together, about the inexorable tie between love for neighbours and for God. Clowns are thus fools with a serious intent, children of Mary who sang of bringing the proud low and raising the humble. The *Magnificat* is their anthem and Utopia their goal.

Utopia—"happy place" (and also "no place")—is the plan for human being, for society, tossed by fools into our serious politics, economics, academics and religion. It offers a different vision, a contradictory hope for our life together. The Jewish hope was formalized as "Jubilee," a word derived from *yobel*, the sound of trumpets. This was the crown

---

9.   See McLelland, *The Clown and the Crocodile* (Richmond, VA: John Knox Press, 1970), pp 79ff.

of religious holy days, the ultimate Festival. Following a sabbath of sabbaths (forty-nine years), the fiftieth was set aside, consecrated, to liberty and celebration. Land would enjoy a fallow season, debts would be forgiven, slaves set free. (See Leviticus 25.) When land and debtors and all sorts of property are "redeemed," we have an occasion of release from bondage, from legal arrangements, from social norms. It is a time of freedom, holiday, carnival. How ironic that the modern "carnival" ("farewell to flesh") has become an extravagant binge before the sombre denials of Lent. Our theme of comic release suggests that Lent may be a denial of gospel, that Christian life is more like a perpetual Carnival, a time of liberation and celebration. Or perhaps better, that in the rhythm of Carnival and Lent mourning must always let joy have the last word.

At last we come to the crucial issue. Is comedy simply the displacement of tragedy, and gospel the opposite of law? Does Easter make Calvary outdated, so that suffering is no longer an appropriate symbol for human being? The excesses of clowns and fools may suggest so, but experience teaches us that their vision too is partial. The utopian vision affords an ultimate perspective on all that we do, but it is not a programme for the present order. It brings hope, and hope means looking to the future. We are to build our new life on that hope, on the expectation of divine presence; we are like doubting Sarah, about to be surprised by Laughter. But our hope does not displace the Cross of Christ; instead it adds a dimension, the extra mile that God went in his Easter revelation. The forty days from Easter to Ascension mark the special time of comic release, the recognition scene in the Garden and the upper room and Emmaus: it is the Crucified who endures. Mary Magdalene, Thomas, the disciples who saw the risen Lord, are comic heroes whose roles are no longer tragic. Now they break up with joy at amazing grace, they arrange banquets and picnics on the shore and rush to tell others the good news. The Cross is not outdated, but placed in a light from the future that shows its ultimate fruit, its power for reconciliation, for new life. It was said of father Abraham that in his testing, "He considered that God was able to raise men even from the dead"—now *that's* faith! (Heb 11:19).

Clowns are outsiders who tell us that someday outside will be in. Meanwhile they bid us remember the future, live as if the power of the new age is already at work among us (Heb. 6:5). We are called to treat our neighbours in the light of God's love and promise. We hope well of all, including our own poor selves. We live in a Jubilee season, heal others and set them free as much as possible, blow trumpets (or the Music Man's seventy-six trombones). If we appear rude and somewhat mad to a suffering world, that is the sign that we are right with God's plan. God will have the last laugh, and so we live and work believing that the whole thing is part of his divine drama. We are in *his* play, and our roles are given us not as fixed assignments but as means of grace, opportunities for celebration. Utopia may be nowhere—yet. But in a sense it is reality, *the Kingdom of Christ*. It is He who reigns in this "meantime," between the old age and the new. His presence is that of the Crucified, but he is liberated from his bondage, freed from the tragic plot. He is therefore subject of both tragedy and comedy, both hero and clown: he survives, but with scars. (Consider the difference between the two transfigurations of Jesus on Mount Tabor and Mount Olivet). We cannot follow him in his vicarious suffering, unique and unrepeatable; but we can follow him in the sacrifice of praise, the life of jubilation.

We started this little play of ideas with Isaac. We saw him as victim and victor, the child named Laughter who survived to play the role of the channel of blessing, the narrow gate through which all covenant folk must pass. This peculiar way of humour or playfulness is not free from suffering, pain, seriousness; but it is that which sustains us along the path despite life's contradictions, despite pains of body, mind or spirit, despite doubt and ignorance and backsliding. Because Jesus once cried out: "Why have YOU forsaken ME?" we can rest in the surety that *we* are never forsaken. Even in our darkest hours, at bedside of the dying or graveside of the dead, in our own pain and loss and fear of death— especially there we may hear the trumpet of victory and hope. Such is the good news from Jesus, descendant of Isaac, doorway to Life. If the biblical witness is correct, the last Act involves a universal recognition scene, a comic and cosmic Revelation. The desire of all nations will be met and Sabbath and Pentecost, Jubilee and Utopia—along with the festive hopes of all peoples on this and possibly other planets—will find their fulfilment in the greater Kingdom of God.

APPENDIX

ADVENTURES IN P-C LAND:
A SAURIAN TESTAMENT

Convocation Morning Address, The Presbyterian College, 1993.

First, my thanks to Principal Klempa and the Faculty for this opportunity of reflecting on our College, its history and reality. The title suggests the sort of Wonderland or even Looking-glass world that every institution becomes. The Academy is especially prone to this phenomenon, since it attracts such characters; the theological academy in particular adds the dimension of holy foolishness that sets seminarians apart—or used to, as we will see. (I've noticed a higher degree of humour among theologues and clergy than other professions. For instance, during a debate on pensions at General Assembly one speaker (glossing Oscar Wilde) complained, "We treat our widows so poorly we don't deserve to have any.") My subtitle warns that this is a personal view, although I hope not too autobiographical.

ALICE ...

One might imagine "Alice in Academia," happening upon our little building in her travels. She has met the White Queen across the street, at the "Royal Institution for the Advancement of Learning," a.k.a. McGill. Naturally the Queen is the university's Royal Visitor and has just solved the budget crisis by firing everyone whose name begins with the letters C through M. This leaves Fred Wisse still tenured, but Robert Culley forced to beg some work from Principal Klempa. Alice finds him in the Library assisting Dan Shute, an interesting experience for them both. Since this is Wonderland, his task is to remove all footnotes that say *Opcit* or *Cf*, since these are forbidden by Royal decree (embodied in the *London Manual of Style*). Alice has already encountered Cathy and George working on obscure machines marked terminal, designing logos for fundraising parties. In a nearby office, someone is playing strange new hymns on a recorder. Entering an upstairs classroom, Alice beholds a wondrous ritual in which several men and women, all dressed alike in grunge, listen to an older man talking in jargon—apocalyptic trajectories, preferential options, self-transcendence—leaving her as bored as the listeners. Suddenly a bell rings, the students dash out, trampling her on their hasty exeunt. Ah! she thinks, they have escaped the torturer at last—only to be trampled again by the professor rushing to get in the cafeteria lineup before the Jello runs out. ...[1]

Well: we could go on with this fantasy, showing the reverse logic of much that we do in theological education. But it breeds too many in-jokes. After thirty-six years on the college faculty, and with memories back to 1955 when I was guest lecturer for a term, I've been around almost one-third of PC history: a dinosaur indeed. I should have used the word "Professaurian" but that would be much too flip for a serious address. Let me be your white rabbit to lead you into a few spots in PC-land.

---

1.   References: Dr Geoff Johnston practiced the recorder in his office; Cathy Bassiano was administrative assistant; George Harper served as general factotum; Principal Klempa insisted on Jello every lunch.

1867 ...

The initial scene in 1867 shows us Erskine Church basement on Ste Catherine Street at Peel, where ten students listen to one of their two lecturers as Presbyterian College is launched. A bold venture, opposed by the already established "Knox's College" (as it was first called) in Toronto. The first professor is Donald H. MacVicar, minister of Côte Street Church, appointed 1868, with 28 students registered.

The original support committee was chaired by Principal Dawson of McGill and included Peter Redpath and other Scots entrepreneurs. It's a far cry from Hugh Maclennan (no friend to Calvinists) concerning Huntly McQueen, the capitalist of *Two Solitudes*. His will left his entire fortune "to found and maintain a new Presbyterian theological college. It was to be located in the heart of the Ontario countryside, to have ample scholarships, and the chairs were to be so heavily endowed the trustees would be able to fill them with the ablest theologians they could import from Edinburgh and Aberdeen."

1873 ...

1873 is a signal year. The McTavish Street building is opened and its Morrice Hall wing added in 1882; it alone remains of the original long hall and two wings; it now houses a sister predestinarian group, the Institute of Islamic Studies.

After a fruitless search for prestigious names in Scotland (as Huntly McQueen had hoped) and the USA, Donald MacVicar is appointed Principal. This is vigorously opposed by a lobby led by none other than Dr Taylor of Erskine Church, who happens to be Chairman of the PC Board and Senate. He resigns in protest. Who said Presbyterians have no sense of humour?

Our College has had only six Principals in its 126 years: MacVicar, Scrimger, Fraser, MacKenzie, Lennox and Klempa. But such is the truculent nature of the place that more than that number have served as Acting Principals during interims, including Ritchie Bell and Donald MacMillan in recent years. Someone too notorious even for this was

John Campbell, professor of Church History and Apologetics. His was the only heresy trial connected with PC (you should always keep an eye on teachers of Apologetics, especially if educated at Knox and Edinburgh—I should explain that the old B.D. diploma had a line marked "Apologeticus" where I used to put my own signature). Perhaps you know the story told by the famous London preacher Joseph Parker: "I mounted the steps to the pulpit today with a special degree of trepidation. A note was handed to me stating, 'I'll be listening to your sermon to test its philosophical insights and logic.' My fears, however, were much mitigated by the fact that the writer spelled philosophy with an 'f'."

Back to John Campbell: when his views on the inspiration of scripture were challenged by conservatives he was charged with unsound teaching. The process in the Presbytery of Montreal was distinguished by having his own Principal as well as Professor Scrimger among the accusers! In good Presbyterian fashion, a compromise was eventually reached in which Campbell was allowed to retain both his chair and his doubts. Naturally he was not made Principal on MacVicar's death, and resigned when Scrimger got the nod in 1904.

There were three burning questions in that Victorian era: how long is eternity? where are the Lost Ten Tribes of Israel? And, who were the Hittites? The first (how long is the biblical "eon"?) caused the near-heresy trial of D.J. Macdonnell of St Andrew's, Toronto; the second spawned the British Israelites—"in England's green and pleasant land"; the third (who are the Hittites?) led our Professor Campbell all the way to Japan! "Every Japanese is *Hito*, 'a man or person,' in other words a Hittite"! [H.K. Markell, *History of The Presbyterian College, Montreal 1865-1986* (1987), 22.] He argued the case in a heavy two-volume work, and received an honorary degree for his pains before the scholarly world rejected his thesis with disdain. (Need I say that the LLD came from the University of Toronto?)

PCland was home to its own French connection also, still a debatable subject. Its original supporters included a lobby for the evangelization of misguided Roman Catholics. For example, the College Board reported to Synod in 1869 that 431 books had been added to the Library during the past year, a number dealing with "popish theology and the career of the Jesuits in the province of Quebec" [Markell, p. 12]. The lobby's finest hour was presumably the acquisition of "Father" Chiniquy with his congregation. Only his hat and cane remain with us as relics of that charismatic if rather un-Presbyterian convert. More serious was the appointment of Daniel Coussirat in 1880 as Professor of French Studies, lecturing in Homiletics, Philosophy and History. But after his death, as Neil Smith's historical sketch remarks, "the French Department, never very vigorous, went into a slow decline and ultimately vanished." [*Presbyterian College Thought* 1967, 5.] So much for the myth that the new United Church was to blame for surrendering our "French work!"

In the 1883 Presbyterian College *Journal* (III.4, p. 44) a different problem surfaced. A brief note entitled "Horse Worship" concerns a certain PC graduate "now in the field ... the god of whose idolatry appears to be horseflesh." Now it is true that horses play a significant part in the taming of the West—the great Robertson, Superintendent of Missions, once remarked that he wished our graduates knew "less Latin and more horse." But in this particular case the poor man apparently discussed horseflesh at every opportunity, "even on the Sabbath day, when his mind is supposed to be full of his message."

Our students of that era boasted a Debating Society (every Friday evening), a Missionary Society and a Philosophical and Literary Society. They had begun their *Journal* in 1881, two years before their friendly rivals at Knox. It provides food for thought and laughter too. Item: "Announcement: If any of you are thinking of marriage, will you please present yourselves to me right after the closing hymn, 'Mistaken souls that dream of heaven'." Item: "The Rev. Mr. Wilkins is something of a faith-healer, and I'm thinking of attending his church for my rheumatism. Is that so? Well I can recommend him for insomnia." Again: "A clergyman left his first charge because the ladies were overly friendly. Meeting his successor he inquired, 'How are you getting along with the ladies?' 'Very well' was the answer, 'there's safety in numbers.' To which he replied, 'I found it in exodus.'" And with unconscious humour, the

Valedictorian for 1884 included a touching reference to his professors: "We will always cherish delectable reminiscences of you all."

1927 ...

Now let's pass to a quite different age, just after Church Union when our PCC is reduced from a large and powerful institution to a struggling remnant—just like today. It is 1927; only one student will graduate and naturally is class valedictorian. But the little group of 44 students start an ambitious *Theological Review*, "published quarterly by the Students' Society of the Presbyterian College, Montreal." Its first editor was none other than C. Ritchie Bell. It opened with a piece by the newly appointed Professor F. Scott Mackenzie, and included articles on "Christianity as the Final Religion" and "The Place of the Church in the Rural Community." These items are still hot in 1993; apparently those worthies thought they too were undergoing a crisis of faith, of confidence, of the other maladies we think came only with the '80s.

Incidentally, that group of students included four future Moderators of General Assembly, one Military Chaplain, John Foote, famous for his action at Dieppe for which he received the Victoria Cross (later he would be nominated for Principal), and W.B. McCodrum who was to become President of Carleton University. In lighter vein, my late colleague and friend "CRB" included a poem entitled *Hyacinths*, concluding with the stanza: "I would marry any woman, / And serve her with a will, / Who, living all alone, should plant / Hyacinths on her sill." I presume his future wife Margaret was the first hyacinth lover he met, fortunately for him. Donald MacMillan, meanwhile, later famous for raising prize gladioli rather than hyacinths, and our own *Systematiker*, was quoted in a page of student sayings: "Curls and that sort of thing are mighty attractive."

1946 ...

Interlude from 1943 to 1946 when the building is rented to the Dept of National Defence, and unsavoury activities are rumoured to occur by the servicemen in residence. Various questionable pictures drawn on the commonroom walls, for instance. After this "Babylonian Captivity" at Knox College, Toronto the little group reassembles. Again there is but one student in that year's cohort—Lorne Lemoine boasts that they reopened the college just for him; there were four students and two professors at the start. But it survives, even thrives under Principal Lennox and his ability to attract scholars from Princeton and overseas. The prestigious Anderson Lectures begin (I was at the very first, given by Emile Cailliet in 1950, when I attended Synod while Ordained Missionary at Val d'Or.)

James Barr, now a world scholar in Old Testament studies, was Lecturer (in *New* Testament!) in the 1950's; Paul Ricoeur was introduced to Montreal through his friend André Poulain, and well before gaining international recognition, gave the Robert Lectures in 1956 (few students could fathom his accent—or his meaning); Dietrich Ritschl, now at Heidelberg, began his teaching career here, as did Michel Despland of Concordia, Charles Scobie of Mount Allison, and Charles Hay later Principal of Knox College. My own trial lectureship in 1955 and appointment from 1957, introduced me to the old building, presided over by rather mature women in the reception desk, library and office. Faculty meetings were few and short. The students were mostly lighthearted, though serious about their vocation of ministry. That vocation seemed clear to both teacher and student in those faroff days: to minister through sermon and visitation. One of Ritchie Bell's sayings was: "a home-going minister makes a church-going congregation."

The library, housed in the octagonal replica of Ottawa's national library, was a delight. I discovered the Sebright collection of antiquarian books, including the only copy of Peter Martyr's *Loci Communes* in Canada. The chance to order books in my area was a challenge. It was the late 'fifties and theology was stirring, particularly with Roman Catholic dogmatic revision. Soon I was confronted by our Librarian, complaining that she was running out of room in the section where these Romans were catalogued. "Which section is that?" I enquired. "Why, *heresy* of course!"

McTavish Street escapades: time would fail me to tell of water fights with rivulets flowing down stairways; of a birthday cake whose chocolate icing was laced with Exlax; of clandestine games played in the supposedly closed Morrice Hall; of afterhours entry through fire escapes, of College Retreats made dangerous by the soccer games sparked by Bob Hill and other Old Countrymen. The advent of women ordinands in 1966 proved a great good for us all, no doubt partly because our faculty had lobbied on their behalf in Assembly committees. We have benefited from the dimension of insight and difference they bring.

And then there were the humorists. James Dickey's portrayal of a very short and nervous David changing his mind about Goliath led to an interview with the Principal. I remember Warren McKinnon's imitation of Tommy Douglas (done in my honour), and the annual marvellous sendups of faculty, particularly our beloved Principal, by the likes of Charles MacPherson and Scott Emery. In fact, this tradition of good humour persists, so that our annual meetings during Assembly are famous (notorious?) for their hilarity, due not least these days to the wry humour of Ian Victor. Knox College has copied us in this shift to lighter vein at its annual luncheon (owing in part to the number of defectors from theirs to ours) as well as in finally introducing daily coffee and weekly student-faculty luncheons.

Presbyterian College has inhabited four different buildings: Erskine Church basement to begin, the McTavish quarters, not so much lavish as impressive, the temporary abode (for two sessions) on Peel Street while our present edifice was abuilding, and for the past thirty years, 3495 University. We have seen many changes, from security of vocation for male servants of Word and Sacraments, through uncertainty about vocation and institutions, to a coeducational enterprise aimed at professional training. From Bachelor of Divinity to Master of Divinity. From bare affiliation with McGill University to full partnership in the Faculty of

Religious Studies.[2] From teaching through lecture and examination to a mixed approach including tutorial, seminar and field-based experience.

Of one thing I am sure. Our little College has more than proved its worth to the Church—and, I hope, the Kingdom. Our tradition has been to put the stress on the vocation of parish ministry; not by downgrading scholarship but by upgrading, to use medieval language, theology as a "practical science." Our graduates (over seven hundred since 1867) have served well in congregations coast to coast, on mission field and military chaplaincy. Of Moderators we have had more than our share. In recent years indeed it's becoming a problem. Since 1983 we've had four graduates and one professor moderating General Assembly. In the past four years three Moderators were our graduates while Linda Bell is a sort of honorary member, especially at our annual meetings. This year of course another graduate is moderator-designate.[3]

More to the point, who's really running the Church? With Tom Gemmel, Glen Davis and Karen Hincke in the three key administrative positions at our Church Offices, assisted by others such as Jean Armstrong, John Bannerman, Ralph Kendall and Ian Morrison, I make the suggestion that we should keep the initials PCinC in front of 50 Wynford Drive, but change the sign (with English 2/3 larger than French) reading: "Presbyterian College in Charge."

Scott Mackenzie once said that a preacher who says "Amen" to his own prayers is like an afterdinner speaker saying "Hear! Hear!" in the middle of his own speech. Therefore now that my before-lunch address is finished I hope you can say either "Amen!" or "Good—let's eat!" And for either one I thank you.

---

2.   Ritchie Bell said we waited 21 years, until the Faculty had come of age; having refused to join the new organism in 1948 it was 1969 before everyone could agree.

3.   I.e., Earle Roberts; in fact, he was followed the next year by another alumnus, George Vais.

BOOKS PUBLISHED

The Visible Words of God: An Exposition of the Sacramental Theology of Peter Martyr Vermigli. Edin.: Oliver and Boyd, 1957; Grand Rapids: Eerdmans, 1965.

The Other Six Days. Toronto: Burns and MacEachern, 1959; Richmond, VA.: John Knox Press, 1960; Tokyo: 1968 (Japanese Trans.); El Paso, TX, 1977 (Spanish trans.)

The Reformation & its Significance Today. Philadelphia: Westminster Press, 1962.

Living for Christ. Richmond, VA: John Knox Press, 1963.

New Look at Vocation. Toronto: Ryerson Press, 1964.

Toward a Radical Church. Toronto: Ryerson Press, 1967; Edin: St. Andrew's Press, 1969.

The Clown and the Crocodile. Richmond, VA: John Knox, 1970.

The New Man. co-ed. with J. Meyendorff. New Brunswick, NJ: Standard Press, 1973.

God the Anonymous: an essay in Alexandrian philosophical theology. Philadelphia Patristic Foundation, 1976. (Greeno, Hadden & Co.)

Peter Martyr Vermigli and Italian Reform. ed. Waterloo: Wilfred Laurier University Press, 1980. (155). Intro. and "P.M.V. — Scholastic or Humanist?"

Doxology: Perpetual Celebration. Toronto: Pres. Church Publication, 1981.

Celebration and Suffering. Toronto: Pres. Church Publication, 1983.

Prometheus Rebound: The Irony of Atheism. Waterloo: Wilfred Laurier U. Press, 1988.

Life, Early Letters and Eucharistic Writings of Peter Martyr. Trans. and ed. with G. Duffield. Appleford: Courtenay Library of Reformation Classics, 1989.

Early Writings, Peter Martyr Library, Vol. I, 1994. Ed.; trans. "Theses for Debate."

Philosophical Works, Peter Martyr Library, Vol. 4, 1996. Trans. & ed.

Peter Martyr Reader, Peter Martyr Library special edition (1999), co-ed.

Oxford Treatise & Disputation (1549), PM Library, Vol. 7, 2000. Trans. & ed.

Martyr's Commentary on Aristotle's Nicomachean Ethics, PML vol. 9. Co-ed. 2006.

Peter Martyr's Loci Communes: A Literary History. Montreal: McGill Printing, 2007.

Peter Martyr Library. General Editor: series of English translations (Series One: 12 vols). Kirksville, MO: Sixteenth Century Journal, Inc.